HRD PRACTICES IN APSRTC

HRD PRACTICES IN APSRTC

A case study with special reference
to Vizianagaram Zone

DR. SANTOSHA PAVANI TAMMINENI

PARTRIDGE

Print information available on the last page.

To order additional copies of this book, contact
Partridge India
000 800 10062 62
orders.india@partridgepublishing.com

www.partridgepublishing.com/india

HRD PRACTICES IN APSRTC

A case study with special reference to Vizianagaram Zone

*Thesis submitted in partial fulfilment of the requirement
for the award of the degree of*

DOCTOR OF PHILOSOPHY

In the faculty of Commerce and Management Studies

By

SANTOSHA PAVANI TAMMINENI
B.Tech., M.B.A.

Under the Esteemed Guidance of

Prof. M. SANDHYA SRIDEVI
M.B.A., Ph.D.
Department of Commerce and Management Studies
Andhra University
Visakhapatnam

DEPARTMENT OF COMMERCE AND MANAGEMENT STUDIES
ANDHRA UNIVERSITY
VISAKHAPATNAM-530 003
ANDHRA PRADESH, INDIA
APRIL - 2014

In Loving Memory of

My Late Beloved Grand Parents

Smt & Sri TAMMINENI SATYAMMA &
PAPA RAO

Declaration

I hereby declare that the thesis entitled **"HRD PRACTICES IN APSRTC - A Case Study with Special Reference to Vizianagaram Zone"** submitted to the Department of Commerce and Management Studies, Andhra University, Visakhapatnam, for the award of the degree of **DOCTOR OF PHILOSOPHY** is based on original research work carried out independently by me under the supervision and guidance of **Prof. M. SANDHYA SRIDEVI**, Professor, Department of Commerce and Management Studies, Andhra University, Visakhapatnam. This work has not been submitted previously in full or a part thereof for the award of other similar Degree, Diploma, Fellowship, Associate ship or any other similar titles in this university or any other university or institution.

Place: Visakhapatnam.   **(SANTOSHA PAVANI TAMMINENI)**

Date: Research Scholar

Certificate

I certify that the thesis entitled **"HRD PRACTICES IN APSRTC - A Case Study with Special Reference to Vizianagaram Zone"** submitted to the Department of Commerce and Management Studies, Andhra University, Visakhapatnam, for the award of the Degree of **DOCTOR OF PHILOSOPHY** is an authentic work done by **Miss. SANTOSHA PAVANI TAMMINENI** under my supervision and guidance. The subject on which the thesis has been prepared is based on her original research work and it has not been submitted earlier in full or a part thereof for the award of any Degree, Diploma or Associate ship or any other similar titles in this or in any other university or institution.

Place: Visakhapatnam.

Date:

(**Prof. M. SANDHYA SRIDEVI**)

Research Director

Acknowledgements

First and foremost, I bow my head in reverence to the almighty for providing me the positive strength and energy to work on this topic and for enabling me to reach far beyond my own restricted ambit of thought and action.

I feel honoured to express my profound regard and deep sense of gratitude to my worthiest and most esteemed research director, **Prof. M. Sandhya Sridevi,** Department of Commerce and Management Studies, Andhra University, for her valuable sagacious and constructive guidance in the completion of this thesis. She provided intellectual and affectionate support to me throughout this research work, without her constant inspiration, I would not have been able to successfully handle this task. Many thanks for her understanding and generous attitude for keeping her doors open to help all the time.

I am happy to express my special gratitude to my doctoral committee member, **Prof. M. Sarada Devi,** Department of Commerce and Management Studies, Andhra University, for her cooperation and accessibility during the course of my work.

I am deeply indebted to **Prof. N. Sambasiva Rao**, Department of Commerce and Management Studies, Andhra University, for his scholarly guidance, inspiring advice and constant help in completing my research work.

My deepest sense of gratitude to **Prof. D. Prabhakar Rao,** Principal, College of Arts and Commerce, Andhra University, **Prof. R. Satya Raju,** Chairman, P.G. Board of Studies, Department of Commerce and Management Studies, Andhra University and **Prof. M. Madhusudana Rao**, Head of the Department, Commerce and Management Studies, Andhra University, for providing me all the required facilities to complete the research work.

I'm very much thankful to **Sri. T. J. V. Govinda Rao,** Retd. Dy. CAO, APSRTC; **Sri. Kaniti Venkata Rao,** Works Manager, Zonal Work Shop,

Vizianagaram zone; **Sri. K.V.V. Prasad,** Personnel Officer, Visakhapatnam; **Sri. Venkateshwar Rao,** Dy. CAO, Head Office, Hyderabad, who rendered extensive support in collecting the data from the employees of APSRTC and provided necessary information as and when I required.

I cannot resist the joy of bowing my head before my mother, **T. Madhavi** and father, **Dr. T. Rama Mohana Rao,** the fountain heads of my inspiration for having attempted to undertake this arduous yet creative task, without their trust, encouragement, emotional and financial support, I could not have been able to complete my thesis work.

I express thanks from the depth of my heart to my uncle **Prof. K. Ramji,** aunty **Dr. K. Saradha Jyothi,** nephew **Chy. K. Sai Venkat Pavan,** and niece **Chy. K. Sai Vaishnavi** for their unconditioned support, love and effection throughout the period of my research. Further, I convey my thanks to my elder uncle **Sri. K. Appala Naidu** and younger uncle **Sri. K. Jagan Mohan Rao** and their family members who helped me a lot by all means in the completion of my thesis. My thanks are also due to my granny, **Smt. K. Kamalamamma** for her blessings.

I feel grateful to **Sri. L. Rama Rao,** Advocate, Hyderabad, **Sri. Pedada Rambabu,** Principal, Government Junior College, Hiramandalam and **Sri. Tirlangi Janaki Ramayya,** Advocate for helping me in the process of survey. I also thank **Sri. Hanumanthu Nagabhushan,** CPO Office, Srikakulam, for providing statistical information.

I express my sincere appreciation and special thanks to my co-scholars, **Malla Pardhasaradhi, Jada Jayendra, Manju Latha** and **Divya** for their encouragement and co-operation at various stages of my research work.

I also place on record, my sense of gratitude to one and all who, directly or indirectly, have lent their helping hand in this venture, which I cannot list them all in this limited space and must ask the forgiveness of those I forgot.

(SANTOSHA PAVANI TAMMINENI)

Contents

Contents

Preface

A complete study on implementation of HRD Practices in APSRTC at Zonal level is rare in number. In contrast to the earlier practices an attempt has been made by the researcher to trace out the impact of HRD practices on employees at zonal level and to investigate whether is implemented in letter and spirit or not, by reviewing operational performance of APSRTC and its financial function. This work is not only an in depth study of HRD practices in APSRTC; the study also presents an overview of Road transport sector in India. With the advent of globalization, transport sectors are confronted with challenges in improving productivity by successfully meeting the intense level of competition from its counterparts. Business today is in a period of change and uncertainty. The success will largely depend on how these challenges are matched with the utilization of human resources which is at our disposal. It has been very unfortunate that the APSRTC has limited its human resource developmental practices for some cadres at apex level only without taking organizational climate of various zones into account while training their managerial personnel. But the need of the hour is to put more emphasis on all the HRD practices at managerial level in the back ground of their level of climate. The researcher looks at the problems of implementing HRD practices in the context of changing technological advancement and government policies. It is an empirical study and is based on both primary and secondary source of information.

The present study is divided into six chapters and the contents of each chapter are as follows:

Chapter - 1 gives a brief introduction of HRD concepts, its evolution, significance, principles, theories, and future perspectives of HRD in modern India.

The preview of research methodology adopted, sample frame, hypothesis, and objectives along with the discussion of other studies done in this field of HRD are discussed in *chapter - 2.*

The origin, evolution of STUs in Road Transport sector in India and performance of STUs till the fiscal year 2012-13 was dealt in *chapter - 3.*

Under *chapter - 4,* Section A covers, APSRTC profile, its origin, physical and fiscal performance of APSRTC during 2002-03 to 2012-13 are assessed and impact of illicit operations and problems of bifurcation to the corporation are presented. Whereas Section B discusses the HRD practices in APSRTC and SWOT analysis was framed to know the Strengths, Weaknesses, Opportunities and Threats of HRD practices in the corporation.

A critical assessment of manager's perspective towards HRD Practices in APSRTC on seven different dimensions was interpreted in *chapter - 5.*

In conclusion, *chapter - 6* gives the summary of the present study along with important findings and observations of the researcher.

This work as a whole would give an overall understanding of the problems faced by APSRTC with reference to the implication of HRD practices at its root levels, financial uncertainties and government policies and few recommendations were offered to be taken by APSRTC in future.

List of Tables

List of Figures

Abbreviations

AC	-	Air Conditioned
ANOVA	-	Analysis of Variance
AOs	-	Accounts Officers
AP	-	Andhra Pradesh
APEC	-	Asia Pacific Economic Cooperation
APPC	-	Andhra Pradesh Productivity Council
APSRTC	-	Andhra Pradesh State Road Transport Corporation
ART	-	Allocation, Recruitment and Training
ARTSCO	-	ARTS Co-operative
ASCI	-	Administrative Staff College of India
ASRTU	-	Association of State Road Transport Undertakings
ASTD	-	American society for training directors
ASTU	-	Association of State Transport Undertakings
ATB	-	Authorized Ticket Booking
AVG	-	Average
BARAT	-	Bus Advanced Reservation Any Time
BD	-	Break Down
BOT	-	Build Operate and Transfer
BSR	-	Bus Staff Ratio
CAD	-	Computer Aided Design
CAT	-	Concessional Annual Travel
CCI	-	Competition Commission of India
CCS	-	Cooperative Credit & Thrift Society
CHRD	-	Comparative HRD

CHRD	-	Critical Human Resource Development
CI	-	Confidence Interval
CIPD	-	Chartered Institute of Personnel and Development
CIRT	-	Central Institute of Road Transport
CIS	-	Centralized integrated Solution
CNG	-	Compressed Natural Gas
CNG	-	Compressed Natural Gas
CPD	-	Career Planning and Development
CPK	-	Cost per Kilometer
CRANET	-	Cranfield Network on International Human Resource Management
CSR	-	Corporate Social Responsibility
DA	-	Dearness Allowance
DM	-	Depot Manager
DMFRF	-	Deceased Members Family Relief Fund
DRF	-	Death Relief Fund
ECT	-	Employees Co-operative Thrift
ED	-	Executive Director
EDLIF	-	Employee's Deposit Linked Insurance Fund
EI	-	Emotional Intelligence
EP	-	Employee Performance
EPB	-	Earnings per Bus
EPK	-	Earnings per Kilometer
EPK	-	Emergency Product Kit
ESMA	-	Essential Service Maintenance Act
FACTIS	-	Financial Accounting Information System
FACTS	-	Finance Accounting Systems
FAPCC & I	-	Federation of A.P. Chambers of Commerce & Industry
GATT	-	General Agreement on Tariffs and Trade
GBT	-	Monthly General Bus
GDP	-	Gross Domestic Product
GIFT	-	Gain Instant Free Travel Scheme
GOM	-	Group of Ministers

GSRTC	-	Gujarat State Road Transport Corporation
HD	-	Human Development
HMA	-	Hyderabad Management Association
HPT	-	Human Performance Technology
HR	-	Human Resource
HRD	-	Human Resource Development
HRDC	-	Human Resources Development Center
HRDC	-	Human Resources Development Climate
HRDP	-	Human Resource Development Practices
HRIS	-	Human Resource Information System
HRM	-	Human Resource Management
HSD	-	High Speed Diesel
HT	-	High Tension
ICE	-	Integrative Intercultural Effectiveness
IEU	-	Independent Education Union
IHRD	-	Integrative Human Resource Development
IHRD	-	International Human Resources Development
IHRM	-	International Human Resources Management
IIM	-	Indian Institute of Management
IIMA	-	Indian Institute of Management Ahmadabad
IIPM	-	Indian Institute of Personnel Management
IJHRM	-	International Journal of Human Resources Management
ILO	-	International Labour Organization
IMC	-	International Mechanical Code
IR	-	Interim Relief
IR&W	-	Industrial Relations and Welfare
IRTDA	-	Indian Roads & Transport Development Association
ISASB	-	Indian Society for Application Behaviour Services
ISO	-	International Organization for Standardization
IT	-	Information Technology
ITI	-	Industrial Training Institute
ITS	-	Intelligence Transport System
JIT	-	Just In Time

JNNURM	-	Jawaharlal Nehru National Urban Renewal Mission
JSO	-	Junior Scale Officer
KM	-	Kilometer
KM	-	Knowledge Management
KMPL	-	Kilometers per Litre
KWH	-	Kilo Watt Hour
L & T	-	Larsen & Toubro
LCD	-	Liquid Crystal Display
LED	-	Light Emitting Diode
LEs	-	Large Enterprises
LLM	-	Low Level Manager
LPG	-	Liberalization Privatization and Globalization
M&A	-	Mergers and Acquisitions
M&E	-	Monitoring and Evaluation
MD	-	Manager Development
MD	-	Managing Director
MDP	-	Management Development Programmes
MDP	-	Management Development Programmes
MGBS	-	Mahatma Gandhi Bus Station
MHCAS	-	Members Handicapped Children Assistance Scheme
MHCES	-	Members Handicapped Children Education Scheme
MIS	-	Management Information Systems
MLR	-	Multi Linear Regression
MNCs	-	Multinational Companies
MOAS	-	Member's Old Age Assistance Scheme
MOs	-	Medical Officers
MOU	-	Memorandum of Understanding
MSRTC	-	Maharastra State Road Transport Corporation
MSTs	-	Mechanical Supervisor Trainee
MSTs	-	Monthly Season Tickets
MV	-	Motor Vehicle
MW	-	Mega Watt
NHRD	-	National Human Resource Development

NILM	-	National Institute of Labour Management
NPC	-	National Productivity Council
NPC	-	National Productivity Council
NSR	-	Nizam State Rail
NSR-RTD	-	Nizam State Rail and Road Transport Department
NVQs	-	National Vocational Qualifications
OC	-	Organization Climate
OCB	-	Organizational Citizenship Behaviour
OD	-	Organizational Development
OLIMS	-	Online Inventory Management System
OLTAS	-	Online Ticket Accounting Systems
OPRS	-	Online Passenger Reservation System
OR	-	Occupancy Ratio
OSC	-	Organization structure and climate
OTE	-	Overall Technical Efficiency
OUT	-	Officer Under Training
OVIE	-	Overall Technical Inefficiency
PA	-	Performance Appraisal
PAAS	-	Pass Automation & Accountal System
PCRA	-	Petroleum conservation Research Association
PFAS	-	PF Accounting System
PG	-	Post Graduation
Ph.D	-	Doctor of Philosophy
PINS	-	Personnel Information Systems
PMS	-	Personnel Management System
PPK	-	Profit per Kilometer
PRC	-	People's Republic of China
PRS	-	Pay Roll System
QWL	-	Quality of Work Life
R & B	-	Roads and Buildings
RFID	-	Radio-Frequency Identification
RM	-	Regional Manager
RMSS	-	Retired Members Security Scheme

ROI	-	Return on Investment
RT	-	Road Transport
RTC	-	Road Transport Corporation
SBR	-	Staff Bus Ratio
SBT	-	Staff Benevolent Thrift Fund
SC	-	Social Capital
SCT	-	Social Cognitive Theory
SD	-	Societal Development
SD	-	Standard Deviation
SDL	-	Self-Directed Learning
SDP	-	Supervisory Development Programmes
SDPP	-	Supervisory Development Programmes
SLT	-	Social Learning Theory
SMEs	-	Small Medium Enterprises
SNA	-	Social Network Analysis
SRBS-	-	Staff Retirement Benefit Scheme
SRC	-	State Re-organization Commission
SRTCs	-	State Road Transport Corporations
SRTU	-	State Road Transport Undertaking
SRTUs	-	State Road Transport Undertakings
SSO	-	Senior Scale Officer
STOINS	-	Stores Inventory System
STU	-	State Transport Undertaking
STU	-	State Transport Undertaking
STUs	-	State Transport Undertakings
SWOT	-	Strengths, Weaknesses, Opportunities, and Threats
T & D	-	Training and Development
TCS	-	Tata Consultancy Services
TD	-	Training and Development
TFP	-	Total Factor Productivity
TIMs	-	Ticket Issuing Machines
TPP	-	Transport Planning Practice
TQM	–	Total Quality Management

TQT	-	Total Quality Transportation
TREATS	-	Travel Regularly and Earn Additional Free Trip Scheme
TSTs	-	Traffic Supervisor Trainee
TWI	-	Training Within Industry
UK	-	United Kingdom
UPA	-	United Progressive Alliance
UPSRTC	-	Uttar Pradesh State Road Transport Corporation
US	-	United States
VAT	-	Value Added Tax
VC	-	Vice Chairman
VEMAS	-	Vehicle Maintenance and Testing System.
VTI	-	Voluntary Turnover Intentions
XLRI	-	Xavier Labour Relations Institute

Synopsis

INTRODUCTION

Road Transport acquired considerable importance in bringing socio, economic development in the context of India becoming independent. Before independence passenger road transport was in the hands of private operators. On the one hand, the private operators could not hold to the expectations of the passengers and on the other hand they were exploiting their monopoly in the transport sector. Such situation gave rise to the demand for the policy of nationalizing passenger transport.

Shortly after independence, the nation embarked on the policy of nationalizing passenger transport. In pursuance of the policy of a nation, Parliament enacted the Road Transport Corporation Act, 1950. In the wake of this enactment, various state governments enacted legislations for nationalization of bus transport and began to implement it in a phased manner, subject to its financial, social and political considerations. APSRTC is one among the nationalized State Road Transport Corporations in India. The first phase of nationalization of State Road Transport service began in Krishna, Guntur and West Godavari districts during 1958-61.

APSRTC was established on 11th January, 1958 under Road Transport Act, 1950. The origin of APSRTC dates back to June, 1932 when it was first established as Nizam State Rail and Road Transport Department (NSR-RTD) – a wing of Nizam State Railways in erstwhile Hyderabad state. It started with 27 buses and 166 employees. It became a full-fledged department of the Government of Hyderabad state from 1st November, 1951 and carried on till 1958 when APSRTC was born.

APSRTC in pursuance of the concept of de-centralization initiated structural reforms once again in May, 1994. Accordingly the corporation was

21

divided into seven zones, each zone covering an average of four revenue districts headed by an executive director. Executive Director has been endowed with vast powers to deal with any eventuality in the operation of bus services and oversee the administration in his jurisdiction or zone. The zone formed at the second level, with region and depot at third and fourth levels in this existing structure. The region otherwise called as revenue district in the plan is under the control of regional manager, whose main function was to streamline the inter - division and inter - depot operations and have a close monitoring of manpower utilization, financial performance, performance of depots in several operations and mechanical engineering parameters. At operational level, depot manager is responsible for the up keep of buses and operations, maintaining passenger amenities to the level of passenger satisfaction. In the scheme of organization, there is a corporation board at the apex level consisting of eight directors, apart from the chairman and vice chairman of the board. Chairman and vice-chairman are also members in the board by virtue of their position. All the policy decisions are taken by the board and implemented by the vice-chairman and managing director of the corporation who acts as a chief executive officer.

Since from inception to till now, APSRTC registered a steady growth in its physical performance with 27 buses to 22477 buses, 166 employees to 1,23,615 employees with 774 bus stations, 213 bus depots and 1881 bus shelters. The corporation buses cover 80.77 lakh kilometers a day ferries almost about 15463 lakh passengers daily to their destinations. It entered in 'The Gunnies Book of World Records' in the year 1999 for having the largest fleet among all the Public sectors in the world. APSRTC is operating buses in 7725 routes connecting 23 revenue regions covering 23388 villages which constitute about 95 percent of road transport. On the other side, financial performance of the corporation shows a grim picture in the last decade. APSRTC to attain competitive advantage in the era of globalization, has to offset loses to the extent of Rs.4800 crore. This competitive advantage can be achieved by developing its most valuable assets i.e. human assets. However, Uday Pareek and T.V. Rao quoted that "HRD is primarily concerned with developing employees through training, feedback and counseling by the senior officers and other developmental efforts". So the management of the corporation has to ensure effective implementation of HRD practices at all levels particularly at managerial level to insulate APSRTC from the existing loses for effective functioning of the organization.

RESEARCH STUDY

A complete study on implementation of HRD Practices in APSRTC at Zonal level is rare in number. In contrast to the earlier practices an attempt has been made by the researcher to trace out the impact of HRD practices on employees at zonal level and to investigate whether it is implemented in letter and spirit or not, by reviewing operational performance of APSRTC and its financial function. This work is not only an in depth study of HRD practices in APSRTC; the study also presents an overview of Road transport sector in India. With the advent of globalization, transport sectors are confronted with challenges in improving productivity by successfully meeting the intense level of competition from its counterparts. Business today is in a period of change and uncertainty. The success will largely depend on how these challenges are matched with the utilization of human resources which is at our disposal. It has been very unfortunate that the APSRTC has limited its human resource developmental practices for some cadres at apex level only without taking organizational climate of various zones into account while training their managerial personnel. But the need of the hour is to put more emphasis on all the HRD practices at managerial level in the back ground of their level of climate. The researcher looks at the problems of implementing HRD practices in the context of changing technological advancement and government policies.

NEED FOR THE STUDY

HRD is an essential component for organizational growth and effectiveness. But it is imperative to mention that the approach of managements towards HRD is still conservative. As a result, the potential of human resource could not be properly gauged and fully tapped for attaining organizational goals in general and the employees in particular. In this regard a required change in the mindset of top management is yet to take place. Unfortunately, HRD policy in most of the undertakings demonstrated a number of loopholes and failed to create desirable work environment and organizational health. So a continuous effort towards HRD is necessary for the development of the organization as whole. This could be achieved through research methods, where in possible development in specific areas may be reviewed and corrective action may be taken.

HRD is a vital area to be focused in an organization when employing huge number of work force. In the organization like APSRTC the HRD policies and practices need a scientific assessment as it employs huge number of nearly 1.3 lakh people of different cadres possessing different skills and performing different functions. But, it is observed that there are no enough studies performed on HRD practices in APSRTC at state level and almost no studies were performed at zonal level. Despite the fact that the performance of the undertaking is influenced by technology, modernization and business strategies, the role of HRD cannot be undermined. So it is appropriate to study the HRD practices of APSRTC at zonal level in order to take appropriate measures to increase employee's efficiency level and productivity.

OBJECTIVES

The basic objectives of the proposed study are:

1. To study the road transportation sector in India and in A.P.
2. To identify the existing HRD practices in APSRTC.
3. To examine the influence of HRD practices on the organization.
4. To suggest measures to improve the performance of employees in the organization.

HYPOTHESIS OF THE PRESENT STUDY

The seven most important dimensions of HRD Practices on which the questionnaire has been divided is the base for developing the hypothesis for the study. The following hypothesis emerges out of the variables selected for conducting research at managerial level in APSRTC.

H_{01}: Training and Development doesn't have significant impact on the employee's performance.

H_{02}: Organizational structure & culture doesn't have significant impact on the employee's performance.

H_{03}: HRD knowledge & Skills doesn't have significant impact on the employee's performance.

H_{04}: HRD Climate doesn't have significant impact on the employee's performance.

H_{05}: Performance Appraisal doesn't have significant impact on the employee's performance.

H_{06}: Counseling doesn't have significant impact on the employee's performance.

H_{07}: Career Planning & Development doesn't have significant impact on the employee's performance.

H_{08}: Overall level of satisfaction on HRD Practices doesn't have significant impact on the employee's performance.

H_{09}: HRD practices don't have significant impact on the designation i.e. level of management.

RESEARCH METHODOLOGY

Research Methodology is the systematic framework within which the research is conducted. In general, Research Methodology describes the overall design of the study, entire data collection process and statistical tools used in the process of data analysis.

DATA COLLECTION

To attain the objectives of the present thesis, the required data is collected from both primary and secondary sources.

PRIMARY DATA

The study is empirical in nature. Therefore the work is largely based on primary data. The survey method through a structured questionnaire was employed for the collection of primary data from the selected sample respondents. The respondents here are top managerial personnel and supervisory cadre employees of Vizianagaram zone of APSRTC.

INSTRUMENT DEVELOPMENT: QUESTIONNAIRE

A structured questionnaire had been developed to get the opinion of the managerial and supervisory cadre employees (Senior Scale Officers-SSO, Junior Scale Officers-JSO and Low level managers - LLM) of APSRTC; To elicit the information from the respondents, questionnaire was designed on practices of HRD as variables on a five point Likert Scale, with 1 for "Not at all true", 2 for "Not so true", 3 for "partly true", 4 for "True" and 5 for "very much true". The questionnaire was divided into three sections. Section A was designed to obtain demographic information of the respondents. It covers qualification, age, gender, present designation, department, monthly salary, length of service, marital status and nature of work. Section B measures the seven most important dimensions of HRD practices like Training and Development, Organizational structure and culture, HRD Knowledge and Skills, HRD climate, Performance Appraisal, Counseling, and Career planning and Development. Section C estimates the overall satisfaction of the respondents towards HRD practices in the organization. In Section C various aspects of HRD practices are measured on a five point Likert Scale, with 1 for "Highly Dissatisfied", 2 for "Dissatisfied", 3 for "Neutral", 4 for "Satisfied" and 5 for "Highly Satisfied". On the basis of these three sections in the questionnaire, the HRD practices have been judged in APSRTC and analysis has been made.

SECONDARY DATA

The secondary data is also used for referring the conceptual aspects and literature review. The data was collected from various sources like published books, libraries, annual reports, both online and print journals, magazines, periodicals, news papers, research surveys, existing works conducted on Human Resource Development and related factors, websites, presentation in seminars and conferences.

PILOT STUDY

The questionnaires were pre-tested with 15 employees. Based on the views and feedback of the respondents changes were made and questionnaire was finalized.

SURVEY METHOD

The survey method used by the researcher for the present study is Census survey. **Census** is the procedure of systematically acquiring and recording information about the members of a given population. A total of 132 (27

Senior Scale officers, 37 Junior Scale Officers and 68 Low level Managers) questionnaires were administered to all the managerial employees in Vizianagaram Zone of APSRTC.

STATISTICAL TOOLS FOR DATA ANALYSIS

The primary data was analyzed using the Statistical Package for Social Sciences (SPSS – 15.0 version). The collected data is processed by using:

1. **Frequency Tabulations** for demographic variables (qualification, age, gender, present designation, department, monthly salary, length of service, marital status and nature of work).

2. **Mean Scores**

It is used to find out item – wise average values of the HRD Practices in APSRTC

3. **Percentage Scores**

The item-wise mean scores of the total sample are presented below:

Since the questionnaire used is a five – point Likert scale, Mean score 4 and around indicates that employees in APSRTC agreed that good human resource development practices are prevailing in the organization. It indicates that human resource development practices are at desirable level, whereas mean score 3 and around indicates an average human development practices are prevailing in the organization and mean score 2 and around indicates poor human resource development practices exist in the organization (APSRTC).

In the present study, in order to make the interpretations easy the mean scores have been converted into percentage scores by using the formula, Percentage score = (Mean Score – 1) X 25. As per this measure the score 1 represents – 0 Percent, 2 represents – 25 Percent, 3 represents – 50 Percent, 4 represents – 75 Percent and 5 represents – 100 Percent. The percent Score indicates the degree to which a particular dimension exists in that organization out of the ideal 100.

4. **Standard Deviation**

Standard deviation is the square root of variance. Standard Deviation method is applied to know the nature of the variations in responses. It is used in human resource development practices to measure the variations in responses of managerial staff in APSRTC.

5. Multiple Linear Regression Analysis

In the present study multiple linear regression analysis is used to find out the impact of HRD Practices on employees of APSRTC.

6. ANOVA Analysis

ANOVA stands for analysis-of-variance, a statistical model meant to analyze data. ANOVA test is conducted to test the significant difference between two mean score among the variables of HRD practices and Demographic variables. ANOVA test is conducted to find the significant difference in the mean score among the respondents of various designations (SSO, JSO & LLM) for the overall opinion of the respondents to the HRD practices in APSRTC. In the present study ANOVA analysis is also used to test further significance level of those items in HRD practices that are resulted as significant.

The statistical results are then interpreted and the findings are compiled to derive pragmatic recommendations in the form of suitable suggestions.

SCOPE OF THE STUDY

The study covers all the important areas of HRD in APSRTC. HRD is broader than human resource management; it consists of several sub-systems such as training and development, employee appraisal, counseling, rewards and welfare, quality of work life, etc. These areas require conceptual clarifications about HR and HRD, organization structure and climate.

The Researcher feels that this study will certainly throw light upon various aspects where the top management in APSRTC needs to work out. The present study covers almost all aspects of HRD practices. The findings and conclusions of the study would be of great help in whipping out some of the undesirable issues that are likely to crop up in the implementation of such HRD practices.

LIMITATIONS OF THE STUDY

Despite of all the earnest attempts made by the researcher to elicit all required data on HRD practices in APSRTC – Vizianagaram Zone from the top management and supervisory cadre employees, the study is subjected to certain limitations due to the fact that the data is based on individual opinion, which may bring in some bias.

1. Undoubtedly, the responses have been collected from the employees of top management and supervisory cadre in APSRTC - Vizianagaram Zone; hence limited analysis could be derived from the study.

2. It is due to this reason that HRD practices are only subjected to managerial cadre, the sample size of the top management and supervisory cadre respondents is confined to 132 only. This is due to lack of permission from the authorities to extend it to other zones for performing a comparative study.

3. In addition to this, most of the respondents were reluctant in expressing their opinion freely without any hesitation and showing lack of interest in responding. This has its own impact to certain extent over the validity of the conclusions drawn.

4. Further, the opinion of some of the employees turns out to be influenced by their peer employees or superiors which might lead to their neutral response to a large extent for several statements.

DESIGN OF THE STUDY

The present study has been articulated by dividing into six chapters and the contents of each chapter are as follows:

Chapter - 1 gives a brief introduction of HRD concepts, its evolution, significance, principles, theories, and future perspectives of HRD in modern India.

The preview of research methodology adopted, sample frame, hypothesis, and objectives along with the discussion of other studies done in this field of HRD are discussed in *chapter - 2.*

The origin, evolution of STUs in Road Transport sector in India and performance of STUs till the fiscal year 2012-13 was dealt in *chapter - 3.*

Under *chapter - 4,* Section A covers, APSRTC profile, its origin, physical and fiscal performance of APSRTC during 2002-03 to 2012-13 are assessed and impact of illicit operations and problems of bifurcation to the corporation are presented. Whereas Section B discusses the HRD practices in APSRTC and SWOT analysis was framed to know the Strengths, Weaknesses, Opportunities and Threats of HRD practices in the corporation.

A critical assessment of manager's perspective towards HRD Practices in APSRTC on seven different dimensions was interpreted in *chapter - 5*.

In conclusion, *chapter - 6* gives the summary of the present study along with important findings and observations of the researcher.

This work as a whole would give an overall understanding of the problems faced by APSRTC with reference to the implication of HRD practices at its root levels, financial uncertainties and government policies and few recommendations were offered to be taken by APSRTC in future.

FINDINGS OF THE STUDY

> The survey results reveal that the managerial staff follow up toward trained employees is neglected, not measured and utilized properly.

> It is observed that teamspirit is high in the corporation.

> It is identified that from the analysis that corporation fails to encourage the practice of self motivation and commitment.

> The study identifies that the employees of the corporation have good initiative and leadership skills.

> It is observed that most of the managerial staff despite of experience still lacks enough skills for designing HRD

> It is observed that when feedback is given to employees they don't take it seriously and use it for development.

> It is observed that Performance Appraisal system doesn't provide an opportunity for each appraisee to communicate the support he needs from the superiors to perform his job effectively.

> Also it is evident that the performance appraisal system failed to assess of employee potential and enables him to select and pursue his future careers.

> It is observed that corporation provides good number of counseling sessions to its employees for their development.

> It is observed that counseling lacks in helping the employees to learn the skills of formulating objectives, framing controlling techniques and the methods.

> It is found that Organization fails to provide facility of assessment center to assist employee's potentialities.

➤ It is found that employees in APSRTC are very much dissatisfied about the existing Library facilities in the organization.

➤ Also it is observed that there is little bit of dissatisfaction regarding the Promotion policy and reward system adopted in APSRTC.

➤ The results of the data reveal that organization structure and climate have no significant impact on the level of management.

➤ It is observed that HRD Practices are not designed based on the zonal level needs.

➤ As a whole it is identified that the HRD Practices adopted by the corporation are satisfactory.

Chapter - I

INTRODUCTION TO HUMAN RESOURCE DEVELOPMENT: CONCEPTUAL EXPOSITION

The thesis aims to focus on the HRD practices in APSRTC with reference to Vizanagaram Zone. In the study, the main objective of the researcher is to examine the road Transport Sector in India, identify the existing HRD practices in APSRTC, the influence of HRD practices on the organization, and suggest measures to improve the performance of employees in the organization. At this juncture, the present chapter deals with the concepts, theories principles, fuctions, evaluation of HRD as an introductory backgroud of the present study.

1. 1. INTRODUCTION

Human Resource Management is perhaps, the oldest and most widely researched subject in management; with technological advances, cultural diversities, and occurance of peoples expectations undergo fundamental shifts towards newer and newer dimensions. In this rapid changing environment, human resources development, a part of HRM plays an important factor to determine an organization's success.

Human resource development is essential for every dynamic and growth oriented organisation. The success of any organisation depends upon the quality and competence of human resources, who will decide, how and when the human resources and other resources are acquired and utilised. Of all the tasks of the management, managing the human component is the central and most important task because all else depends upon how well it is done[1]. "Human resources" may be thought of as "the knowledge, skills, creative abilities and benefits of an organisation's work force, as well as the values, attitudes and benefits of an individual involved... It is the sum total of inherent abilities, acquired knowledge and skills represented by the talents and aptitudes of the employed persons."[2] Unlike other resources like money or physical equipment, human resources are the most valuable assets of an organisation. Human resources have most potential and versatile capabilities; utilisation of human resources to the maximum possible extent, helps the organisation in achieving its goals.

A country may possess abundant and inexhaustible natural and physical resources, and the necessary machinery and capital but, unless there are men who can mobilize, organise and harness resources for the production of goods and services, it cannot make rapid strides towards economic and social advancement[3]. Galbraith, a renowned economist, stated that well-educated and well trained workforce is not only an economic resource, but is also nation's greatest form of capital[4]. Despite technological advancement, the rate of increase in human capital is vital for developing nations to accelerate the pace of economic growth. No country can generate income and wealth of its nation without human power. So developing human resources should be part of country's economic planning.

1.2. Definitions of HRD:

Human resource development (HRD) is defined in various ways by different authors. Few important definitions were discussed hereunder:

> According to Leonard Nadler, "Human resource development is a series of organised activities, conducted within a specialised time and designed to produce behavioural changes[5]."

> In the words of M. N. Khan, "HRD is the process of increasing knowledge, skills, capabilities and positive work attitude and values of all people working at all levels in a business undertaking[6]".

> Dr. Len Nadler says, "HRD means an organized learning experience, with an objective of producing the possibility of performance change[7]".

> According to Uday Pareek, 1991, "HRD is a new systematic approach to proactively deal with issues, related to individual employees and teams, and organizations and a movement to develop organizational capability to manage change and challenge[8]".

> Ellen Dowling said that Human Resources Development (HRD) refers to the function (or discipline) that focuses on the people who work for a company. HRD specialists (both internal employees and external consultants) use a variety of performance assessment and management tools to help the company's workers improve their job skills, increase their job satisfaction and plan for a full and rewarding future[9].

Human resource development is a conceptual framework of acquiring or sharpening capabilities required to perform various functions associated with their present and future roles. It helps the employees develop their personal and organisational skills, knowledge and abilities. HRD includes employee training and development, performance management and development, employee career development, coaching, mentoring, key employee identification and organisation development.

1.3. History of HRD:

The HRD function has gained a lot of momentum in the last decade. The term "Human Resource Development" was coined by Leonard Nadler, Professor Emeritus at George Washington University and author of "The Handbook of Human Resource Development." Nadler first publicized the term at the 1969 American Society for Training and Development conference in Miami. With his wife, Zeace, Nadler has since written many books about training and development, including "Every Manager's Guide to Human Resource Development[10]."

Human Resources Development (HRD) as a theory is a framework for the expansion of human capital within an organization through the development of both the organization and the individual to achieve performance improvement.

Adam Smith states, "The capacities of individuals depended on their access to education[11]". Human Resource Development is the integrated use of training, organization, and career development efforts to improve individual, group and organizational effectiveness. HRD develops the key competencies that enable individuals in organizations to perform current and future jobs through planned learning activities. Groups within organizations use HRD to initiate and manage change. Also, HRD ensures a match between individual and organizational needs[12].

1.4. Evaluation of HRD

The evoluation of HRD can be discussed in 2 stages:

1. A global perspective
2. An Indian perspective

1. At global level we have:

-   Emergence of apprentice-ship training program and collective bargaining mechanisms;
-   Emergence of vocational training program and factory schools;
-   Training programs for semi – skilled workers; and
-   Emergence of training as a profession.

2. An Indian perspective:- growth and development of HR in India.

-   Emergence of apprenticeship training programs and collective bargaining mechanisms:
    In America, during seventeenth century, skilled artisans used to produce almost all household article like utensils, furniture, shoes, clothing etc. With these articles they operated small shops. At the beginning, it was a one man show, there after when demand for the products increased, the artisans appointed additional workers.
    At that time, as there were no schools available to train the workers the artisans (shop owners) themselves turned into trainers and trained the workers (apprentices).

The apprentices thus mastered all the crafts were called as "yeomen". Yeomen's at this stage if they wished to start a new shop could leave the artisans. But as the yeomen were paid very little wages they were unable to mobilize sufficient funds to establish a shop of their own.

The growth in business led to the development of a number of yeomen by the craftsman. In order to limit the growing number of yeomen, master craftsmen established "craft guilds" to regulate the aspects relating to working, wages and apprentice testing procedures, etc. The craft guilds, also grew in power, making it still more difficult for the yeomen to establish their own craft shops.

Yeomen, on the other hand, counter balanced the powerful craft guilds by establishing "yeomenaries". This yeomenary served as a collective voice in negotiating higher wages and better working conditions from the craftsmen. Modern labour union movement has its start here[13] (Desimone, 1998)

Emergence of vocational training program and factory schools:-

Early vocational education programs:-
Dewitt Clinton's manual school was established in NewYork in 1809. In 1863, President Licoln signs the land grant act promoting A & M College. Smith Hughes Act, 1917 provides funding for vocational education at the state level. These early vocational education programs provide occupational training to unskilled young people who were either unemployed or had criminal schools.

Early factory schools:
The factory systems were started with the advent of industrial revolution in the late 19th century. This began to replace the hard tools of the artisans with scientific management principles in this period. The products were produced using machines by semi – skilled workers. Semi – skilled workers produced more qualitative and quantitative products than those of skilled workers in a small craft shop by using machines.

The growth of factories increased the demand for skilled workers, engineers, machines and skilled mechanics to design build and repair the machines. Consequent to the growing demand for skilled workers, factories had to create factory schools that offered mechanical and machine training programs. These factory schools in a short duration focuses on the skills needed in a particular job and imparted training to its workers to the extent needed.

Emergence of training program for skilled and semi – skilled workers:-

In 1913, Ford motor company launched its first mass production model T- Cars, it was using assembly line. Due to its mass production, the cars were made affordable to a large segment of public and resulted in great demand for these cars. This situation led the ford company to design more assembly lines and increased the need for semi and skilled works for its new assembly line. The mass production success in Ford Company was copied by most of the automobile manufactures occurred more demand for semiskilled workers.

With the outbreak of First World War, all the factories which produce non-military goods had to retool their machinery and retrain their semi – skilled and unskilled workers to produce military items. Charles Aller, director of training of the US shipping board, introduced a four step instructional training method called as "show, tell, do and check" - for all the training programs offered by the shipping board[14] (Miller, 1987). Later this training was called as job instruction training.

Emergence of training as a profession:-

The outbreak of Second World War also forced industries to retool their factories to support the war effort. The federal government in order to help in this process established training within industry (TWI) service to co-ordinate training programmers across defense related industries. TWI also trained company instructors to teach their programs at their plant. After the end of the world war, TWI had trained around 23,000 instructors, 2 millions certified supervisors[15], (Miller, 1987) etc.

Many defense related companies established their own training departments with the trained instructors from TWI. These departments were responsible for designing, co-coordinating and implementing training programs in their organization.

In 1942, the American society for training directors (ASTD) was established to maintain certain standards within the emerging training profession. The members for this society were people who had experience in training or related field or a college student related to this profession.

Slowly the transformation took place in the role performed by the professional trainers during 1960s and 1970s. Professional trainers realized that their role is not confined to train employees but also to coach and counsel employees. This additional enhancement role led to rename the society as American society for training and development (ASTD).

During the period 1970s and 1980s ASTD organized several conferences discussing the emerging field of training and development. This resulted in ASTD approving the term HRD in recognition for the growth and development in that field.

Indian perspective of growth & development of HR In India:-

In India, after the completion of First World War the state felt necessity to protect the welfare of workers. This resulted in the emergence of trade union movement and finally gave a formal recognition to the Trade Union Act, 1926. Tata group and many others factories introduced labour welfare activities like provident fund and leave rules.

In India, this can be considered as the beginning of HR as a field. Later in 1982 by the recommendation of royal commission labour welfare officers were appointed to deal with the selection and grievance related to the handling of the employees. After the introduction of factories Act, 1948 it was made mandatory for factories to have welfare officers in establishments having more than 500 workers. All these developments laid the foundations for the personnel function in India[16][17] (Balasubramanian, 1994, 1995). In 1950s to help the development of HR, two professional bodies namely Indian Institute of Personnel Management (IIPM) at Kolkata and National Institute of Labour Management (NILM) at Mumbai were established.

During 1960s, the personnel function was transformed as personnel management by slowly shifting its focus from welfare activities to IR and personnel administration.

During 1970s, with the advent of heavy industries after independence the concern for welfare was shifted to the concern for efficiency. In 1980s, professionals began to know the importance and started talking about HRM and HRD etc. During this time professional bodies IIPM and

NLPM were merged to form National Institute of Personnel Management (NIPM) at Kolkata[18]. NIPM is a professional body that conducts conferences, seminars, courses in distance mode and also publishes a journal on personnel Management.

1.4.1. Emergence of HRD:

In the early 70s two consultants Uday Pareek and Prof.T. V. Rao from the Indian Institute of Management were approached by L & T for a review exercise of their performance appraisal system. In 1974 the consultants studied the system and made recommendations for improving it. Prof. Rao & Pareek felt that a development oriented performance appraisal system may not achieve its objective unless accompanied by other sub – systems like employee counseling, potential appraisal, career planning and development training, Organization Development etc. Thus, a new HRD System was introduced at L & T in the year 1975.

They recommended that "performance appraisal, potential appraisal and counseling, career development, career planning and training & development get distinct attention as unique parts of an integrated system which we call the HRD system[19]". In India, this was the first of its kind. The new system established the linkages between various personnel related aspects such as performance appraisal, employee counseling, potential appraisal, training etc.

By the recommendations of Rao and Pareek, separate HRD development was created in the L & T Organization. Later, State Bank of India and its associates followed the recommendations of the two consultants. In 1978, Bharat Earth Movers Limited, Bangalore, one of the large public sector companies in India, established an HRD department. The HRD function started spreading in the year 1979, when IIM, Ahemadabad held first HRD workshop to discuss its concept and issues. Subsequently a series of work-shops were held to develop HRD facilities by IIMA and Indian Society for Application Behaviour Services (ISASB). HRD thus gained its importance in India.

In 1986, the Government of India established a separate ministry of HRD. It was a logical culmination of the realization of the importance of developing Human factor[20] (Ashok Kumar, 1991). The seventh five year plan 1985 – 1990) emphasized the need of HRD by stating that the productive forces of the economy can be strengthened only by realizing the creative energies of all groups of society.

The governments initiative had led a few organizations to introduce the HRD department in their organizations where as some organizations renamed their personnel department as HRD department. Thus, the term HRD also became popular in the Indian scenario.

In 1985, a national seminar was jointly organized by XLRI centre for HRD and HRD department of the L & T in Mumbai. The national HRD network took birth during this seminar to develop and facilitate learning among HRD Professionals. In 1990, this gave birth to the academy of HRD as an academic centre for training, research and extension services in HRD field.

With the LPG in 1991, the competition from overseas increased the pressure and expectation from the HR function that plays a strategic role and becomes an active player in achieving the corporate goals. The liberalization of economic policies and the increased level of competition by overseas firms have put a lot of pressure on human resource function in domestic firms in order to prepare and develop their employees to compete with international firms on efficiency and skill base[21] (Venkata Ratnam, 1995). Also these domestic firms were depending on human resource development rather than human resource management to support them[22] (Ramaswamy and Schiphorst, 2000). Thus HRM was made to play a leading role in the organizational development and meeting the competitive world.

Rao and Abraham[23] (1989) conducted a study on 'HRD practices in India', in eight different organizations and concluded that the HRD fanctions are not well structured as envisaged in mid 1970s. It was found to be more convenient driven than system driven. Later on organizations and confederations recognizing the importance of HR and HRD activities for their growth and success.

Today, in India, most of the larger public and private sectors are using the techniques and approaches of HRD to develop their work force for the achievement of organization goals along with individual satisfaction and growth. Thus, HRD movement has unique history in both Indian and Global scenario[24].

1.5. Pre-requisites of Effective HRD

Human Resource Development helps in the process of enabling organisation culture in an organization. Organization culture means creating an environment where employees are motivated to take initiative and risk, they feel enthused to experiment, innovate and they make things happen. In order to attain effective HRD, the following pre-requisites are essential:

1) **Approach of Top Level Management**: The main objective of HRD is to develop the skills and capabilities of each employee as an individual, in relation to the present and future job roles. This objective of HRD can be achieved only by having knowledge of capabilities, limitations and problems of the employees concerned. Obviously this information can be collected by top level management by being in touch with the employees at all levels. Top executives should frequently visit the work place of the workers and spend time with them to know the capabilities and problems of the workforce. By adopting this approach top management can better utilize the capabilities of the available workforce by creating trust among the people of the organization. This helps in reducing the communication gap and resolve grievances, if any, between workforce and management.

2) **Communication System and Feedback**: A proper communication system should be developed and implemented. It should provide all important information to the employees from the beginning to the end. This system should communicate both formal and informal information by getting feedback from the employees. As we know when a communication system is connected with feedback, a reliable feedback system should be structured.

3) **Conditions for growth and Development:** Human Resources are considered as the most important assets in an organization. They can be developed to an unlimited extent in order to create healthy organizational climate (openness, trust, collaboration etc). To achieve this, the progress of the company must be shared with the employees, their efforts should be appreciated and recognised by giving them rewards, promotions, incentives etc. Their excellence should be rewarded in an appropriate and acceptable way. So as to create the

condition for the development of the workers, a balanced environment amongst all these should be maintained.

4) **Investment in HRD Programme:** There is no shortcut for success. The maintenance of a healthy working climate and the development of its human resources is a very complicated process. In order to attain desired results, the top management and HRD professionals must invest proper time, funds and energy in each and every programme related to HRD. The top level management must create the path, create a development climate and help the employees to realize their potential.

5) **Proper Utilization of Human resource Skills:** HRD managers must try to make optimum utilization of available and potential human resource skills. Manpower planning and right sizing of human resources may be used for this purpose.

6) **Decentralization:** A system can be designed for the involvement of employees at all the levels of management. Giving importance to each and every employee in the organisation can create a sense of belongingness and commitment among the employees. Although major policy decisions, may be centralized but other important decisions should be decentralized with the involvement of various subordinates. Thus a balanced approach should be maintained in the centralization and decentralization.

Hence by adopting the above pre-requisites in the organization, even ordinary people can produce extraordinary results. The people in the concern grow and help the organization to realize their goals and progress. (Khurana et al, 2009)

1.6. HR and HRD

The terms Human Resource or Human Resource Development are frequently used by management experts, while talking about managing business or industrial organizations. Beer, Spector, Lawrence, and other professors of the Harward Business School, and Michael Poole, the chief editor of International Journal of Human Resources Management (IJHRM) consider the "People as the most important single asset of any organization"[25].

Jane Weightman in his book, 'Managing Human Resources' writes that "managing human resources is an extremely important part of making organisation work well". According to him "managing human resources implies acknowledging that the humans are the most important factor in an organization[26]".

Today HRD is treated far beyond the traditional personnel function. HRD and many other are subsets of HR function. The traditional personnel function which had been more of a maintenance function with very little growth, focus now transformed into more pro-active and change-oriented. Udai Pareek in a talk at the National Institute of Personnel Management Convention, 1978 on 'Personnel Management in search of a soul' stated that the modern HR function has HRD at its core; HRD is its soul. According to T. V. Rao, the HR function, as it is evolved in India, consists of three main subfunctions, HRD, Industrial Relations and worker affairs and human resource administration. All three can be combined to form human resource management (HRM). However, HRD includes all aspects of competence, commitment and culture building. Earlier some aspects of HR function that mattered like in culture, commitment and competence building are not included as a part of HRD are now included as contextual factors of HRD. The Traditional HRD function had limited space with manpower planning, recruitment and placement, despite they are significant with the influence of factors in that context. Hence, the HRD function cannot be administered without HR and also HR cannot be dispense without HRD in the present global business backdrop. As a matter of fact, both HRD and HR are processed together to attain competitive advantage. An extended definition of HRD includes a number of elements of the HR function, whereas a focused and narrowed down definition of the HR function can mean HRD[27].

HRM and HRD both are very crucial topics of management because of its relavance with the organisation. The tasks Human resource management and human resource development can be differentiated on the following grounds:

- The human resource management targets towards maintenance of human resources whereas human resource development is targeted towards development of human resources.

- In case of organisation structure, human resource management is independent whereas human resource development creates a structure, which is inter-dependent and inter-related.
- Human resource management mainly focuses to improve the efficiency of the employees whereas HRD focuses at the development of the employees as well as organisation as a whole.
- Responsibility of human resource development is given to the personnel/human resource management department and specifically to personnel manager whereas responsibility of HRD is given to all managers at various levels of the organisation.
- HRM motivates the employees by giving them monetary incentives or rewards whereas human resource development stresses on motivating people by satisfying higher-order needs[28]. (Khurana et al, 2009)

1.7 Theoretical Foundations of HRD:-

In the organizational context, the field of Human Resource Development (HRD) has been borrowed from other disciplines such as Psychological theory, Economic theory, and Systems theory. A theory is a set of statements or principles devised to explain a group of facts or phenomena, especially one that has been repeatedly tested or is widely accepted and can be used to make predictions about natural phenomena. The main intention of discussing these theories is to acknowledge the fact that HRD should continue to develop as a discipline and the integration of economic, psychological and system theories serve as a unique theoretical foundation of Human Resource Development.

Figure 1.1: HRD Theories

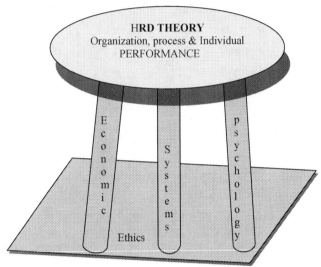

Source: Richard A. Swanson, March, 2006

• **Economic Foundation of HRD**

In the beginning stages of human civilization, business traced its roots in one form or the other. Every business activity is necessarily an economic activity, to give and take has been the two aspects over which the base of the business lies. Previously, it was carried out on an individual basis and with the passage of time, it was transformed in the shape of a formal organized structure which is familiar as 'Organisation'. The below figure depicts the economic justification of having HRD in the organizational context.

Figure 1.2: Economic Foundation of HRD

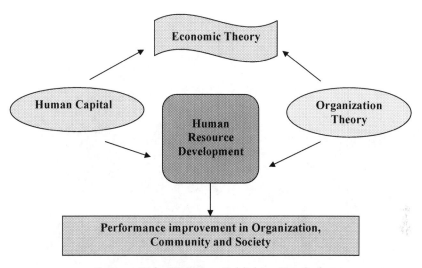

Source: Deb: 2010, Ane Publishing Pvt. Ltd.

An organisation is a structured entity through which business activity is carried out for achieving economic objectives of the organisation. From the above figure it is clear that in the organizational context economic theory holds the epicenter position in the evolution of the concept of Human Resource Development. Economics is the study of how scarce resources are optimally allocated and utilized. It consists of certain concepts of efficiency which could help in designing a framework for ensuring maximum societal well-being. So, economics is considered to be the theory of human behaviour.

• **Psychological Foundation of HRD**

In the organizational context, psychology is concerned about the individual behaviour at work. From the global scenario, organization to be effective and well-organized in the present competitive edge; it must take care of maintaining a cohesive working environment where the working conditions are integrated with the talents and skills of the human resource. The practical application of psychological tools to solve problems of the employees working in the organizations facilitates their integration with the organizational climate and results in enriched and enhanced performance.

Figure 1.3: Essentials of a Psychological Theory

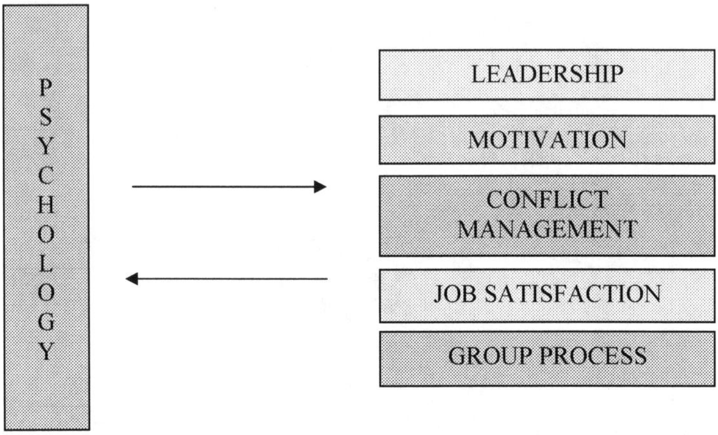

Source: Deb, Ane Publishing Pvt. Ltd., 2010.

The theory is operated at the individual level as well as at a group and at organizational level. It explicits the way how the perceptions, attitudes, behaviour of an individual can affect upon the technologies, internal sub-systems, processes, goals and objectives of the organization. Understanding the psychological perspective is critical to the organizational performance because it brings key skills and perspectives that effectively facilitate change in culture and shifts in strategy to address the complex challenges and risks facing organizations. To sustain organizational effectiveness, there is a need to strike a balance between the individual needs and goals with that of the organization. Human considerations such as adapting with the dynamic changes of time, organizational decisions based on the performance of the employees, perceived equity has immense impact on individual performance and ultimately sways over organizational performance. The working environment should be so congenial that the employees working there should feel relaxed and satisfied.

- **Systems Foundation of HRD**

Systems theory was founded in the midst of 1940s-1970s by Ludwig Von Bertalanffy, William Ross Ashby and others. This theory was derived from principles of philosophy, sociology, organizational theory, management, and economics and among other fields. It sees the world in terms of 'systems' where each system is a 'whole' that is more than the sum of its parts, but also itself as a part of larger system. System theory or general system theory is an interdisciplinary field that studies the systems as a whole.

Organizations maintain a synchronism between the internal affairs of the organization and the business environment by interacting with the external environment; it is termed as an open system. The theory is based on the assumption that an organization or an individual cannot develop in vacuum, they have to expose themselves to the external world for their growth and development. In the organizational aspect, HRD is a subsystem and a system of its own because human resources are prime movers of all the other physical resources and transform those input resources into valuable output in the form of useful products and services. This process of transformation involves a host of human resource development processes, because of the reason that human efforts are required to augment the performance by familiarizing changes in human behavior. To describe the systems model, diagrammatic model is shown.

Figure 1.4: Systems Model of Organization

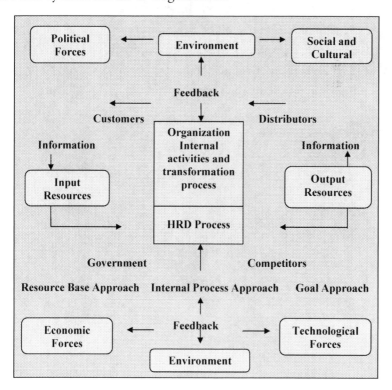

1.8 HRD Process

HRD is a process, not merely a set of techniques and mechanisms. The techniques and mechanisms such as training and development, performance appraisal, counselling, and organization development interventions are used to accelerate this process in a un-ending way. As the process has no boundary, the mechanisms may need to be examined at regular intervals to see whether they are promoting or hindering the process. In order to facilitate this process of development, organisations have to plan and allocate organisational resources for the purpose, and by exemplifying an HRD philosophy that value of human beings in the organisations can promote development.

HRD Process and Hrd Climate

Human Resource Development Practices leads to development of desired Human Resource Development Climate or Process. HRD culture is a crutial part of organizational climate. HRD processes facilitate the development of an HRD culture in the organization. In the words of T. V. Rao, "Human Resource Development Climate is the perception of the employees about the Human Resource Development Culture in the organization". HRD experts mostly use "OCTAPACE" to state the important features of HRD climate. The following figure presents the salient features of HRD Culture.

Figure 1.5: HRD Process

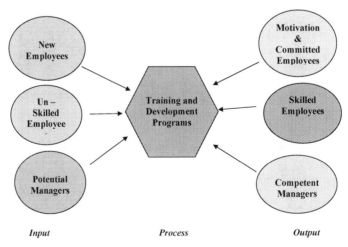

Input   *Process*   *Output*

Figure 1.6: Features of HRD Climate

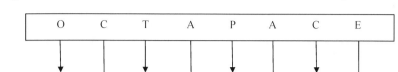

In an organisation, HRD Climate is reflected by its role clarity, openness, trust, team – work, Pro- active orientation, planning for the development of every employee etc. Human Resource Development climate and processes are dependent on personnel policies, investments on HRD, top management commitments, line manager's interest, culture etc. To sum up the relationship between HRD mechanism and HRD processes and climate can be explained as under:

a) HRD Practices/ mechanisms are most useful instruments/ interventions to develop a healthy HRD Climate.

b) HRD instruments are used to develop desired HRD processes. For instance, Performance and Potential Appraisal help to assess and determine the competence required for job performance. Reviews, Discussions, Feedback, Counselling Session help in building trust and better senior – subordinate relations. Role Analysis exercises result in role – clarity in the organization. Training and Potential Development exercises have proactive orientation. Job enrichment is a deliberate exercise of upgrading risk and responsibility in work – group. OD exercise helps to manage change and problems in the organization. It promotes openness, effective communication, inter – departmental collaboration in the organization. it aims at providing a climate for human growth and Development.

c) HRD Climate is dependent on HRD mechanism as well as personnel policies, top management styles etc.,

d) HRD mechanism and personnel policies should be periodically reviewed to create/ develop desired HRD Climate.

1.9 HRD PRACTICES / SUB-SYSTEMS/ MECHANISMS:-

The main objective of HRD practices in an organization is to train the existing employees to develop their skills and knowledge and is also oriented toward socializing the new employees in the organization by providing required skills and abilities to handle present and future job goals more efficiently.

The term human resource development has been used at micro and macro level. At the macro-level, in the context of improving the quality of human life, it takes wealth, capabilities, skills, attitudes of people which are more useful to the overall development of the organisation and nation's as well. At the micro level, HRD represents the improvement in quality of employees so as to achieve higher level of productivity. The objective is to develop certain new capabilities in people to help them perform present job in a better way and to accept future job challenges[29].

HRD practices in an organization are classified into primary practices and secondary practices. Primary practices include, training and development; organizational development and career development. In order to perform organizational goals more efficiently, these primary practices are linked with secondary practices. Secondary practices consist of role analysis and development; performance appraisal; potential appraisal; performance counseling employee orientation; succession planning, quality circles, information sharing; participative devices & QWL, quality circles; HRIS and research. The following figure shows the model of HRD functions.

Training and Development:

Training involves the process of providing the knowledge, skill and abilities required for an individual to perform a specific job or task. Development deals with preparing the individual to perform the current job in a better way and also to handle future responsibilities.

Training and Delopment function starts right from the time an employee joins an organization and continues until the individual leaves the organisation. At the time of joining, the individual is given orientation training that includes input as to the norms and values of the organisation and how to function within the job. Later, the individual is put to technical or skill training which helps him to develop the skills needed to perform the job.

Once the individual is set in the job, HRD activities focuses on the development aspect of the individual. Development may take the form of coaching, councelling and putting an individual through management development and training programs. These training programes help the individual to takeup higher responsibility and also do the work alloted to them in a more efficient way.

Organization Development:

It can be defined as applying behavioural science concepts to bring about planned change in the organisation. The aim of OD is to bring about organizational effectiveness by indulging in micro and macro level changes. Some of the micro level changes are team – building, conflict resolution etc. Macro level changes are structual reorganization, cultural transformation etc. Amongst these changes, HRD professionals role is to act as a change agent.

Career Development:

Career Planning involves activities performed by an individual to access his skills and abilities. Career management involves all the steps taken to achieve this career plan. Career Development consists of both Career Planning and Career Management. It is a process by which an individual progresses through a series of stages each of which is characterized by a relatively unique set of issues, themes and tasks.

Individuals can progress in their career through proper training and development. Organisations are now planning their training and development programs not only with the organizational point of view but also according to the individual career growth needs.

Role analysis and development:

Role studies are very important to the development, training and professionalization of HRD[30] (Nadler and Nadler, 1969). They may be used to define a role more clearly so as to avoid ambiguity in the expectation from that role. This helps in:

1. Clarifing the role for the role occupant
2. Preparing the role description and
3. Reduces role ambiguity

This secondary function has to be performed by the HRD person in order to carry out appraisal, identify training and development needs of the role occupant etc. When roles are analysed, other such systems may follow; It will also bring about increased role clarity, increased accountability, and a feeling of significance among the occupants of the roles.

Employee Orientation:

Employee orientation builds up the new employees to contribute more quickly to the business. It is also essential to help the employees to meet the challenges they face in coping with the radical change and organizational restructuring, or the challenges of adapting to new work pattern.

Effective orientation is implicated with motivating people to become productive in the shortest time and to stay with the organization. A comprehensive and succesful orientation scheme is one that meets the needs of employees as they progress into their organization. Initially, they will be made to know about the industrial safety, security, health, comfort and welfare. Subsequently, they will be made aware of the role and responsibilities expected of them. Finally, they would be shown their role in the team and how they can make a contribution to the organization and its objective.

The role of the HRD staff in employee orientation is in developing an effective and quicker training program and assisting with a process that is essentially controlled by the various line managers in an organization.

Performance Appraisal:

Performace Appraisal is the assessment of individual's performance in a systematic way and used developmental tool for all round development of an employee and the organization. It allows decision-making for particular purpose which includes:

1. **Clarifying expectations and reducing ambiguity about performance:** When an employee's performance is appraised, he is made clear regarding his / her performance areas more lucidly and gets clarity about the deviations in the expectations from his job.

2. **Improving Individual Performance:** The clarity an individual obtains from his appraisal will help him to identify areas of strengths and weaknesses. This provides him an opportunity to work on his shortcomings.

3. **Determination of rewards:** The identification of gaps between actual performance and expected standards helps the organizations in fixation of rewards and incentives.

4. **Improving motivation and morale:** The Provision of rewards and incentives and the clarity of work expectations would facilitate an individual to improve the standards of performance and help in motivating him and boosting his morale.

5. **Identifying training and development opportunities:** The gap identified between the actual and expected performance through the appraisal process clearly depicts the areas of improvement. This helps in planning the necessary training and development activities for the individual.

6. **Selecting people for promotion:** The target achievement analysis undertaken through the performance appraisal process is one of the important inputs which guides the organization to identify the deserving candidates to shoulder higher responsibilities.

7. **Managing careers:** During the individual's career life cycle in an organization, the performane exercise helps to reinforce the achievements and shortcomings at a particular period of time. This helps in monitoring the career progression of an individual and plan further career activities.

8. **Counselling:** The performance appraisal exercise forms the basis for the higher ups in the organization to guide and counsel the subordinates to identify their lacunae and proceed in the right direction.

9. **Discipline:** An individual's performance progression is checked through performance appraisal which helps to discipline his work activities.

10. **Planning remedial actions:** Remedial actions could be worked jointly by the organization and the individual based on the results of the appraisal process.

11. **Setting goals and targets:** Inputs drawn from past performance helps to fix fresh targets for the forthcoming years.

Thus, it is understood that performance assessment and appraisal are not only used as a control mechanisms but also used for performance improvement of the individual employee and as a tool for competitive advantage for both the individual and the organization.

Potential Appraisal:

The term 'potential' refers to the hidden talent and skills possessed by an employee. The employee might or might not be aware of them. Potential appraisal is a future – oriented appraisal whose main objective is to identify and evaluate the potential of the employees to assume higher positions and responsibilities in the organizational hierarchy. Many organizations consider and use potential appraisal as a part of the performance appraisal processes. The appraisal is carried out on the basis of:

(i) Supervisor's observations,
(ii) Data retrieved from the earlier performance of the employee's,
(iii) Performance on roles in simulated settings related to a new position.
(Rao, 2005)

Performance Counselling:

Performance Counselling refers to the help provided by a manager to his subordinates in analysing their performance and other job behaviour in order to increase their effectiveness in the job. Potential Appraisal can be made development oriented only when it is followed by proper performance counselling. So the focus of performance counselling is to identify the development needs of the employees based on his or her performance appraisal. It acts as an important function in HRD by facilitating the Performance Appraisal process and improving its effectiveness.

Succession Planning:

Succession planning is a process for identifying and developing internal employees with with the potential to fill key business leadership positions in the organization.

The benefits that organizations derive due to succession planning include:

1. Succession planning engages senior management in a disciplined review of leadership talent.
2. It guides development activities of key executives.
3. It brings selection systems, reward systems and management development into alignment with the process of leadership renewal.
4. Assures continuity of leadership.
5. Avoids transition problems.

Human Resource Information System and Research:

Another secondary function of HRD department is proper and systematic maintenance of information about every employee. This may be used for counselling, training and development, career planning, promotion etc. This information can also be used as a base for research on employee performance.

The "government as prime mover" in development was reinforced by the realization in the late fifties that insufficient entrepreneurship was leading to serious absorptive capacity constraints to the provision of foreign aid and the undertaking of the government – sponsored investment projects. In the second phase, lasting from 1979 to about 1996, was a continuation of then Neoclassical "getting price right" line of thought. Neo-classical trade theorists (Krueger, and Bhagwati), who came to dominate the field of economic development, suggested that international trade can provide a substitute for low domestic aggregate demand. Governments should also remove price distortions in domestic factor and commodity markets ("get prices right") to induce suitable movement of factors among sectors, encourage the adoption of appropriate technology, and increase capital accumulation. In this view, domestic and international liberalization programs would suffice to bring about sustained economic growth and structural change[31]. (Adelman, 1999)

HRD is an essential component for growth and economic development. Government can play a vital role in the development of human resource. The enhancement of HRD of a country is dependent on the government and national policies, while at the firm or micro level HRD can happen through training and efficient utilization of resources. In India, we have a full fledged separate ministry for the purpose of covering education, health, sport etc. But there are certain loopholes like bureaucracy, red-tapism etc. which are needed to be filled up in the light of substantial development for the nation. Policies should be framed in a manner that is capable of tackling the objectives of HRD. There should be task forces, rotating employees in various sections and sub sections to become familiar with the entire system. They should work efficiently and take a lead in HRD because government's investment in the field will be of autonomous nature i.e. without any profit motive. It will also induce the private sector to make large investments in this area. Human resources of any country is the national asset and they need developments from time to time to meet the edge of growing competition at a global level. Overall progress of a country depends largely on its developed workforce. Hence they should be helped in developing their potential to shoulder responsibility of Nation's development (Sheikh, 2009).

1.12. Future HRD Perspectives

After globalization, industries and firms are bound to face the challenges of the new times. To survive in this era of fierce competition, organizations require bold, innovative and dynamic workforce or else they are eased out of the main stream of management in the corporate world. The main responsibility of the HRD strategists is that they should have a farsighted vision in framing, formulating, and implementing strategies which could exploit the opportunities available in the present scenario to beat out the competition. Thus, an HRD manager must broaden his horizons of creativity and innovations to trace out the better prospects for growth of HRD. Hereunder, few perspectives have been analyzed and discussed.

- Advanced Technology.
- New and Diverse customers.
- Changes in the sources of raw materials and financial resources.
- Corporate Restructuring
- Modification in the Structure of Industries.
- Changes in the regulatory framework of government regarding corporate governance.
- Downsizing of organizations/ enterprises.
- Mergers and acquisitions.
- New and revised corporate strategies.
- Work simplification methods/ processess.
- Exploration of newer markets and alteration of existing markets.
- Diversification of products and services[32] (Swarajayalakshmi, 2005).

In the changing global competitive environment, Human resources constitute the most valuable asset in the context of development and growth perspective of the organization. The quality of human element contribution is dependent on the relative performances of nations, regions of economy, industrial Sectors as well as corporate enterprises[33]. Therefore, it is the vital responsibility of the HRD managers to look after the desired areas of concern for the persistence of development of skills and knowledge of the work force by making arrangements to make sure that these necessary developments take place in a cohesive and well – organized manner.

1.13. CONCLUSION

The present chapter has dealt with the concepts, theories and origin of HRD at length along with its theories, principles and sub-systems of HRD. The next chapter would deal with the review of literature pertaining to HRD and different aspects associated with HRD. The succeeding chapter also focuses on literature connected to APSRTC and other SRTU's.

Chapter - II

REVIEW OF LITERATURE

The present chapter portrays the entire framework of the research construct. The chapter gives a preview of research methodology adopted, sample frame, hypothesis of the study, objectives and limitations of the study. The researcher's objective in this chapter is to present and discuss few studies that are done retrospectively in the field of Human Resource Development and Road Transport Industry.

INTRODUCTION

Any research is incomplete if it doesn't take literature review into account. The present review includes several research Papers, Books and Thesis in order to provide an insight into the academic endeavors' pertaining to the concept of HRD and factors relating to HRD. The discussion covers varied arguments and meaningful findings pertaining to the previous studies. The following cited reviews are few important studies conducted by various researchers in the field of HRD in India and foreign countries.

2.1 Retrospective Reviews on Human Resource Development

Alexander E. Ellinger and Andrea D. Ellinger[34] **(2014)** through their study propose that organizations can create and maintain competitive advantage by leveraging the expertise of human resource development (HRD) professionals to provide a range of developmental and change-oriented interventions related to critical supply chain manager skill sets that are currently in short supply.

Anushree Banerjee[35] **(2014)** identified that the major issues that restrain the industry from achieving high economic value are shortage of qualified personnel, shortage of tourism training institutes, shortage of well qualified trainers, working conditions for the employees. Policies which can help the employees to work in supportive environment are also a point of concern. So the author in this article attempted to judge the work done by the HRD team of the tourism industry with special reference to Jet Airways India Ltd.

Peter McGraw[36] **(2014)** article outlines, analyzes, and comments on the pattern of HRD from the mid-1990s to the present day with reference to economic turbulence and responses to it, especially since the beginning of the global financial crisis in 2007. The central themes of the review are the emergence of more "performance" oriented approaches toward HRD assessment and evaluation, the HRD practices of multinational companies (MNCs) operating in Australia compared with locally owned organizations, and HRD practices within foreign owned MNCs from different home countries. Data for the article is drawn primarily from the analysis of three iterations of the Cranfield Network on International Human Resource Management (CRANET) Australia survey in the years 1996, 1999, and 2009.

Clíodhna MacKenzie et al[37] **(2014)** with their study on Global Financial and Economic Crisis starting in 2007 tried to find the solution for the contribution of Human Resource Development (HRD) strategies and practices to the crisis. The study with its primary focus on the development of human resources, argued that HRD aligned itself too closely with the strategic goals of organizations, often times profit centric, and failed to provide leaders with the skills, knowledge, and values required to question the decisions made by organizations in the pursuit of profit goals and the development of a culture of risk taking. The study found that HRD strategies, practices, and processes are factors which may have contributed to a culture of excessive risk taking and ineffective decision making. The authors also outline the implications for HRD theory and practice.

Maura Sheehan[38] **(2014)** analysis shows that T&D investment is highly sensitive to uncertainty, especially general T&D. Given the importance of T&D—especially general T&D for sustained competitive advantage—it is absolutely essential that investment is sustained, even in the presence of uncertainty. Viewing and treating T&D as an investment, rather than its current accountancy configuration, as "expenditure," can help to ensure T&D investment is maintained. Practitioners need to become more confident and competent in demonstrating that T&D is an investment, with the potential to generate significant returns for organizations, especially in relation to sustained competitive advantage.

Jie Ke and Greg G. Wang[39] **(2014)** analyses the linking China's ethical dilemmas to traditional cultural beliefs and values is necessary to understand the ethical issues in dealing with increased uncertainty in future development. Three major cultural beliefs/ideologies that influence ethical behaviors in China are analyzed: Confucianism, Taoism, and Capitalism. Ethical imperatives derived from cultural analysis and HRD implications are presented at the national, organizational, and individual level.

Saul Carliner[40] **(2014)** in his research on 'Human Performance Technology and HRD' stated that Performance—the achievement of results—is central to definitions of HRD. Human Performance Technology (HPT) refers to a systematic methodology for developing performance in individuals and organizations. Through a systematic process, HPT explores issues at the organizational, unit, and individual level and several advantages of HPT.

Dr. Leigh Burrows[41] **(2014)** explores the outcome when they pretend that emotions and spirit do not exist. The author also highlights the potential of mindfulness to contribute to personal, interpersonal and structural/organizational elements of workforce development. Within the emerging areas of spirituality and mindfulness it is entirely possible to transfer new knowledge across industrial and/or professional sectors, even when the contexts and processes are different, if the emphasis is placed on stimulating reflection and learning.

Dr. Jim Stewart and Dr. Sally Sambrook[42] **(2014)** examined recent developments in 'critical HRD' (CHRD). The concept of human resource development (HRD) is first explained as an alternative to 'workforce development'. This includes the argument that HRD is broader in scope and so encompasses the more limited term 'workforce development'. Then CHRD is explored as a term that denotes a shift in theorizing and research on HRD which aims to question and challenge conventional understandings of the purpose and means of facilitating learning in work organizations. This is preceded by a section explaining the relationship of CHRD with the broader critiques of organization and management studies adopted in critical management studies (CMS), which provides some of the context of CHRD.

Melinde Coetzee and Dries (A.M.G.) Schreuder[43] **(2014)** explores the relevance of Schein's career anchor theory to contemporary career development by presenting an overview of various research findings that show how people's career anchors influence their subjective experiences of their work and careers.

Atluri Bala Saraswathi[44] **(2013)** stated that to reach organizational effectiveness and development at the end, and to face the challenges that they confront with organizations therefore have to upgrade their ethics, methods, technological and managerial skills and finally the HRD Culture. While there has been a great deal of concern on how to usher the environmental changes for organizational effectiveness, by putting systems in place that foster work culture, skills, capabilities and behavioural aspects to meet the challenges, arriving at the same is well within the realm of HRD that forms the crux of organizational reengineering, which is the core of this exploratory study under a case study design.

Asad Abbas and Ali Madni[45] **(2013)** carried out research in the field of HRM and HRD. Researchers found out that there is a gap in body of knowledge that there is no comprehensive business process model for human resource development field. The article sets out to examine the relationship between current business process reengineering activities and Human Resource Development. This research's objective is to give a model explaining business process approach of Human Resource Development.

Sheema Tarab[46] **(2013)** in her study highlights the gaps that have been analyzed on the basis of responses retrieved by the employees of BSNL and Reliance at managerial and non-managerial level such as, the inappropriate psychological climate, lack of arrangements for specific training programmes, performance appraisal, less autonomy in working for employees at lower levels, awareness of policies followed in the concerned organizations, participative management etc.

Bhaskar Purohit and R.K. Verma[47] **(2013)** assessed the perception of 42 Medical Officers (MOs) about the overall importance given to various dimensions of the HRD climate. The study instrument measured 10 HRD dimensions. The instrument had 27 statements that were based on a 5-point

Likert scale. Each statement represented one of the 10 HRD dimensions and higher averages/score indicated a better perception of the HRD climate for that particular dimension. The study findings indicate that 'Participation' is given the least importance followed by 'Succession Planning'. The study also found that 'Rewards and Welfare' was perceived to be given the highest importance. It can be concluded that the overall HRD climate from the viewpoint of MOs needs improvement. Such improvements are possible if there is a genuine focus in development of people and if there is a dedicated HRD Department in the Health System that treats various sub systems of HR like appraisal, counseling, rewards and welfare, etc., as interdependent rather than independent.

Hee Sung Lee and Jeong Rok Oh[48] *(2013)* propose a conceptual model for a community of practice, which is the core of knowledge management, by conducting an integrative literature review. Community of practices can effectively solve business problems or achieve specific objectives by generating and sharing powerful knowledge. The conceptual model suggests successive approaches to develop community of practice, starting with accomplishing the fundamental dimension of motivating employees, through creating an organizational culture, and culminating in the strategic dimension of providing organizational support. The model also indicates potential barriers when implementing knowledge management interventions, such as cultural issues, internal fear of criticism, external confidentiality issues, lack of time, and shortage of technology. Based on the conceptual model, implications and recommendations for HRD practitioners seeking to optimally implement communities of practice in their organizations are presented.

Dan Li[49] **(2013)** states that under current retirement policy, a large number of Yong Retirees' HRD do not continue to be developed and human resources are idle or waste. In the view of this, firstly, this article analyzes the retirement policy and the present situation of young retiree human resources development and the conclusion is that part of the quantity and the proportion of this resource are growing rapidly, but the structure is not balanced. Secondly, this paper analyzed the utilization effect from the angle of economic effect and social effect, and then concludes that, on one hand the development of the old human resources can meet the needs of social and economic development. On the other hand, to meet the needs of the elderly themselves the human resources development strategy is put forward.

Pi-Chi Han[50] **(2013)** attempts to propose an integrative intercultural effectiveness (ICE) model, modified from Han's (2012) study, as the guidelines for reexamining the structure and content of IHRD programs for developing global management and international workforce, to conceptualize intercultural competence, to identify the cross-cultural learning processes for acquiring initial and optimal learning outcomes, and to advance IHRD professionalism in the theoretical understanding of developing ICE for the global workforce and management. The author through this paper recommends IHRD needs to take a progressive approach for the organizations. They must move from reactive to proactive role and facilitate continuous learning in the cross-cultural arena. Most importantly, a call to manage change, to facilitate intercultural competencies, and to develop global talent for IHRD becomes crucial for organizations to be globally competitive.

Dr. Rinku Sanjeev et al[51] **(2013)** found that effectiveness of training and development program in FMCG organization can be influenced by different factors like clarity in setting the objective of training program, day-to-day feedback and discussion of trainee's performance, etc. The result also shows that the effectiveness of the training program to a large extent depends on the training need identification and assessment.

Deepakshi Gupta and Neena Malhotra[52] **(2012)** made a study on Human Resource Development Climate in Information Technology Organizations and gives dimension-wise analysis of human resource development climate in the different organizations that were covered. These dimensions are: rigorous selection procedure, value based induction, comprehensive training, team-based job design, working conditions/environment, employee friendly work environment, compensation, development oriented performance appraisal, career development and value added incentives.

Daniel Eseme Gberevbie[53] **(2012)** study was primarily carried out to empirically examine the impact of HRD and OC on employee performance in the Nigerian financial sector. The study provides an insight into the relevance of HRD and OC and how they impact on employees' performance in the workplace. However, the study shows that although HRD and OC impact strongly on EP; but this is not totally sufficient for sustainability and growth to be achieved in the Nigerian banking sector. This implies that in spite of the positive impact of HRD and OC on EP, there is also the need to tackle the issue of unethical behaviour – corruption amongst banks staff at all levels to guarantee sustainability and growth of banks in the country. The paper therefore recommend among others the enforcement of stiffer penalty for bank employees found engaging in unethical practices as a way of overcoming the challenge of unethical behaviour of staff for sustainable growth in Nigeria.

Akintayo DI[54] **(2012)** investigated the influence of human resource development programmes on job security among industrial workers in Nigeria. The purpose of investigation is to ascertain the relevance of human resource development programmes, as an alternative approach to human capital formation, to job security among industrial workers in Nigeria. The findings reveal that there is significant association in job security among industrial workers. It was also found that only three independent variables (computer skill training, labour relations skill training and interpersonal treatment skill training) have significantly influenced workers' job security. However, it was found that management skill, conflict skill, and communication skill training programmes were not as significant in influencing workers' job security in work organization. Based on the findings of study, it is recommended that human resource development programmes should be given priority by all establishments in order to forestall job security for all level of workers.

Gary N. Mc Lean et al[55] **(2012)** in their article on 'Capacity Building for Societal Development: Case Studies in HRD', Stated that traditionally, the core of human resource development (HRD) has focused on corporate settings and emerged primarily in the United States. This article presents case studies in which HRD principles and theories have been used for societal development—the general improvement of the welfare of people usually outside of the workplace, primarily in communities. At least one of the coauthors, and usually two or more, have been either involved in or reported on all of the cases included. It is critical for HRD academics and practitioners to understand this evolving, broad-based perspective of HRD and participate in its practice, theory development, and research.

Clíodhna A. MacKenzie et al[56] **(2012)** posed an important question for human resource development (HRD) concerns how its practices may have contributed to the global financial crisis. Commentators have highlighted that HRD must take some of the blame. First, they considered whether HRD's traditional role of contributor through performance-based development interventions, may have facilitated questionable practices in organizations. Second, they reflected on whether HRD was an irrelevant spectator through being benign and impotent; rather than challenging the status quo in organizations. Third, they contemplate the protagonist role and argue that HRD practitioners pursued short-term performance-based wealth maximizing objectives with scant regard for the long-term organizational or societal impact. Finally, they conclude by considering how HRD scholars can engage tomorrow's business leaders in critical reflection and how HRD practitioners can pursue a strategic decoupling position which allows for challenging the status quo without alienating their professional status in the organization and ethical standing in practice.

Tami S. Moser and Michael Williams[57] **(2012)** constituted a study on 'Considering A Market-Driven Human Resource Development Approach in Small Business: Succession Management Systems for Strategic Continuity and Excellence'. This research study addresses the unique challenges faced by small business leaders and human resource managers in the creation of dynamic succession management systems that acknowledge the resource limitations inherent to small businesses. A phenomenological methodology was used to investigate this issue within the small business community. The explorations lead to the suggestion that a market-driven approach to human resource development was a first step in creating excellence in succession management systems that ultimately lead to business continuity.

Peter Stokes and Ewan Oiry[58] **(2012)** paper is to identify the epistemological and ontological paradigms on which these approaches are couched in a British historical socio-cultural context. To put into light what this alternative perspective on competencies could add to reflection and practice, this paper realizes an in-depth two-year ethnographic study (employing participant-observer methods) of a consultancy delivered training programme for customer service competency based vocational qualification in a water utilities company based in the north of England. Based on a wide literature review on competencies, the first main result of this paper is to show that many of competencies approaches are underpinned by an empirical, pragmatic and ultimately modernistic, positivistic predilection. In an attempt to reappraise this rigid and highly structured representation of competencies, the paper draws on the resources of critical management approaches and notions of "lived experience". The main empirical result is that competencies are richer than competencies (especially NVQs) usually suppose be and those critical perspectives are valuable in seeking to address these lacunae.

Thumwimon Sukserm and Yoshi Takahashi [59] **(2012)** took a study to explore the relationships between learning and ethical behavior with mediation of self-efficacy. The current study is distinguished from previous studies by its investigation of the relationships of three variables such as learning, self-efficacy, and ethical behavior based on the four-level model of Kirkpatrick and transfer of training by the application of the social cognitive theory of Bandura through the analysis of human resource development (HRD) in corporate social responsibility (CSR) activity in local Thai firms. This study aims to encourage organizations to prepare and construct "ethical behavior" through CSR activity. The major finding was that self-efficacy mediated the relationship between learning (KSA change) and ethical behavior.

Nada Trunk Sirca et al [60] **(2012)** in their paper aimed to describe the role of HR practices in the area of HR development theoretically and empirically. The study conducted on a sample of Slovenian employees from various organizations shows that at least four different types of HR development system is implemented and perceived by the employees. The HR system that encompasses the whole process of HR development: training, career management, performance and reward management is most strongly and positively connected with employee's overall job satisfaction. Surprisingly, also less holistic development system that includes only training and the financial support of formal education is positively related to job satisfaction.

Julie Gedro et al [61] **(2012)** in their article on Recovered alcoholics and career development: Implications for human resource development presents three issues regarding alcoholism, recovery, and career development. First, alcoholism is a disease that creates health and wellness problems for those it afflicts. It also impacts individual and workplace productivity. Second, alcoholism has a persistent stigmatization. As a result, those alcoholics who are in recovery face challenging choices around self-disclosure. Disclosure of one's identity as a recovering alcoholic could be perceived as risky, since it could be seen as a negative. Third, because of such risk, and because of the paucity of research within the field of human resource development around alcoholism and recovery, there is a gap in the literature regarding these issues.

Ellen Scully-Russ[62] **(2012)** draws upon the theory of the risk society to develop three propositions, argue that Human resource development (HRD) and sustainability lie in a mutually co-constructive relationship. While many have critiqued HRD for its scant attention to sustainability, this paper identifies how three models of HRD including strategic HRD, critical HRD, and holistic HRD currently respond to the ideologies that vie to define the sustainability project. It is argued here that if HRD scholars and practitioners are more deliberate in their relationship with sustainability, they will encounter new and powerful conceptual and ethical frameworks to address the long standing tension in the field. As HRD grapples with sustainability they will need to address its own developmental dilemmas, which may give rise to a new HRD; one that is more aligned with the dilemmas of today's complex, global society.

Greg G Wang and Judy Y. Sun[63] **(2012)** advocated a formal language approach for human resource development (HRD) theory building. To this end, it develops a theoretical framework for comparative HRD (CHRD) within the form of a formal language system. Through a review of existing HRD literature in comparative research, the authors generalize the research into three axioms of CHRD expressed to offer insight for future research in comparative realms with each axiom focusing on a particular comparative facet. Combining the axioms, they formally provide a definition of CHRD and further derive implications for future HRD research and address related challenges in existing CHRD research.

Namhee Kim[64] **(2012)** states that although current human resource development (HRD) theory does not adequately address the issues and challenges faced by larger contexts, the methods originating from traditional HRD have been increasingly recognized as useful and effective interventions to deal with problems and issues that occur beyond a single organization or group of organizations. To address the gap between traditional HRD frameworks and the social reality of complex and large system change projects, this article identifies major issues that encompass typical use of HRD for societal development (SD), including community development, international development, and organizations' social responsiveness, and emphasizes the usefulness of organization development approach for SD.

Muhammad Tariq Khan et al[65] **(2012)** presents an organizational model of HRD encompassing all the aspects of human resource development from organizational point of view. It is considered by management professionals, as sub discipline of HRM, but many researchers have, broadened the scope and integrated the concept of HRD by looking at it from socioeconomic angle and giving it other dimensions such as physical, intellectual, psychological, social, political, moral and spiritual development.

Vilmante Kumpikaite and KestutisDuoba[66] **(2012)** analyzed the factors impacting global human resource development, globalization's impact on human resource development process. Intensive global competition, higher customer expectations and greater focus on quality have resulted in much greater requirements placed upon employees today than decades ago. The challenge has been to internalize a new type of organizational behavior in order to operate successfully under unfamiliar conditions.

James. M. Kilika et al[67] *(2012)* used the existing theoretical literature to provide empirical evidence on the design of HRD Infrastructures among universities in Kenya. The study relied on the nature of the knowledge intensive organizations and the philosophy of Human Resource Development (HRD) to propose a conceptual model for the design of HRD Infrastructures for organizations in this sector. The findings of the study reveal a significant correlation between Organizational Development (O.D) needs and HRD values that exist between HRD values and organizational learning orientation. The findings provide an important insight into the situational positioning of HRD in Kenya and a major step towards understanding HRD infrastructures for the knowledge intensive industries.

Sylvia N. Naris and Wilfred I. Ukpere[68] **(2012)** evaluated staff development and training at a higher institution in Namibia to offer suggestions where there are shortcomings in the staff development and training strategies. The analysis revealed that training and development is not a standalone function, it requires involvement by all stakeholders. Changes in the external environment have led to organizations realizing that their competitive advantage depends on skills and knowledge of their human resources. In other words, training and development has become such an important aspect for both organizations and individuals. The authors are of the view that all staff development and training activities should be linked to the strategic goals of organizations.

Akinyemi Benjamin[69] **(2012)** study aims to examine the relationships among human resource development climate (HRDC), organizational citizenship behaviour (OCB) and voluntary turnover intentions (VTI) in the banking sector. Questionnaires were distributed to working adults in Nigerian commercial banks to increase the employees' individual perception, and thus data obtained was treated as an individual data source. The results indicate that the HRDC has a significant relationship with OCB and VTI. However, OCB shows no significant relationship with VTI.

Gibb S.J.[70] **(2011)** stated that Human Resource Development meets the needs of students studying both undergraduate and specialist postgraduate modules in learning and development and human resource management, as well as CIPD students. It provides students with the tools to analyze develop and implement learning and development strategies for the workplace.

Myungweon Choi and Wendy E. A. Ruona[71] **(2011)** examine the concept of individual readiness for organizational change as well as its relationship to change strategies and organizational culture. A review of literature on change strategies and a learning culture suggests that individuals are more likely to have higher levels of readiness for organizational change when they experience normative-re-educative change strategies and when they perceive their work environment to have the characteristics associated with a learning culture.

Raavi Radhika[72] **(2011)** in her survey on 'HRD Processes at Singareni Collieries Company Limited Kothagudem (A.P)' examines the impact of HR practices on the human resource development process at Singareni Collieries Company Limited. The study mainly focuses on different development programmes conducted in the organization, studies various HRD methods and their relevance in meeting training objectives and to measure the 'effectiveness' of development programmes in the organization. Finally, through this study the author suggested that improvement of induction training to employees is required whenever the changes take place by transfers to new technologies at all levels.

Deepakshi Gupta[73] **(2010)** in her study concludes that information technology industry selects its employees through several fair interview and test rounds in organizations, so that they can get skilled and efficient employees.

Thomas N. Garavan and David McGuire[74] **(2010)** article argues that societal HRD (SHRD) can make an important and long-lasting contribution to CSR, sustainability, and ethics through its capacity to question a continual focus by organizations on efficiency and performance. The article outlines a framework of activities that HRD may use to reorient the agenda, hold organizations accountable, provide leadership on CSR, sustainability, and ethics, and at the same time ensure that the organization is profitable and successful. The article summarizes the six articles that are included in this issue.

K. Peter Kuchinke[75] **(2010)** argues for the relevance of the HD frameworks for HRD. This is done by briefly reviewing the role of values for professional fields in general and HRD in particular, followed by a summary of the justifications for and definitions of HD as reciprocal obligations between social institutions and individuals. The central part of the paper argues for the conceptual proximity of the two fields and proposes that the moral and ethical value stance of HD can provide a solid philosophical foundation for HRD.

Thomas G. Reio Jr. and Rajashi Ghosh[76] **(2009)** through their study state that for the physical health model, establishing relationships with co-workers and positive affect positively contributed to perceived physical health, while organizational incivility negatively contributed to the dependent variable. As for the job satisfaction model, establishing relationships with coworkers and supervisors and positive affect positively predicted satisfaction, whereas negative affect and incivility made negative contributions to the regression equation. In all cases, the magnitude of effect ranged from medium to large, supporting the theoretical, empirical, and practical relevance of understanding the detrimental effects of uncivil behaviors on organizational outcomes. HRD researchers and professionals are highlighted as possible means for reducing uncivil workplace behaviors and improving organizational performance.

Ronald L Jacobs and Yoonhee Park[77] **(2009)** focused on two major components: formal training and informal learning. These components have become the defining features of workplace learning. This article proposes a conceptual framework of workplace learning that is comprised of the interaction of three variables: 1) the location of the learning; 2) the extent of planning that has been invested in developing and delivering the learning experiences; and, 3) the role of the trainer, facilitator, or others during the learning process. The need for the proposed framework stems from two concerns. First, formal training and informal learning represent incompatible levels of discourse, making it difficult to have a cohesive understanding of workplace learning. Second, workplace learning appears to exclude a large segment of HRD practice, particularly when formal training programs occur in the work setting.

Laura L. Bierema[78] ***(2009)*** *in* this *article* tries to critique human resource development's (HRD) *dominant* philosophy, practices, and research; illustrate how they negatively affect women HRD practitioners and recipients; and recommend alternative conceptualizations of the field. This article is grounded in a critical feminist theoretical framework, draws on critical theory and critical management studies, and is inspired by the author's ongoing disenchantment HRD's over reliance on "performative" ideas and practices.

Mustapha M. Achoui[79] **(2009)** study is to highlight the challenges of human capital development in the Gulf Arab countries in general and in Saudi Arabia in particular. The main challenges are: high dependence on oil and the petrochemical industry; high dependence on foreign labour; a low rate of female participation in employment; and a weak link between educational system output and the needs of the economic sectors, especially those of the private sector, which requires skilled and professional labour.

Irakli Gvaramadze[80] **(2008)** paper will argue that current HRD strategies have an individualistic role rather than an interactive and interpersonal influence for better knowledge sharing and organizational learning. The research implies that HRD should change its interventions in terms of how the individual is conceptualized to make knowledge actionable in social contexts to create favourable conditions for knowledge sharing and organizational learning.

Alan Clardy[81] **(2008)** proposed three strategic roles for the HRD function in core competency management and discussed about participating in strategic planning, developing core competencies, and protecting them. Author also proposed Specific tasks for each role.

Dingie HCJ van Rensburg et al[82] **(2008)** studied on the patterns of planning, recruitment, training and task allocation associated with an expanding ART programme in the districts of one province, the Free State. The introduction of the ART programme has revealed both strengths and weaknesses of human resource development in one province of South Africa. Without concerted efforts to increase the supply of key health professionals, accompanied by changes in the deployment of health workers, the core goals of the ART programme – i.e. providing universal access to ART and strengthening the health system – will not be achieved.

Thomas N. Garavan and Alma McCarthy[83] **(2008)** in their article outlines that collective learning is important to both human resource development

(HRD) researchers and practitioners. Collective learning is a broad term and includes learning between dyads, teams, organizations, communities, and societies. Most of the collective learning highlights the characteristics such as relationships, shared vision and meanings, mental models and cognitive and behavioral learning. Collective learning processes pose challenges for both HRD research and practice.

Tara Fenwick and Laura Bierema[84] **(2008)** explore the engagement of HRD professionals in corporate social responsibility (CSR), examining one central question: how do HRD professionals perceive their roles and challenges in implementing CSR in organizations that claim CSR to be a key focus of their corporate identity and operation? The evidences in the study shows that their engagement tends to focus on employee learning and promotion, employee ownership of development, and employee safety and respect. Overall, however, HRD appeared to be only marginally involved or interested in the firms' CSR activities. The article concludes with an argument for greater engagement of HRD in CSR and offers suggestions for research and practice towards this end.

Greg G. Wang and Richard A. Swanson[85] **(2008)** focuses on the areas agreement between two recent and seemingly disparate Human Resource Development Review articles by Wang and Swanson (2008) and McLean, Lynham, Azevedo, Lawrence, and Nafukho (2008). The foundational roles of economics in human resource development theory and practice are highlighted as well as the need for comparative studies. A framework for conducting comparative human resource development policy studies is proposed.

Jens Rowold[86] **(2008)** aims to explore the simultaneous impact of employees' participation in non-technical training, technical training, and coaching on subsequent job performance, job involvement, and job satisfaction. The study found that non-technical training impacted subsequent soft skills and that technical training predicted subsequent hard skills as well as job involvement. Moreover, employees' participation in coaching predicted job satisfaction.

Brian Nicholson and Sundeep Sahay[87] **(2008)** paper provides an analysis of the human resources issues facing policy makers in less developed countries engaged in software exports policy formulation. The complexities are highlighted through the case study of Costa Rica, where there is an ongoing national strategic planning effort to increase software exports.

Alan Clardy[88] **(2008)** in the study shows that there is not yet a standard research protocol for how to research core competencies. A framework for studying core competencies is proposed here based on four questions: Does the firm have a competitive advantage? If so, is it based on capabilities? What is the nature of the specific core competencies involved? Does the competition have core competencies, and if yes, what are they? The implications of this model for researchers and practitioners are discussed.

Lynn Perry Wooten and Erika Hayes James[89] **(2008)** in their study highlight that many neglect the other leadership responsibilities associated with organizational crises. This may result from lack of formal training and on-the-job experiences that prepare executives to lead crises. Executives who enable their organizations to recover from a crisis exhibit a complex set of competencies in each of the five phases of a crisis—signal detection, preparation and prevention, damage control and containment, business recovery, and reflection and learning. In this article, through the use of qualitative research design and the analysis of firms in crises, author examined leadership competencies during each phase of a crisis. In addition, this article links the important role of human resource development to building organizational capabilities through crisis management activities.

Holly M. Hutchins and Jia Wang[90] **(2008)** explore the role of HRD in organizational crisis management. Specifically, the authors review the theoretical underpinnings of organizational crisis management research, identify opportunities for HRD to be involved in crisis management processes, and explore how HRD research and practice may contribute to supporting organizations' crisis management efforts.

Anne H. Reilly[91] **(2008)** argues that effective crisis communication is one of the key components of effective crisis management, and this article describes key human resource development (HRD) competencies that facilitate crisis communication. Research from organization development, crisis management, and crisis communication is used to provide an integrated framework for studying crisis communication that emphasizes the role of HRD in coping with crises. A repertoire of techniques for crisis communication is provided, together with recommendations for companies seeking to enhance their firms' crisis management capacities through communication. Implications for HRD practice, theory, and research are provided.

Xiaohui Wang and Gary N. McLean[92] **(2007)** said that from the beginning of the use of the term human resource development (HRD) to describe our field, there have been struggles over the meaning of the term and, even more broadly, of the field itself. In recent years, there has been increased attention to the question of the field's definition, in general, as well as attention to the emerging field of national HRD. This article moves this exploration one more step toward an exploration of the dilemma of defining international and cross-national HRD. A beginning definition is offered, not as a definitive answer but to facilitate ongoing discussion in the dialogue on HRD definitions.

Peter Holland et. al.,[93] **(2007)** in the paper developed the argument that in an environment characterized by increasing levels of skilled labour shortages organizations need to design employment systems that prioritize human resource development to enable competitive advantage. Our findings suggest that employers are addressing issues related to attraction - recruitment and selection. However, in critical HR development areas associated with retention such as training, job design, skill development, careers management and team building, results indicate a lower level of resource allocation. Finally, conclude that this lack of resource allocation is of concern for Australian organizations that are struggling to compete both domestically and internationally for skilled workers.

Abdullah H. et al[94] **(2007)** examined the concepts and nature of human resource development (HRD) at the national level in Malaysia. In examining HRD from the national perspective, writer utilizes a review of documentary evidence from relevant Governmental reports and documents. The author discussed plans, policies, strategies, roles and responsibilities in HRD at the national level.

Lincoln **et al**[95] **(2007)** described four additional criteria are proposed; namely, compellingness, saturation, prompt to action, and fittingness. The task of developing such criteria from different paradigms of inquiry while ensuring paradigmatic congruence holds particular challenges, some of which are discussed.

Ritva Laakso-Manninen and Riitta Viitala[96] **(2007)** in their book entitled 'Competence management and human resource development-A theoretical framework for understanding the practices of modern Finnish organizations'; the project was rewarding and also showed how two different writers, sometimes approaching the topic from different directions, could quite easily arrive at a joint understanding about the key challenges facing the field of competence management and human resource development today.

Salvatore Parise[97] **(2007)** article describes how social network analysis (SNA) can contribute to the knowledge management (KM) efforts of human resource development (HRD) professionals in organizations today. The author provides three cases to illustrate how SNA can aid HRD analysis and interventions involving (a) knowledge creation and innovation, (b) knowledge transfer and retention, and (c) knowledge associated with job succession planning. The author concludes by discussing the implications for HRD of utilizing SNA in the organization.

Kenneth J. Zula and Thomas J. Chermack[98] **(2007)** article examines the literature surrounding human capital, human capital planning, and the implications for human resource development (HRD). The research reports an in-depth justification and rationale for the incorporation of human capital planning into practice and research to determine the impact on HRD interventions and organizational performance through the use of a model and process for human capital planning.

Carole Tansley and Sue Newell[99] **(2007)** in this article, consider how project leadership knowledge and behaviour influence project team trust and social capital development and use in the context of a global HR information systems project. The study highlights ways in which a PL can foster the development of trust in the context of complex cross-cultural, cross-functional IS project teams. The study identifies how there are different types of trust that need to be generated and how this depends on good internal, external and hybrid PL leadership. PLs need to apply knowledge in three areas in order for trust to develop within the project team (external leadership, internal leadership and hybrid leadership), which in turn is a necessary pre-condition for the development and exploitation of social capital, a significant influence on project success.

Grugulis and Irena[100] **(2007)** in their book make a critical perspective in exploring a number of key issues associated with how people are 'developed' at work. Using many empirical studies on skills and training from recent years as a basis, the author explains how skills, or the lack of them, are viewed in the contemporary workplace. Questions considered in this text are: Will workers of the future all be knowledge workers? If training and development are so important, why do employers invest so little in them? And is there such a thing as 'bad training'?

Jonathon R. B. Halbesleben and Denise M. Rotondo[101] **(2007)** outlines that in light of research, significant links between social support and human resource outcomes, managers concerned to develop social support. One solution is to examine the experiences of a group of employees with extremely high work—life integration, same-career couples, to develop lessons for human resource development. Same-career couples are employees who work in the same workplace or in the same occupation as their partner. From their experiences and research concerning social support, the authors suggest mechanisms to develop social support with the intention of improving human resource outcomes.

Andreas Schmidt and Christine Kunzmann[102] **(2007)** highlights that competency-oriented approaches are gaining ground in human resource development. Key technology to cope with the complexity of fine-grained approaches is ontology's. By having a formal semantics, many competency-related tasks can be partially automated on a technical level. In this paper, the authors want to show that ontology-based approaches also foster the sustainability of such approaches on an organizational level by providing connections between the operational and strategic level. Authors present reference ontology and a reference process model which have been applied in a hospital case study.

Thomas N. Garavan, David O'Donnell, David McGuire and Sandra Watson[103] **(2007)** present a brief justification for adopting a multi perspectival approach to theory and practice in human resource development (HRD). It is argued that such an approach has the potential to add theoretical depth and breadth to HRD discourse as well as contributing to reflective HRD practice.

S Girma et al[104] **(2007)** states that there is no policy specific to human resource development (HRD) for health and no proper mechanism to manage the existing health workforce. A number of measures are being taken to alleviate these problems. The enrollment of students has been increased in different categories and new trainings started in professions like dentistry. The process to develop policy and strategy for managing human resource for health has been started. The implications of these for HRD by 2015 are explored briefly.

Claire Valentin[105] **(2006)** paper argues that mainstream research in management and human resource development (HRD) is dominated by a positivist paradigm. In a theoretical discussion and review of literature on management, human resource management, HRD and organization studies, it explores critical perspectives in research, which draw on postmodernism and critical theory. It examines how they have contributed to the emergence of a critical HRD and discusses the features of a critical HRD research.

Barry-Craig P. Johansen1 and Gary N. McLean[106] **(2006)** pin points that the workplace, classrooms, and the world in general are becoming increasingly diverse. Globalization, communications technology, immigration, an increased focus on religion and spirituality, and the ease of both domestic and international travel offer an opportunity to work, learn, and interact with people whose backgrounds differ from our own. To be effective, HRD practitioners must recognize how cultural background, assumptions, and view of the world influence an understanding of adult learning. The dangers of not developing such an understanding include inconsistent and/or a theoretical practice, misunderstandings, miscommunication, and the dangers of cultural imperialism.

Liam Brown et al[107] **(2006)** in their paper compares and contrasts the current attitudes towards, awareness of and take-up of eLearning in large and small organizations and outlines the implications for human resource development (HRD) professionals. The study focused on awareness; perceptions; technology support infrastructure; and current and planned involvement, most frequent and most preferred methods of delivery, benefits, barriers, the motivational factors and overall attitudes to eLearning. The comparison describes a number of similarities and a number of differences both within the large organization sector and within the SME sector and between the two sectors. Finally, the implications for HRD professionals are also discussed.

Jia Wang and Greg G. Wang[108] **(2006)** examined current MD-related policies and practices at national, organizational, and individual levels. The analysis found that although much effort was made at multiple levels for developing managers, China's approach to MD tended to be fragmented and lacked coherence. The study further offered critical implications for China MD practice and recent emerging NHRD research. In discussing future NHRD research directions, the study calls for HRD scholars to be mindful of the discipline and theory building in exploring new HRD research frontiers.

Arif Hassan et al[109] **(2006)** aim of the study was to measure employees' perception of human resource development (HRD) practices, to explore whether ISO certification leads to any improvements in HRD system, and to examine the role of HRD practices on employees' development climate and quality orientation in the organization. Results indicated large inter-organizational differences in HRD practices. In general, however, employees' ratings were moderate. ISO certified companies, compared to others, obtained higher means on some HRD variables. Organizations with better learning, training and development systems, reward and recognition, and information systems promoted human resource development climate. Quality orientation was predicted by career planning, performance guidance and development, role efficacy, and reward and recognition systems.

Kit Brooks and Fredrick Muyia Nafukho[110] **(2006)** aims to offer a theoretical framework that attempts to show the integration among human resource development (HRD), social capital (SC), emotional intelligence (EI) and organizational productivity. The literature review provides evidence that it is logical to assume that the relationship among HRD, social capital, emotional and organization productivity is highly integrated. This finding influenced the authors to conceptualize an integrated model that illustrates the interconnectivity of HRD, social capital, emotional intelligence and organizational productivity with internal and external environmental factors.

Ani B. Raidén and Andrew R.J. Dainty[111] **(2006)** tried to present case study research of the HRD strategy, policy and practice of a large UK-based construction contractor in relation to the concept of LO. The analysis suggests that the organizational project-based structure and informal culture combine to form a "chaordic LO". A "chaordic enterprise" comprises a complex organisation that operates in a non-linear dynamic environment. However, it appears that this approach has evolved unintentionally rather than as a result of targeted strategic human resource management (SHRM) policies, which in turn reflects a genuine commitment to advanced HRD.

Noordeen Gangani et al[112] **(2006)** in their article explore some of the major issues in developing and implementing a competency-based human resource development strategy. The article summarizes a brief literature review on how competency models can be developed and implemented to improve employee performance. A case study is presented by American Medical Systems (AMS), a mid-sized health-care and medical device company, where the model is being used to improve employee performance and gain a competitive advantage.

Tracy Wilcox[113] **(2006)** argued that the economic and political power enjoyed by contemporary corporations brings with it an associated set of responsibilities and duties, particularly in the light of issues emerging in the global and local political environment. These issues arise in part from a shifting of the regulatory ground from the achievement of 'social good' to 'economic good', and the shifting of risk from business organizations to individuals and communities. The paper considers the impact of these changes on human resource development. Some of the areas in which an organization's social and ethical responsibility can encompass HRD practices are explored and possible HRD responses to the issues and concerns raised are discussed.

Susan A. Lynham1 and Peter W. Cunningham[114] **(2006)** in this article propose a number of comparative discoveries about the necessary role and nature of national human resource development in its context. One such discovery is the influence of the political, economic, and socio-cultural environments on the necessary nature and role of national human resource development in each country. A second is that context and intent shape and inform what makes for responsible human resource development. Another is that discoveries from this and other studies suggest emerging models and necessary attributes, components, and dimensions useful for informing an integrative and collaborative theoretical and sense-making framework for future study and practice of national human resource development. These and other discoveries pose numerous challenges to the human resource development profession.

Mary E. Graham and Lindsay M. Tarbell [115] **(2006)** through their study state that recent specification of HR competencies has the potential to influence the professional development of all HR practitioners. It is possible, however, to master the competencies and still underperform. This disconnect may occur because current competency work reflects the perspective of top management clients of human resources to the neglect of the employee perspective. In addition, competencies have become linked so tightly to firm outcomes that normative influences in competency development are lost. Focus groups confirm that credibility dimensions vary across stakeholders, with employees emphasizing trust, management emphasizing expertise and effective relationships, and top management emphasizing the achievement of results. The study concludes that, more broadly defined competencies for HR professionals are necessary.

Andreas Schmidt and Christine Kunzmann[116] **(2006)** study express that on the organizational level, competence management uses competencies for integrating the goal-oriented shaping of human assets into management practice. On the operational and technical level, technology-enhanced workplace learning uses competencies for fostering learning activities of individual employees. It should be obvious that these two perspectives belong together, but in practice, a common conceptualization of the domain is needed. This paper, present such a reference ontology that builds on existing approaches and experiences from two case studies.

Consuelo L. Waight[117] **(2005)** through this article sets the stage for exploring the connections between creativity and human resource development (HRD). It signals the significance of exploring creativity and HRD by looking at knowledge workplaces, workforce projections, work values, occupation projections, on-the-job training, and entrepreneurship. The article also shows how research on creativity and HRD has examined similar learning and performance variables.

Greg G. Wang and Elwood F. Holton III[118] **(2005)** article reviews economic theories and models pertinent to HRD research and theory building. By examining neoclassical and neo-institutional schools of contemporary economics, especially the screening model and the internal labor market theory, it is argued that economic theories not only provide a foundation but also have important implications to HRD theory, research, and practice. Broadening research directions may be fruitful and provocative in expanding HRD's theoretical base as well as practical applications in organizations.

Susan K. Lippert and Paul Michael Swiercz[119] **(2005)** generates 11 propositions exploring the relationship between Human Resource Information

Systems (HRIS) and the trust an individual places in the inanimate technology (technology trust) and models the effect of those relationships on HRIS implementation success. Specifically, organizational, technological, and user factors are considered and modeled to generate a set of testable propositions that can subsequently be investigated in various organizational settings. Eleven propositions are offered suggesting that organizational trust, pooled interdependence, organizational community, organizational culture, technology adoption, technology utility, technology usability, socialization, sensitivity to privacy, and predisposition to trust influence an individual's level of trust in the HRIS technology (technology trust) and ultimately the success of an HRIS implementation process. The summary of the relationships between the key constructs in the model and recommendations for future research.

Greg G. Wang and Dean R. Spitzer[120] **(2005)** the authors delineate M&E development into three stages, discuss the relative features in each stage, and propose an integrated approach for researchers and practitioners working together to further advance M&E in HRD. To this end, this issue is dedicated to addressing a gap in the HRD M&E literature by presenting a set of theories, models, and practical approaches as a starting point of the third stage of M&E development for HRD research and practices.

Jinyu Xie[121] **(2005)** in this paper discusses HRD roles, required competencies, and outcomes. Role analysis is crucial to the professionalization and education of HRD. Using ASTD's HRD model as a reference, this study examines HRD roles across China. Results support the ASTD HRD roles model, and offer a useful profile of HRD roles in China.

Darlene Russ-Eft and Hallie Preskill[122] **(2005)** article argues that, in many cases, ROI (Return on Investment) does not provide the kind of information needed by decision makers. What is needed is a systems model that examines the effect of organizational and environmental factors on the intended outcomes of an HRD initiative or program. Author states that such a model can help to frame any evaluation, including one that focuses on ROI.

Sarah A. Hezlett and Sharon K. Gibson[123]**(2005)** in this article examine past theory, research, and practice on mentoring through the lens of HRD, in order to identify gaps, the authors summarize key issues that have been studied regarding mentoring and career development, organization development, and training and development, proposing new directions for future research. The authors conclude with a research agenda that identifies where researchers need to go with mentoring research and HRD to better inform the practice of mentoring in organizations.

Greg G. Wang and Jia Wang[124] **(2005)** address the limited supply of methodologies and techniques, the authors conquered three barriers: the analytical barrier, the business barrier, and the technical barrier. Sprouting from an analysis of HRD systems interactions, the author proposes a systems approach to tackle these three barriers. This article discusses the role of theory building and market trends in HRD M&E.

Richard J. Torraco[125] **(2005)** examined six theoretical perspectives on work design for their contributions to understand how work is organized and designed in organizations: socio-technical systems theory, process improvement, adaptive structuration theory, the job characteristics model, techno-structural change models, and activity theory. A critique of these theories raises concerns about their ability to explain the design of work in new work environments. The critique highlights the need to eliminate the discontinuity in how theory explains the structure and articulation of work among system levels. The implications of this study for further research on work design theory and for human resource development practice are discussed

<u>**Colin Fisher**</u> Dr[126] **(2005)** paper challenges the assumption that HRD practice is necessarily good or benign. It recognizes that HRD involves moral choices and provides a conceptual exploration of the matter, enlivened by anecdotal illustration. The semiotic square is the chosen tool for the task. It has been built around a descriptive matrix of HRD roles and four ethical stances. All the roles have been argued to possess potential ethical limitations and the conclusion is reached that HRD practice is not ethically uniform and is not necessarily an unambiguously good thing. However, the main benefit of the semiotic square analysis is that it enables the ethical limitations of HRD to be described and mapped.

Laird D. McLean[127] **(2005)** the majority of the literature on creativity has focused on the individual, yet the social environment can influence both the level and frequency of creative behavior. This article reviews the literature for factors related to organizational culture and climate that act as supports and impediments to organizational creativity and innovation. The work of Amabile, Kanter, Van de Ven, Angle, and others is reviewed and synthesized to provide an integrative understanding of the existing literature. Implications for human resource development research and practice are discussed.

Kimberly S. McDonald and Linda M. Hite[128] **(2005)** in their study address the dearth of discourse and practice from the perspective of human resource development (HRD). The authors suggest a framework for reintegrating career development into the HRD function and offer specific learning activities better suited to the needs of individuals and organizations in this turbulent environment. Recommendations for future action are provided.

Norma D'Annunzio-Green and Helen Francis[129] **(2005)** present findings of an exploratory study of managers' experiences of an emotion management leadership programme in a large retail company. Drawing on the concept of the psychological contract, authors explore the signaling by the programme of a shift from a transactional to relational contract and how this influenced managers' perceptions about what the organization expected of them and what they could expect in return.

Beverly Dawn Metcalfe and Christopher J. Rees[130] **(2005)** paper contributes to these theoretical explorations by attempting to map out the terrain of IHRD theory and activity. Drawing on international HRM (IHRM), development economics and development sociology writings propose that international HRD in the global arena can be categorized under three headings: 'global HRD', 'comparative HRD' and 'national HRD'. The authors presented a development model as a way of analyzing HRD. It is argued that this model can be viewed as a heuristic device that may be used to break down the components of IHRD and, in doing so, contributes to IHRD theory formulation and a greater understanding of HRD organization policy and practice within an international context. Our theoretical discussion stresses the broader social development orientations of education and HRD.

Aahad M. Osman-Gani and Ronald L. Jacobs[131] **(2005)** study investigated the human resource development practices of organizations in Singapore, where companies are continuously responding to rapid technological changes in order to remain competitive. The results show similar patterns of responses across business sectors; however, some differences were found in the transport and communications sectors. On-the-job training was reported as the most frequently used training method to address organizational change needs. The discussion and recommendations focus on the need for improved change management approaches.

Jon E. Lervik et al[132] **(2005)** in this paper, contrast the dominant perspective 'Implementation as Replication' with a perspective of 'Implementation as Re-creation'; through four stages of the implementation process, identifies and discusses how these contrasting perspectives yield different implications for how firms go about introducing HRD best practices. First, when firms take up a practice, is this a process of adoption or translation? Second, is it assumed that new knowledge can be implanted directly and lead to new behaviour, or is active experimentation a necessary precondition to gain new knowledge? Third, are deviations from the intended plan considered errors to be corrected or sources for learning? Fourth, are introduced best practices treated in isolation or as integral parts of the firm's management system? The researchers argue that implementation efforts guided by the re-creation perspective increase the prospects of HRD best practices succeeding as a useful tool in the receiving firm.

Arvind Kumar Purohit[133] **(1996)** stated that HRD essentially involves the creation of environment in which the flower of human knowledge, skills, capacities and creativity blooms. Research also mentions that HRD cannot be a single system or activity, but a package of systems and processes through which information, knowledge, skills, insight, foresight, maturity and wisdom can be cultivated and enhanced among the people to enable them to do the best for LIC organization.

2.2 Retrospective Literature Review on SRTUs and APSRTC

The following reviews include several research Papers, Books and Thesis dated from pertaining to the studies undergone on STUs and APSRTC. The discussion covers varied arguments and meaningful findings regarding those previous studies. The following cited reviews are few important studies conducted on STUs and APSRTC by various researchers.

Sanjay K. Singh[134] **(2014)** examines the cost structure of publicly owned State Transport Undertakings (STUs) in India. To examine the cost structure, the author estimates a translog cost function. The study found that the cost function is fully separable between time (technology) and its other arguments, i.e., technological progress experienced by STUs are (Hicks) neutral. Furthermore, average cost curve for STUs is U-shaped and it is increasing for the mean firm, i.e., large and medium size STUs are operating on diseconomies of scale whereas small size STUs are experiencing economies of scale.

D. Paul Dhinakaran and Dr.M.Rajarajan[135] **(2014)** focused to measure the various problems and suggest ways to reduce problems and to provide higher perception, in addition to identifying the level passengers' perception towards service quality in Tamilnadu state transport corporation (Kumbakonam) limited, Kumbakonam.

Srinivas D[136] **(2013)** study reveals that despite of socio-economic importance and the potential, public sector transport in India suffers from serious problems of operation, finance, capacity and quality. Moreover, the increased competition, management crisis, absence of long-run perspective, lack of commitment crisis, absence of long-run perspective, lack of commitment and customer orientation etc., being problems of falling occupancy, economic inefficiency, deteriorating service quality etc., inspite of problems, leakages, losses, there is a great scope and need for the public sector road transport corporations to operate in the market in view of the demand for the service, social good and as obligation of the government. The author quotes the case with the Indian Railways which used to sustain losses and which turned around to the efficiency. Author states that it should also be the case with road Transport Corporation to catch up the operational efficiency, financial stability and economic viability.

Srinivasa Rao S[137] **(2013)** attempted to know about the latest trends in APSRTC and more appropriately the status of dynamic HR profession and its role in the present day. The study helps to know the HRM practices existing in the organization and would further support in giving necessary inputs for better world.

P. C. Reddy et al[138] **(2013)** in their study intends to examine the information system policies and practices in APSRTC, to highlight the inadequacies, lapses, if any, therein and provide constructive suggestions to rectify those problems to improving the overall managerial performance.

Narasimha Rao[139] **(2013)** attempt to examine the turnaround management strategies in APSRTC. In the study he reviewed the credibility building actions implemented by A.P. State Road Transport Corporation for its turning around. The study found that the APSRTC could not convert its revenue into net profit due to under utilization of assets till 2003. However, it is evident that there was marginal improvement of net profit during the period 2004-10. APSRTC adopted retrenchment, re-positioning, re-organization and financial strategies in its turnaround management process.

TarakeswaraRao[140] **(2013)** examines working of trade unions and representation of labour may prove to be particularly crucial in the management of the most innovative organizations like APSRTC. He opined that there is a need to focus on organizing the unorganized and reach out to the new generation of workers, the e-generation. Delivery of services to members is another key issue. Trade unions need to reinvent themselves as e-organizations to survive and prosper.

Chandran Vijaya[141] **(2013)** opined that for any organization, Union - Management relations is very important for its effective functioning. Doing a job effectively can be done by employees only when they are satisfied. and when both Employee Satisfaction and Union –Management Relations are in good manner then it will have its good impact on Customer Satisfaction as they will be (that is Employer and Employee) in a position to do their jobs effectively in serving customers (passengers). The study makes an analysis on Employee Satisfaction and Union – Management relations and its impact on Customer Satisfaction.

Srinivasa Rao[142] **(2013)** makes an attempt to know about the latest trends in APSRTC and more appropriately the status and role of HR profession in the present day. The study helps to know the existing HRM practices in the organizations and would further support in giving necessary inputs for better functioning of the organization. The study examines the satisfaction levels of employees on specific human resource management practices followed in APSRTC. However, the author analyzed the perceptions of sample respondents with regard to the recruitment, selection and training undergone by them and enquired into the opinions on wage, salary procedures, the welfare measures of APSRTC and its impact on employees. Finally, he evaluated that APSRTC may adopt many modern strategies to achieve better efficiency but the employer and employee relations are based on existing HRM functions/activities of APSRTC, the reduction in possible wastage can be achieved through better resource utilization.

John Wesly[143] **(2013)** explores the depth of the current crisis in the trade union movement by focusing on some strategic economic, social and political dimensions. The study of trade unions and politics in the light of economic reforms is carried on with a view to analyze the performance of trade unions in spite of constitutional safe guards and protections under various labour legislations such as Trade Unions Act, Industrial Disputes Act etc. With regard to Indian conditions, trade union affiliation with political parties failed to create confidence in the minds of workers and could not attract the attention of the ninety five per cent of the workers in the unorganized sector to become the members of the trade unions. Statistics show that there are below five per cent of workers in the organized sector.

Dharma Naik[144] **(2013)** made a study on need for sound performance appraisal in APSRTC and suggested that the onus of appraisal should be on the appraisee. The superior's role should be to help the subordinates in relating their self appraisals, their targets, and plans for ensuring period to realities of the organization. Naik also examined the effectiveness of the Corporations organizational setup. Finally, said that Customer feedback could be thought of as an input in the system of performance appraisal.

Anita D'Souza[145] **(2012)** in her paper on A Study on Employee Satisfaction (With Special Reference to A.P.S.R.T.C Sangareddy Bus Depot) demonstrates the significance of employee satisfaction and how companies can successfully implement a program to positively impact both organizational culture and ultimately bottom line profits. She found that leadership skills directly related to employee satisfaction include: having a clear direction for the group; having realistic and clear objectives; and being able to give appropriate feedback, recognition, and support.

Trinadh Babu M.[146] **(2012)** made a survey on Marketing Operations of APSRTC - A Study With Reference To Vizianagaram Zone. In that study the researcher had presented the entire marketing operations adopted in APSRTC. Though his study he tries to gave several measures in reducing several costs pertaining to APSRTC.

Jawahar Suresh[147] **(2012)** made a research on the topic entitled Human Resource Planning in Andhra Pradesh State Road Transport Corporation (APSRTC) – A Study of Karimnagar Zone of Andhra Pradesh. He undertook this present study with a view of the importance of Human Resource Planning and need to have an effective Human Resource Planning for ensuring smooth planning especially in a service oriented organization like APSRTC. The Author attempted to understand and analyze the role of present setup of the Human Resource Planning in sound planning of the organization.

Udai S. Mehta[148] **(2012)** research focuses on road transport sector identifies and list provisions in different statutes, rules, policies and practices, which limit competition or have the potential to limit competition in a sector. Finally the study recommends changes in the regulations and their implementation procedures to address the competition related issues. The study also has come up with few suggestions to promote and protect competition in the road transport sector. The study also advocates for the reformation of State transport undertakings and curbing of cartels in transport sector by the Competition Commission of India (CCI). As part of reformation the study underlines the need for deregulation of tariffs, restructuring and commercialization of STUs, elimination of STU monopoly rights, changes in the tax regime to achieve uniformity of tax treatment of all buses operating in the inter-city markets.

Sawinder Kaur and Navkiranjit Kaur[149] **(2012)** made a survey on Growth and Pattern of Bus Service in Punjab to have an overview of bus service in the State of Punjab and to study the growth in number of buses held by different bus operators.

Vijay and Durga Prasad[150] **(2011)** made a comprehensive analysis of elicited information from selected passengers on the different amenities and facilities provided by APSRTC both at bus stations and on board the bus. They also examine whether the existing amenities provided by APSRTC are sufficiently catering the needs of the passengers. Finally, they aimed to suggest some strategies and measures that would go long way for improvement of passenger amenities of APSRTC.

Kanagaluru Sai Kumar[151] **(2011)** studied on consumption pattern of materials in Andhra Pradesh State Road Transport Corporation by analyzing various items that constitute materials such as stores & spares, springs, tyres & tubes, lubricants, and HSD oil. The study also aimed to find the consumption pattern of materials in relation with number of vehicles and the number of kilometers operated as well as its influence on the losses of the corporation. The results indicated that the materials management practices of the corporation were good and have not shown any impact on the losses of the corporation.

Agarwal and Pramod Bhargava[152] **(2011)** analyzed the financial distress in State Road Transport Undertakings (SRTUs). The study is useful in judging the profundity of financial distress in undertakings and identifies the variables, which are influencing and determining the financial distress in SRTUs. The analysis found that the SRTUs understudies are very likely to face bankruptcy, if corrective steps are not adopted immediately. The probability of bankruptcy in APSRTC is .99 which is close to the peak probability of bankruptcy. The accounting variable with a negative coefficient responsible for this situation is the debt ratio. Immediate efforts need to be promptly taken to avoid this situation.

Prasada Rao and Bayyarapu[153] **(2011)** in their study describes that Andhra Pradesh State Road Transport Corporation (APSRTC) is the sole public transport provider in the State of Andhra Pradesh. It is a pioneer in setting up various innovative methods and systems in public transport like integrated depot management system, night express services, depot computerization, nonstop services, luxury services for city operations (Metro), one man services and electronic ticket issuing machines. It carries 14 million commuters per day with a fleet of 22,129 buses. APSRTC is in forefront in pollution control and reduction of Green House Gas (GHG) emissions by adopting several innovative methods. All the buses under operation are Euro-III/IV compliant. It also uses alternate fuels like Compressed Natural Gas (CNG) and bio-diesel blends for urban transport.

Panduranga Murthy and Sathyavathi[154] **(2011)** undertook a field survey to understand the present marketing practices or business strategies of APSRTC and chronicle them to enable the enthusiastic sister organizations working in the same / similar industry to utilize them, so that the wheel need not be reinvented. The study also endeavors to find gaps if any, in the organization and made required recommendations depending on the obtained statistical results.

Shivi Agarwal et al[155] **(2011)** measures the technical efficiency of public transport sector in India. The study makes an attempt to provide an overview of the general status of the State Transport Undertakings (STUs) in terms of their productive efficiency. It is concluded that the performance of the STUs are good but still very far from the optimal level. The mean overall technical efficiency (OTE) is 83.26% which indicates that an average STU has the scope of producing the same output with the inputs 16.74% lesser than their existing level. Significant variation in OTE across STUs is also observed.

Prakash et al[156] **(2011)** undertaken a study to understand the present marketing practices or business strategies of APSRTC and chronicle them to enable the enthusiastic sister organizations working in the same/similar industry to make use of them so that the wheel need not be reinvented. The study also endeavors to find gaps, if any, in the organization and to make required recommendations. The emergence of marketing concept in respect of services is a recent phenomenon. Their purchase does not result in ownership of something physical. They are often described as ephemeral and experiential. A substantial portion of our purchasing is of services. The customer pays for an experience, or a service provided by a service firm. Service in most cases involves transfer of some intangible benefits which result from the activities of service providers.

Sai Kumar[157] **(2011)** studied on the practices of scrap management of Andhra Pradesh State Road Transport Corporation. The effectiveness of scrap management policies is measured in terms of obsolete materials, number of vehicles scrapped, revenue on the materials scrapped, and the revenue realized on the sale of scrap materials and vehicles, the share of scrap revenue in the total non-operating revenue and in the total revenue, and percentage of scrap inventory in the total inventory. The data have been analyzed using various statistical tools. The results indicate that the scarp management practices of the corporation were good.

Sai Kumar[158] **(2011)** presents a study on the quality of services offered by the Andhra Pradesh State Road Transport Corporation (APSRTC). As the corporation incurred continuous losses in the past, this study highlights whether the losses affected the quality of services offered to the traveling public. Quality of services is measured in terms of number of trips operated, regularity, breakdowns, rate of accidents, and the number of vehicles off the road. In addition, he also examines the quality of services offered in relation to inventory maintenance.

Rajesham[159] **(2009)** made a remarkable study of incentive schemes in passenger Transport Industry at various levels in the organization. The effect on performance level of various sections was bought out by him. At the same time, he also analyzed distribution of savings between the management and the workers in APSRTC during 1989-90s.

Prakash et al[160] **(2008)** made a study on Training in A.P.S.R.T.C - an empirical study. The authors in their study observed and opined that Training is an essential component in the overall strategy of efficient and cost effective service. The need for training of personnel to face the new and emerging task of planning and development and achievement of social economic objectives has been emphasized in successive five years plans. The training sector has been given a new impetus and focus during the last few years and the emphasis has been to evolve a new administrative set up with stress on competence, commitment and performance.

Ravichandran and Surya Prasad[161] **(2007)** examined in detail the reasons related to the declining operating and financial performance of Gujarat State Road Transport Corporation (GSRTC). The contribution of various environmental and governance issues related to the decline of GSRTC are identified. Based on the diagnosis, a detailed revival plan consisting of a set of actions to be undertaken by the management is proposed. The responsibilities of the government, the management, and the employees in implementing the revival plan are briefly discussed. This article concludes with set of strategic priorities that need to be examined by government in reviving GSTRC and other similar state-owned public utilities.

Vishnuprasad Nagadevara and Ramanayya[162] **(2007)** examined the Factors Affecting Passenger Satisfaction Levels – A Case Study of Andhra Pradesh State Road Transport Corporation. The factor analysis of commuter expectations reveals that "Comfort and convenience" and "Quality and Reliability" are the two major dimensions for ensuring customer satisfaction. On the other hand, the factor analysis on actual experiences of the commuters suggests that "Crew Behavior" is a major dimension in the minds of the commuters. Same is the case of "Costs and Reliability". It suggests that the factors contributing to customer satisfaction are different in different regions of the state. Consequently the Corporation have to adapt different strategies in different regions. Crew behavior is important in all the regions; it has to concentrate more on convenience aspects in the Hyderabad Region. It has to concentrate on comfort in the bus and seat availability in Rayala Seema and Coastal Regions.

Satyanarayana[163] **(2006)** guided for the thesis on organizational climate in State Road Transport Corporation in 2006 has rightly suggested that efficiency. The study suggests that efficiency of RTC can be measured in relation to capital productivity, labour productivity, and vehicle productivity cost of operation, quality of service and total costs and benefits. In all measures that are given above, standards are to be fixed by the corporation, with regard to quality of service it can be measured either with reference to the punctuality or with reference to the optimum service index. Accidents or a breakdown affects the punctuality of the buses.

Metri[164] **(2006)** addressed the importance of TQM for transportation organizations. He defined "Total Quality Transportation (TQT)" and applied Deming's 14-point model for aiding TQT implementation. An organization structure and an implementation model have been proposed for its successful implementation. The model is designed to guide top management in adopting TQT in their organizations.

Kane and Tony[165] **(2005)** said that the ultimate purpose of measuring performance is to improve transportation services for customers. Two important motives for measuring performance are to understand customers' desires and improving services to fulfill those desires. Both of these emphases underlie most of the reasons cited in the literature for the increasing importance of performance measurement to transportation agencies.

Kondayya[166] **(2003)** made a survey on the topic entitled HRD in APSRTC – A Study with reference to managerial personnel. In the study he examined the organization structure, managerial performance appraisal, practices and climate for managerial training and its contribution to HRD practices. He analyzed the HRD support practices, i.e. stead techniques for building managerial competencies and tried to find out the outcomes of HRD from the standpoint of managerial personnel and organization.

Karne et al[167] **(2003)** did their study on Analysis of productivity and efficiency in MSRTC and examined the issue of splitting MSRTC into smaller regions to find out whether it would actually help in its financial recovery as like as Karnataka Road Transport Corporation. Also, they observed the possibility of improvement in financial profitability by means of enhanced input productivity.

Pollappa[168] **(2000)** studied on Industrial Relations – Need to have an Effective Grievance Handling Machinery – A Case Study of Cuddapah Zone of APSRTC – 2000. In his study he observed that the total number of grievances could have been minimized if the employees and their leads were adequately educate about the rules and the degree of the severity of the grievance policies must be framed without any ambiguity.

Sunil Kumar[169] **(1999)** attempted to gauge the extent of technical efficiency in 31 state road transport undertakings (SRTUs) operating in India and also to explore the most influential factors explaining its variations across SRTUs. The key findings of the DEA analysis are only five SRTUs define the efficient frontier, and the remaining 26 inefficient undertakings have a scope of inputs reduction, albeit by the different magnitude; the extent of average overall technical inefficiency (OTIE) in these SRTUs is to the tune of 22.8 percent, indicating that the sample SRTUs are wasting about one-fourth of their resources in the production operations; managerial inefficiency (as captured by the pure technical inefficiency) is a relatively more dominant source of OTIE; and operation in the zone of increasing returns-to-scale is a common feature for most of the undertakings. The multivariate regression analysis using Tobit analysis highlights that the occupancy ratio is the most significant determinant for all the efficiency measures, and bears a positive relationship with overall technical, pure technical and scale efficiencies. Further, scale efficiency is also impacted positively by the staff productivity.

Ghosh[170] **(1999)** observed that the SRTUs are facing tremendous challenge from the private bus operators. The government support is not forthcoming, under these circumstances, SRTUs are required to frame strategies in order to survive and grow. To make these strategies workable, workforce need to be geared up through proper Human Resource Development strategies. **Ghosh (1998)** studied on Human Resource Development Climate in State Transport Undertakings to elaborate the prevailing state of the HRD Climate in SRTUs to gear up the employees for meeting the challenges - It is required that SRTUs should develop good HRD Practices. His survey revealed that the state of development climate in SRTUs is not up to the mark and needs immediate attention. He suggested that continues development of people through various HRD instruments should be given high priority. **Ghosh (1997)** attempted to find out the extent to which training of officers is effective in SRTUs. He suggested that the exercise of identifying the training needs must include employees and the performance appraisal should be made at least partly open and used as a tool to identify training needs.

Gawhane and Sudarsanam Padam[171] **(1999)** observed that the percentage share of SRTUs in the market is declining year after year due to the process of liberalization of permits. The private operators' buses are coming on the road with unprecedented growth whereas SRTUs' buses are stagnated. They suggested that SWOT analysis at corporate level in the SRTUs is necessary and accordingly aggressive marketing, modernization of fleet, computerization for creating passenger friendly environment, changing promotional policies and HRD and other strategies should be adopted by SRTUs.

Rajeswari[172] **(1998)** examines the performance of Andhra Pradesh State Road Transport Corporation both at the state and regional levels. It particularly deals with the pricing policies of the transport service as being implemented by the corporation. The organizational set up of the corporation along with its various features like capital investment and staffing has been described in full length. Both financial and social performance were examined using indicators like cost per kilometer earnings per kilometer, load factor and arrived at gross margins for the survey period. Through this study she observed certain facts like the Government of Andhra Pradesh has not been allowing APSRTC to revise fares vis-à-vis cost escalation. On some occasions the government took away the surplus in the form of increased motor vehicle tax/ surcharge. In both cases the corporation has been incurring losses, starting from late 1970s. When the charges of APSRTC are compared with railways, the fares charged by APSRTC are on the higher side range between 17 to 37% in selected routes. However, route length needs to be considered here. Also when APSRTC is compared with other state corporations it revealed that the fares charged by APSRTC are lower than Karnataka and Maharastra and higher than Tamil Nadu and Kerala.

Made Gowda[173] **(1996)** in his paper aimed to test the hypothesis that the employees of SRTUs are not much inefficient as generally conceived by the public. He commented that the poor performance of SRTUs cannot be attributed to the inefficiency of the Human Resource alone.

Rama Rao[174] **(1996)** focused attention on the bus services provided by APSRTC to the rural masses and its consequential affect on socio-economic development of rural household in Visakhapatnam district.

Saxena[175] **(1994)** conducted a study on few selected State Road Transport Corporations in India regarding the aspects of their financial management.

In his study with special reference to Uttar Pradesh State Road Transport Corporation (UPSRTC), the techniques of financial analysis were applied to study financial structure and sources of income in the organization.

Prem Babu[176] **(1993)** studied the role of Human Resource Development in greater Manchester busses, U.K., with special reference to training and development of middle level managers and supervisors including the assessment of training need and design and content of training programs. He observed that the training program developed for managers and supervisors was more purposeful and relevant to their specific needs for overall improvement in the performance of the company.

Vaidya[177] **(1983)** in her study on Inter-State routes with Special reference to Punjab focuses on route –wise costs, organizational set up, profitability analysis, and physical performance aspects like vehicle utilization, staff productivity and quality of service. He also stressed the contribution of Inter – State routes and their role in maximizing over-all revenue as well as minimizing losses.

Sudarsanam padam[178] **(1994)** attempted to reflect on the imperatives of HRD from the point of view of the passenger, road transport industry, which is not only highly labour intensive but has a preponderance of non-economic objectives. He felt that it can only be the government which could help the unorganized sector of the passenger road transport industry by providing educational facilities to upgrade human and technical skills at the induction level with the hope that competitive market force will nurture further progress. In the organized sector, there has to be a three-pronged approach to tackle the motivational needs to the workers, supervisors and managers, not only through formal training but through a bias for better performance and higher productivity.

Agarwal[179] **(1992)** analyses the financial performance of State Road Transport Corporations (SRTCs) of Rajasthan and Uttar Pradesh. This was done in terms of various ratios like liquidity ratio, leverage ratio, activity ratio were compared. The study covers bus services operated by public and private sector undertakings in Punjab. It is disclosed that the performance by the private sector was better than that of public sector. Increasing of operations in public sector cannot be done without increasing costs, and hence increases in loses. On the contrary, private operations can increase their operations, whereby they would increase their profits without incurring any loss. There has been rapid increase in movement of people from one place to another, because of economic development and the consequent urbanization. Hence, to meet the growing demand for road transport, more investment on road transport sector is required.

Gangappa[180] **(1991)** studied the organizational structure and operational efficiency of the Ananthapur Depot of APSRTC and analyzed various associated factors. He also made a study of the performance of Urban Passenger Road Transport Service with reference to the services run by APSRTC in the twin cities of Hyderabad and Secunderabad. The focus was on matters of operational performance and cost-fare relationships.

Raman[181] **(1990)** in his article has outlined many issues but he particularly stressed that Urban bus transport is a rational choice for public monopoly and often there is a need to provide transport as a social service, at rates affordable to urban settlers. He has also proved and supported this view with the instance that in United States 74% of operating cost has been covered by the fare in 1971 and 65% in 1990 while in Japan no PSUs are making profit though they are operated with maximum efficiency and productivity. This shows that in almost all the countries, PSUs are rendering social service though they are running in loss.

Sudarsanam Padam[182] **(1990)** examined the organized structure of four major SRTUs in the country. He also measured the performance of these undertakings in relation to their structure.

Rama Mohan Rao[183] **(1989)** in his study dealt with the turnaround achieved by APSRTC through improved and innovative operations Management. Several studies have focused their attention on the role of transport in the development of national economy.

Kulshresta[184] **(1989)** in his work examined different problems regarding management in Several State Transport Undertakings (STUs) in India. He made an analysis of various aspects of internal administration, operational management, and management of maintenance as well as service, personal and commercial administration. His study includes with one chapter on performance and efficiency of APSRTC.

Mishra and Nandagopal[185] **(1988)** suggest that, with the severe and continuing resource problems besetting the Indian economy, and with the pressure on policy makers to increase economic growth, there is a need to privatize State Transport Undertakings (STUs). Points out that whether

STUs should undergo sweeping reforms, or privatized, has assumed serious proportions. They attempted to study the reasons for and against nationalization of passenger Road Transport business in public sector at the time of takeover. Aims to contextualize this sector in the country's planned economic development, outlines a profile of STUs, evaluates their operations, and indicates the scope and methods for reform and privatization.

Vijayaraghavan[186] **(1988)** attempted to assess the present strategic position of the SRTUs through an elaborate SWOT analysis and to chalk out the strategic options for them in the present emerging environment of changing needs and attitudes. The diagnosis shows that the SRTUs in India are not really competing well in an industry which is becoming more and more unstable. He suggests competitive types of strategies emphasizing the importance of service marketing approach.

Ganagadhar Rao M[187] **(1987)** attempted to study the human factor in APSRTC with a focus on the conductors. Conductors are the promoters of the organizational image as well as they are the primary source of feedback from the public about the organization. so the study has its own impact on the organization.

Patankar[188] **(1986)** analyzed various aspects that have an impact on operational efficiency as well as financial performance of State Transport Units (STUs) and few recommendations were made. The study is not only on the development of transport but also made a reference to the performance of transportation system.

Phaniswara Raju[189] **(1986)** made a study on 'Materials Management in APSRTC' and examined the materials management practices and purchasing systems on the basis of various parameters like material consumption per vehicle, material consumption per kilometer, inventory per vehicle, inventory in terms of number of month's consumption etc. The study revealed the increasing levels of materials consumption in APSRTC as compared to other undertakings. He observed the absence of the use of important analytical techniques like value analysis and network techniques in the purchasing system of APSRTC. He mainly suggested the reclassification of stores items based on the - 45 -criticality, the re-fixation of reorder level and reorder quantities. The study also showed the wastage caused by maintenance of unnecessary stock records relating to items, which were no longer used.

Satyanarayana[190] **(1985)** undertook a comprehensive study of different aspects concerning the working of APSRTC. He evaluated the organizational structure of APSRTC and suggested suitable modifications to make the existing structure, effective. He has also thrown light on the financial policies and practices, personnel policies and procedures and management information system of APSRTC.

Santosh Sarma[191] **(1985)** in his study of productivity in Road Transport Corporation explained and suggested some of the modern management techniques to be followed by the passenger Road Transport industry.

Mahesh[192] **(1982)** made a review of 25 public Road Transport Undertakings regarding financial performance. It is to be noted that they were managed as corporations and companies from 1975 to 1980. However, their position regarding performance was decided based on their performance were cost based.

Jamwal[193] **(1978)** underlined the principles to be kept in mind while framing the organization structure for transport undertakings. He stressed that the management should have a basic philosophy or a set firmly held convictions towards various aspects of the organization.

Rahi Kishore[194] **(1977)** made an evolution of trends of profits, its objectives was on efficiency in operations; returns on invested capital, total effective kilometers operated, total cost etc. The performance of Punjab roadways was compared with that of Amba Bus Syndicate private Limited, on the basis of profits earned and efficiency of management.

Chaturvedi[195] **(1976)** measures the operational efficiency of Rajasthan State Road Transport Corporation from different dimensions. Some research studies at micro level on the specific functional area of a State Transport undertaking were carried out and most of them were unpublished.

Sastry[196] **(1974)** conducted a study of various State Transport Undertakings He examined many aspects like vehicle utilization, personnel productivity, quality and reliability of services as well as profitability from these services.

Krishna Murthy[197] **(1969)** gave a sketch of the origin of APSRTC and outlined the statistics reckoning fixed as well as variable costs, gross as well as net income and cancelled as well as delayed trips for different districts in the State. He explained economic, technical financial angels, and the punctuality of the buses.

Ramanadham[198] **(1955)** study covered the aspects like pricing, rail-road coordination, organization structure and finances of nationalized road services in Hyderabad. The study pertaining to APSRTC is concerned special mentions.

Rajesh Pilot[199] once marked that the image of the STUS depends largely on the passenger comforts they provide to the travelling public. So they should provide safe, comfortable and reliable services. They should inculcate among their crew, a sense of discipline and an attitude to be courteous and helpful to the passengers.

2.3. RESEARCH GAP

The foregoing review of literature sheds light on key gaps in the preceding researches carried out in the field of HRD. The researcher from her review of literature had found that there are many studies conducted on HRD and its related aspects in different organizations except in transport organization. There is a study entitled, 'HRM Practices in APSRTC – A study on Vizianagaram Zone', conducted by **Srinivasa Rao, S.,** focused on management of human element in the organization. The study could not survey the development practices of human resources. And another study carried out by **Kondayya, K.V.N.R.S.,** in the year 2003 on the topic entitled 'HRD in APSRTC – A Study with reference to managerial personnel'. In that study the researcher has focused about HRD aspects in APSRTC i.e. on the entire state. As HRD is a vital element in every organization, it should be developed from the grass roots level. As he did not concentrate on the impact of HRD aspects at Zonal level, this provides at the disposal of the researcher to access the research gap for the present study.

Due to this reason the present study has been designed to look into HRD practices followed by APSRTC at zonal level. The case study of Vizianagaram zone which has been chosen by the researcher for presenting the survey results is on the basis of performance and contribution of Vizianagaram zone with respect to various other existing zones in APSRTC. (See Table 4.9)

2.5. NEED FOR THE STUDY

HRD is an essential component for organizational growth and effectiveness. But it is imperative to mention that the approach of managements towards HRD is still conservative. As a result, the potential of human resource could not be properly gauged and fully tapped for attaining organizational goals in general and the employees in particular. In this regard, a required change in the mindset of top management is yet to take place. Unfortunately, HRD policy in most of the undertakings demonstrated a number of loopholes and failed to create desirable work environment and organizational health. So a continuous effort towards HRD is necessary for the development of the organization as whole. This could be achieved through research methods, where in possible development in specific areas may be reviewed and corrective action may be taken.

HRD is a vital area to be focused in an organization when employing huge number of work force. In the organization like APSRTC the HRD policies and practices need a scientific assessment as it employs huge number of nearly 1.3 lakh people of different cadres possessing different skills and performing different functions. But, it is observed that there are no enough studies performed on HRD practices in APSRTC at state level and almost no studies were performed at zonal level. Despite the fact that the performance of the undertaking is influenced by technology, modernization and business strategies, the role of HRD cannot be undermined. So it is appropriate to study the HRD practices of APSRTC at zonal level in order to take appropriate measures to increase employee's efficiency level and productivity.

2.6. OBJECTIVES

The basic objectives of the proposed study are:

1. To study the road transportation sector in India and in A.P.
2. To identify the existing HRD practices in APSRTC.
3. To examine the influence of HRD practices on the organization.
4. To suggest measures to improve the performance of employees in the organization.

2.7. HYPOTHESIS OF THE PRESENT STUDY

A hypothesis can be defined as an assertion or conjecture about the parameter or parameters of a population, for example the mean or the variance of a normal population. They may also concern the type, nature or probability distribution of the population. It is categorized in two types that are as follows:

➢ Null Hypothesis (H_0)
➢ Alternative Hypothesis (H_1/ $H\alpha$)

2.7.1. Null Hypothesis (H_0)

The Null Hypothesis typically corresponds to a general or default position. For example, the null hypothesis might be that there is no relationship between two measured phenomena or that a potential treatment has no effect. It is important to understand that the null hypothesis can never be proven. A set of data can only reject a null hypothesis or fail to reject it. It only means that there is no enough evidence to reject the null hypothesis. A null hypothesis is denoted as H_0.

2.7.2. Alternative Hypothesis (H_1/ $H\alpha$)

In hypothesis testing, a proposition that is accepted if the null hypothesis is rejected is known as an Alternative Hypothesis. In other words, alternative hypothesis is the "hypothesis that the restriction or set of restrictions to be tested does not hold". It is often denoted as H_1 or $H\alpha$.

2.7.3. Level of Significance

The significant level is usually denoted by the Greek symbol α (lowercase alpha). Popular levels of significance are 10 percent (0.1), 5 percent (0.05), 1 percent (0.01), 0.5 percent (0.005) and 0.1 percent (0.001). If test of significance gives p-value lower than the significant level α, the null hypothesis is rejected. Such results are informally referred to as 'statistically significant'.[200]

As sample size is small, the Confidence Interval (CI) chosen for the present study is 90 and 95 percent for which level of significance is 0.1 and 0.05 percent

The seven most important dimensions of HRD Practices on which the questionnaire has been divided is the base for developing the hypothesis for the study. The following hypothesis emerges out of the variables selected for conducting research at managerial level in APSRTC.

H_{01}: Training and Development doesn't have significant impact on the employee's performance.

H_{02}: Organizational structure & culture doesn't have significant impact on the employee's performance.

H_{03}: HRD knowledge & Skills doesn't have significant impact on the employee's performance.

H_{04}: HRD Climate doesn't have significant impact on the employee's performance.

H_{05}: Performance Appraisal doesn't have significant impact on the employee's performance.

H_{06}: Counseling doesn't have significant impact on the employee's performance.

H_{07}: Career Planning & Development doesn't have significant impact on the employee's performance.

H_{08}: Overall level of satisfaction on HRD Practices doesn't have significant impact on the employee's performance.

H_{09}: HRD practices don't have significant impact on the designation i.e. level of management.

2.8. RESEARCH METHODOLOGY

Research Methodology is the systematic framework within which the research is conducted. In general, research methodology describes the overall design of the study, entire data collection process and statistical tools used in the process of data analysis.

2.8.1. DATA COLLECTION

To attain the objectives of the present construct, the required data is collected from both primary and secondary sources.

2.8.1.1. PRIMARY DATA

The study is empirical in nature. Therefore the work is largely based on primary data. The survey method through a structured questionnaire was employed for the collection of primary data from the selected sample respondents. The respondents here are managerial and supervisory cadre employees of Vizianagaram zone of APSRTC.

2.8.1.1.1. INSTRUMENT DEVELOPMENT: QUESTIONNAIRE

A structured questionnaire has been developed to get the opinion of the managerial employees (Senior Scale Officers-SSO, Junior Scale Officers-JSO and Low level managers - LLM) of APSRTC. To elicit the information from the respondents, questionnaire was designed on practices of HRD as variables on a five point Likert Scale, with 1 for "Not at all true", 2 for "Not so true", 3 for "partly true", 4 for "True" and 5 for "very much true". The questionnaire was divided into three sections. Section A was designed to obtain demographic information of the respondents. It covers qualification, age, gender, present designation, department, monthly salary, length of service, marital status and nature of work. Section B measures the seven most important dimensions of HRD practices like Training and Development, Organizational structure and culture, HRD Knowledge and Skills, HRD climate, Performance Appraisal, Counseling, and Career planning and Development. Section C estimates the overall satisfaction of the respondents towards HRD practices in the organization. In Section C various aspects of HRD practices are measured on a five point Likert Scale, with 1 for "Highly Dissatisfied", 2 for "Dissatisfied", 3 for "Neutral", 4 for "Satisfied" and 5 for "Highly Satisfied". On the basis of these three sections in the questionnaire, the HRD practices have been judged in APSRTC and analysis has been made.

2.8.1.2. SECONDARY DATA

The secondary data is also used for referring the conceptual aspects and literature review. The data was collected from various sources like published books, libraries, annual reports, both online and print journals, magazines, periodicals, news papers, research surveys, existing works conducted on Human Resource Development and related factors, websites, presentation in seminars and conferences.

2.8.2. PILOT STUDY

The questionnaires were pre-tested with 15 employees. Based on the views and feedback of the respondents, changes were made and questionnaire was finalized.

2.8.3. Survey method

The survey method used by the researcher for the present study is Census survey. **Census** is the procedure of systematically acquiring and recording information about the members of a given population[201]. A total of 132 (27 Senior Scale officers, 37 Junior Scale Officers and 68 Low level Managers) questionnaires were administered to all the managerial employees in Vizianagaram Zone of APSRTC.

2.8.4. STATISTICAL TOOLS FOR DATA ANALYSIS

The primary data was analyzed using the Statistical Package for Social Sciences (SPSS – 15.0 version). The collected data is processed by using:

1. **Frequency Tabulations** for demographic variables (qualification, age, gender, present designation, department, monthly salary, length of service, marital status and nature of work).

2. **Mean Scores**

It is used to find out item – wise average values of the HRD Practices in APSRTC

3. **Percentage Scores**

The item-wise mean scores of the total sample are presented.

Since the questionnaire used is a five – point Likert scale, Mean score 4 and around indicates that employees in APSRTC agreed that good human resource development practices are prevailing in the organization. It indicates that human resource development practices are at desirable level, whereas mean score 3 and around indicates an average human development practices are prevailing in the organization and mean score 2 and around indicates poor human resource development practices exist in the organization (APSRTC).

In the present study, in order to make the interpretations easy the mean scores have been converted into percentage scores by using the formula, Percentage score = (Mean Score – 1) X 25. As per this measure the score 1 represents – 0 Percent, 2 represents – 25 Percent, 3 represents – 50 Percent, 4 represents – 75 Percent and 5 represents – 100 Percent. The percent Score indicates the degree to which a particular dimension exists in that organization out of the ideal 100.

4. **Standard Deviation**

Standard deviation is the square root of variance. Standard Deviation method is applied to know the nature of the variations in responses. It is used in human resource development practices to measure the variations in responses of managerial staff in APSRTC.

5. **Multiple Linear Regression Analysis**

In the present study multiple linear regression analysis is used to find out the impact of HRD Practices on employees of APSRTC.

6. **ANOVA Analysis**

ANOVA stands for analysis-of-variance, a statistical model meant to analyze data. ANOVA test is conducted to test the significant difference between two mean score among the variables of HRD practices and Demographic variables. ANOVA test is conducted to find the significant difference in the mean score among the respondents of various designations (SSO, JSO & LLM) for the overall opinion of the respondents to the HRD practices in APSRTC. In the present study ANOVA analysis is also used to test further significance level of those items in HRD practices that are resulted as significant.

The statistical results are then interpreted and the findings are compiled to derive pragmatic recommendations in the form of suitable suggestions.

2.9. SCOPE OF THE STUDY

The study covers all the important areas of HRD in APSRTC. HRD is broader than human resource management; it consists of several sub-systems such as training and development, employee appraisal, counseling, rewards and welfare, quality of work life, etc. These areas require conceptual clarifications about HR and HRD, organization structure and climate.

The Researcher feels that this study will certainly throw light upon various aspects where the top management in APSRTC needs to work out. The present study covers almost all aspects of HRD practices. The findings and conclusions of the study would be of great help in whipping out some of the undesirable issues that are likely to crop up in the implementation of such HRD practices.

2.10. LIMITATIONS OF THE STUDY

Despite of all the earnest attempts made by the researcher to elicit all required data on HRD practices in APSRTC – Vizianagaram Zone from the top management and supervisory employees, the study is subjected to certain limitations due to the fact that the data is based on individual opinion, which may bring in some bias.

1. Undoubtedly, the responses have been collected from the employees of top management and supervisory cadre in APSRTC - Vizianagaram Zone; hence limited analysis could be derived from the study.

2. It is due to this reason that HRD practices are only subjected to managerial cadre, the sample size of the top management and supervisory cadre respondents is confined to 132 only. This is due to lack of permission from the authorities to extend it to other zones for performing a comparative study.

3. In addition to this, most of the respondents were reluctant in expressing their opinion freely without any hesitation and showing lack of interest in responding. This has its own impact to certain extent over the validity of the conclusions drawn.

4. Further, the opinion of some of the employees turns out to be influenced by their peer employees or superiors which might lead to their neutral response to a large extent for several statements.

2.11. DESIGN OF THE STUDY

The study has been articulated as:

Chapter I: Introduction to Human Resource Development: Conceptual Exposition

Chapter II: Review of Literature.

Chapter III: Glimpses of Road Transport Sector in India

Chapter IV: APSRTC – An overview

Chapter V: Analysis of the Data

Chapter VI: Summary, Major findings, Conclusion and Suggestions.

2.12. CONCLUSION

In the present chapter, the researcher has flashed a broad outlook of the study spectrum by discussing the review of literature which helped in estimating the research gap. In addition to that the objectives of the study, hypothesis, scope, sample size and limitations of the study are also dealt in this section. The next chapter has been designed to give the glimpses of growth and development transport sector in India.

Chapter - III

GLIMPSES OF ROAD TRANSPORT SECTOR IN INDIA

Passenger Road Transport is basically a service industry and its financial performance is influenced by costs, revenues and physical performance. However, the present chapter mainly deals with the aspects of Physical and Financial performance of reported SRTUs in India. Physical aspects like fleet utilization, vehicle productivity and man power productivity of reported SRTUs were discussed in this chapter. Financial performance of SRTUs includes comparative financial performance, Total expenditure etc., of reported SRTUs for a specific time period, seized a place for analysis in this chapter.

3.1. Transport in General

India's transport sector is large and diverse; it caters the needs of 1.1 billion people[202]. A well knit and coordinated system of transport plays an important role in the sustained economic growth of a country. The sector in 2011-12 contributed about 6.5 percent to the Nation's GDP with Road Transportation contributing about 4.8 percent a lion's share[203]. The share of various sub sectors of the Transport in the GDP is given in the table 3.1.

The transportation system in India comprises a number of distinct modes and services notably railways, road transport, ports, in-land water transport, coastal shipping, and air-lines. Of all the modes of transport road transport and railways are the dominant means of transport. In the early 50's, road transport primarily served as a mode complimentary to the railways. However, in course of time it became competent with the railway transport[204].

Table 3.1: Shows the Percentage share of Transport
Sub – sectors in the GDP.

Sector	2003-04	2004-05	2005-06	2006-07	2007-08	2008-09	2009-10	2010-11	2011-12
As Percentage of GDP (at factor cost and constant prices)									
Mode of Transport:	6.4	6.7	6.7	6.7	6.7	6.6	6.5	6.4	6.5
Railways	1.0	1.0	1.0	1.0	1.0	1.0	1.0	1.0	1.0
Road Transport*	4.6	4.8	4.8	4.8	4.7	4.8	4.7	4.6	4.8
Water Transport*	0.2	0.2	0.2	0.2	0.2	0.2	0.2	0.2	0.2
Air Transport*	0.2	0.2	0.2	0.2	0.2	0.2	0.2	0.3	0.3
Services*	0.5	0.5	0.5	0.5	0.5	0.4	0.4	0.4	0.4

*- Unadjusted Financial Intermediation Services Indirectly Measured (FISIM).
Source: Central Statistical Organization.

Table 3.2: Shows Freight Movement by
Road Transport & Railways: 1999-2000 to 2011-12

(Billion Tonnes Kilometres)

Year(s)	Road Transport	Railways
1999-2000	467.0 (60.5)	305.2 (39.5)
2000-01	494.0 (61.3)	312.4 (38.7)
2001-02	515.0 (60.7)	333.2 (39.3)
2002-03	545.0 (60.7)	353.2 (39.3)
2003-04	595.0 (61.0)	381.2 (39.0)
2004-05	646.0 (61.1)	411.3 (38.9)
2005-06	658.9 (59.9)	441.8 (40.1)

2006-07	766.2 (61.4)	481.0 (38.6)
2007-08	851.7 (62.0)	521.3 (38.0)
2008-09	920.2 (62.5)	551.4 (37.5)
2009-10	1015.1 (62.8)	600.5 (37.2)
2010-11	1128.4 (64.3)	625.7 (35.7)
2011-12	1212.4 (64.5)	667.6 (35.5)

Note: Figures in the parenthesis denote percentage to the respective total.

Source: Road Transport Year Book, transport research wing, Ministry of Road Transport & Highways, Government of India, New Delhi, (2011-12).

Figure 3.1: Chart shows the percentage of Freight Movement by Railways and Roadways

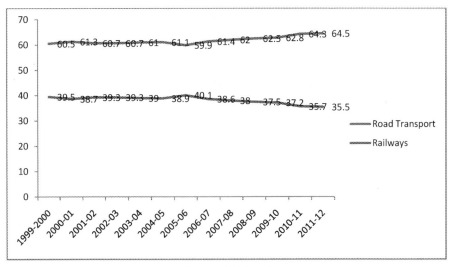

Source: Table 3.2

The table 3.2 speaks about the Freight Movement by Road Transport sector in India had increased from 60.5 percent in 1999 – 2000 to 64.5 percent during 2011 – 2012. Except in 2005 – 2006 the freight movement by railways was decreasing from 39.5 percent to 35.5 percent in 1999 – 2000 to 2011 – 2012 respectively. In 2005 – 2006 it was recorded as 40.1 Percent which is marginal.

From the table we can understand that people preferred freight movement by road transport because of the increase in road connectivity between mofussil areas and cities during 1999 – 2000. It can also be inferred that preference of freight movement by road is due to the faith and belief that goods will reach the destination in time with less cost compared to railways.

Table 3.3: Represents Passenger Movement by
Road Transport & Railways: 1999-2000 to 2011-12

(Billion Passenger Kilometers)

Year(s)	Road Transport	Railways
1999-2000	1,831.6 (81.0)	430.7 (19.0)
2000-01	2,075.5 (82.0)	457.0 (18.0)
2001-02	2,413.1 (83.1)	490.9 (16.9)
2002-03	2,814.7 (84.5)	515.0 (15.5)
2003-04	3,070.2 (85.0)	541.2 (15.0)
2004-05	3,469.3 (85.8)	575.7 (14.2)
2005-06	4,251.7 (87.4)	615.6 (12.6)
2006-07	4,251.7 (86.7)	694.8 (13.3)
2007-08	4,251.7 (86.3)	770.0 (13.7)
2008-09	4,251.7 (86.1)	838.0 (13.9)
2009-10	4,251.7 (85.2)	903.4 (14.8)

2010-11	4,251.7 (85.0)	978.5 (15.0)
2011-12	4,251.7 (85.0)	1,046.5 (15.0)

Note: Figures in the parenthesis denote percentage to the respective total.

Source: Road Transport Year Book, transport research wing, Ministry of Road Transport & Highways, Government of India, New Delhi, 2011-12.

The table 3.3 shows that the passenger movement by road transport was increased from 81 percent to 85 percent during 1999 – 2000 to 2011 – 2012 respectively. The table also reveals that passenger's preference towards railway transport is decreasing from 19 percent in 1999 – 2000 to 15 percent in 2011 – 2012.

It can be inferred that this change of passenger transport from railways to road transport may be because of the enhancement of road connectivity between villages, villages and towns and towns and cities during the above period, 1999-2000 to 2011-2012.

Figure 3.2: Chart shows Passenger Movement by
Road Transport & Railways: 1999-2000 to 2011-12

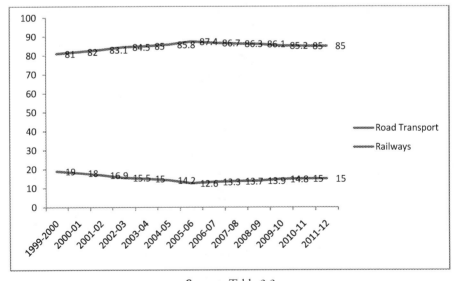

Source: Table 3.3

3.2. Road Transport in India

Road Transportation plays a pivotal role in India in bringing about greater mobility both within and between rural and urban areas. Through increased mobility, it also immensely contributes to social and economic development of different regions of the country. Realizing the importance of this link, the Government of India, in course of time has lucratively invested in the development of network of passenger transport services to linkup towns and villages all over the country.

India has one of the largest networks in the world, aggregating to about 4.1 Million Kilometers at present[205]. The country's road network consists of National Highways, State Highways, Major District Roads and Rural Roads. The National Highways has about 70,934 kilometers length and comprises only 1.7 percent of the total length of the roads. It carries over 40 percent of the total traffic across the length and breadth of the country[206].

Figure 3.3: Exhibits Network in India: National Highways Map.

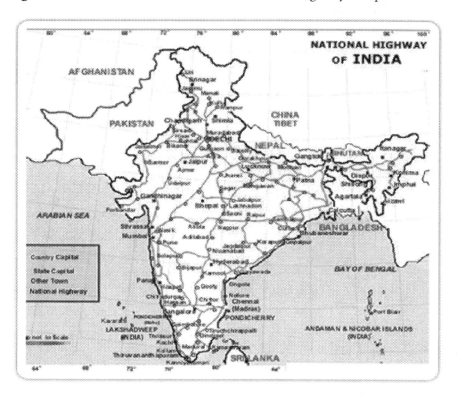

Table. 3.4: Shows Roads in India

National Highways/ Expressways	70934 KMs
State Highways	1,54,522 KMs
Major and other District Roads	34,17,000 KMs
Rural Roads	26,50,000 KMs

Source: Manorama Year Book, "Transport", P. 629, 2013.

The National Highways have been further classified depending on the carriageway width of the Highway. Generally, a lane has width of 3.75 Meters in case of single-lane and 3.5 Meters per lane in case of multiple National Highways[207]. The brake-up of National Highways in terms of width is as under[208].

Table. 3.5: Shows National Highways in terms of width

Single Lane	17,089 KMs (24%)
Double Lane	36,651 KMs (52%)
4 Lane/ 6 Lane/ 8 Lane	17,194 KMs (24%)

Note: Figures in the parenthesis denote percentage to the respective total.

Figure 3.4: Exhibits Renumbered National Highways Map of India.

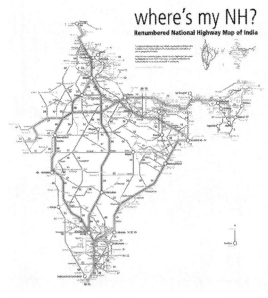

Source: www.wikipedia.com/ Transport in India

The density of India's highway network at 0.66 KMs of Highway per Square Kilometers of land is similar to that of the United States (0.65) and much greater than china's (0.16) or Brazils (0.20)[209].

Roads are the dominant mode of transportation in India today. They carry almost 90 percent of the country's passenger traffic and 65 percent of its freight[210]. Over the four decades the share of road transport in all over traffic flows, has been continually increasing with the substantial shift from rail to road was observed in table 3.3. This mode is currently estimated to have a share of 80 percent in passenger transport and 60 percent in freight transport[211].

Private operators have been a complementary role and they have been aggressive by occupying the space vacated by the state operations and run through all major centers of the country. The reach of private operators is even more, if we include un-authorized operators like Jeeps, Maxi-Cabs and Trucks. Since STUs were caught between two opposite corporate objectives of plying the services on commercial considerations on one hand and social consideration on the other, they are in quandary, and cease to operate on uneconomical routes depriving the rural masses of access to various goods, services and facilities. This situation gave way to private operators to exploit rural masses. In this context the study throws light upon the utility of rural bus transport services and makes STUs to give a policy orientation and convinced the State Governments of its constitutional obligation of the need to give all possible support for the continuation of such services in rural areas.

Classification of Transport Services

The passenger Road Transport services in general could be broadly divided into four different categories as follows:

1. Inter State
2. Inter District
3. Intra district & Rural
4. Urban operators

The characteristics of each of these services vary widely with respect to vehicle utilization, time of operation, crew requirements, profitability and major players for the types of services.

Table 3.6: Shows various types transport services in India

Category	Vehicle utilization (KMs/days)	Service type	Different Players	Profitability	Main Competitors to STUs
Inter State	>600	Volvo, Luxury, Deluxe	Public & Private	Very High	Private
Inter District	300-450	Volvo, Luxury, Express	Public & Private	Moderate & High	Private
Intra District	250-350	Express, Ordinary, Limited Halt	Public mostly Private, Autos & Maxi Cabs	Low & Loss making	Illegal contract buses, Maxi cabs
Urban Operators	200-250	Ordinary Limited Halt	Mostly Private (Autos)	Mostly Loss making	Illegal contract Buses, Autos Maxi cabs

Source: cistupiisc.ernet.in

The table 3.6 depicts that there is competition between public and private buses in inter – state and inter – district services. Private buses secure edge over public transport buses in the above stated categories because they manage profit making routes in convenient timings of the passengers by influencing transport department. Benz, Volvo, Luxury, Deluxe and Express buses are used in vehicle utilization between 300 - 450 and more than 600Kms per day. In the category of intra district and urban operators there is a competition between public and private illegal contract buses – Maxi cabs are maintained. It is evident from the table that with regard to profitability, vehicle utilization in the above category between 250 – 350 and 200 – 250 Kms per day mostly resulted in losses or making less profits.

3.2.1. Importance of State Transport Undertakings (STUs)

In India, investment in Road Transport is treated as a public provision of services as in many parts of the world. One of the key objectives of this provision has been to meet the public transport needs at an affordable, safe and reliable bus services to the people both in rural and urban areas. Accordingly, the Road Transport Act, 1950 gave boost to rural mobility. The promulgation of RTC Act enables states and Central Government to take initiative to form the Road Transport Corporations. The RTC Act thus made bus transport an integral part of social and economic infrastructure. Following the course the Motor Vehicles Act, 1950 was subsequently amended to make special provision for State Transport Undertakings (STUs). This Act was further amended in 1969 for promoting the state monopoly in passenger Road Transport services expeditiously[212].

The 38 reported Public sector transport undertakings (STUs) in India today own- 1,33,823 bus fleet, provide direct employment to 7,28,569 people and carry about 2,527.16 crore passengers[213].

The STUs in the country are set up under four forms as under:

i.   Undertakings formed under the Road Transport Corporation Act, 1950.
ii.   Undertakings formed as companies under The Companies Act, 1956.
iii. Undertakings working as Department of the State Governments.
iv.   Undertakings working as Municipal Undertakings.

Figure 3.5: Exhibits forms of SRTUs

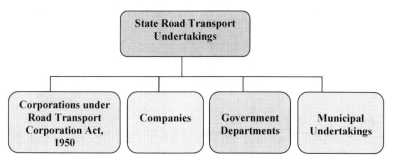

The SRTUs operating in India are further classified into three categories:

1. SRTUs operating in the plain areas.
2. SRTUs operating in hilly areas.
3. SRTUs operating in cities.

Figure 3.6: Classification of SRTUs

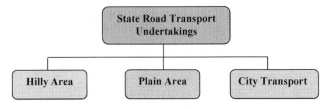

Table 3.7: Shows No. of SRTUs in India during 2002-03 to 2012-13.

Year	No. of SRTUs
2002-03	43
2003-04	43
2004-05	36
2005-06	36
2006-07	32
2007-08	36
2008-09	37
2009-10	35
2010-11	38
2011-12	38
2012 - 13	38

Source: 1. Review of Performance of SRTUs 2009-10 to
2012-13, Ministry Roads & Highways – Annual Report

Figure 3.7: Shows No. of SRTUs in India during – 2002-03 to 2011-12.

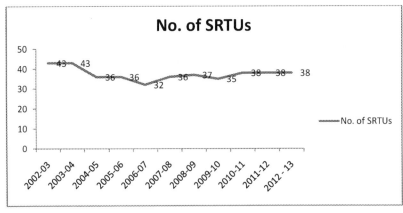

Source: Table 3.7

3.2.2. Performance of STUs

The present study brings out the performance of State Road Transport Undertakings (STUs) across the country during 2002-03 to 2012-13. It deals with the overall share of STUs in public transport, their financial position, operational performance together with the analysis of cost components, restructure of business models for tapping non-traffic revenue sources and monitoring by top management. The study provides a clear picture of public transport in India and helps policy makers to analyze the performance of STUs and infuse desired improvements in the State Road Transport Sector.

3.2.2.1. Physical Performance of STUs

Table 3.8: Shows Fleet utilization of STUs during 2002-03 to 2012-13

Percentage of fleet utilization of STUS	Average Fleet held (No's)	Average Fleet operated	Difference	Percentage of fleet utilized
2002-03	98090	90468	7622	92.22%
2003-04	103302	95997	7305	92.92%
2004-05	109611	101168	8443	92.29%
2005-06	101273	93610	7663	92.43%
2006-07	107821	99395	8426	92.18%
2007-08	113649	104991	8658	92.38%
2008-09	117879	108931	8948	92.40%
2009-10	118768	109785	8983	92.43%
2010-11	130563	118154	12409	90.49%
2011-12	131824	119209	12615	90.43%
2012-13	133823	121751	12072	90.97%

Source: 1. Performance of STUs, CIRT, Pune, 2002-03 to 2012-13
2. Review of Performance of SRTUs 2009-10 to 2012-13, Ministry Roads & Highways – Annual Report
3. http://data.gov.in/catalog/physical-performance-srtus

Fleet Utilization, is the proportion of buses, put on road to the buses held by the SRTUs. The table 3.8 expresses the overall fleet utilization of SRTUs during 2002 – 2003 to 2012 – 2013. Although percentage of fleet utilization seems decreased from 92.22 percent in 2002 – 2003 to 90.97 percent in 2012 - 2013, actually the table reveals during 2002 – 2003 to 2009 – 2010, the fleet utilization percentage was not a considerable variation except fraction of fluctuations. In the reference period, the percentage of fleet utilization is uniform except a degree difference.

It is evident from the table, that percentage of fleet utilization decreased by some extent i.e. 1 or 2 percent marginal difference is observed during 2010 – 11 to 2012 – 13 being 90.49 percent and 90.97 percent respectively. It may be the reason that there is no replacement of buses for the condemned old buses.

Table 3.9: Shows total accidents occurred during 2002-03 to 2012-13

Year(s)	No. of accidents	No. of fatal accidents
2002-03	20445	3852 (18.84)
2003-04	21444	4127 (19.24)
2004-05	21197	4632 (21.85)
2005-06	20241	4107 (20.29)
2006-07	21866	4471 (20.44)
2007-08	24863	4936 (19.85)
2008-09	23610	4567 (19.34)
2009-10	21547	4621 (21.44)
2010-11	22760	4767 (20.94)
2011-12	20783	4378 (21.06)
2012-13	19464	4080 (20.96)

Note: Figures in the parenthesis denote percentage to the respective total.
Source: 1. Performance of STUs, CIRT, Pune, 2002-03 to 2012-13
       2. Review of Performance of SRTUs 2009-10 to 2012-13, Ministry Roads & Highways – Annual Report

The table 3.9 portrays that there is an increase in fatal accidents from 3852 in 2002 – 2003 to 4080 in 2012 – 2013, with some fluctuations in between under the review period. As evident from the table, the percentage of fatal accidents range between 18.84 percent (2002 – 2003) to 21.44 percent (2009 – 2010).

The reduction in the percentage of fatal accidents in proportion to the total accidents during the years may be because of counseling given to the public by the police and transport departments. Personal awareness of individuals about traffic rules also support the fall in fatal accidents percentage from total accidents during the period of reference.

Figure 3.8: Shows Graphical representation of fatal accidents occurred during 2002-03 to 2012-13

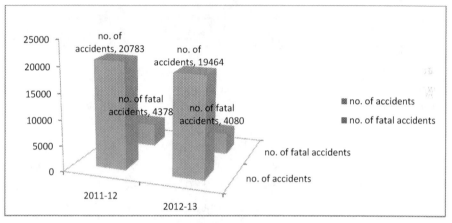

Source: Table 3.9

Table 3.10: Shows No. of buses owned by the Public and Private Sector in India from 1961-2012

(In thousands)

Year (as on 31ˢᵗ March, 2012)	Public sector buses	Private sector buses	Total	Percentage of public sector buses
1961	18	38.8	56.8	31.69014
1966	26.5	47.0	73.5	36.05442
1971	-	-	-	-
1976	52.2	62.8	115	45.3913
1981	69.6	92.3	161.9	42.9895
1986	84.0	143.3	227.3	36.95557
1991	106.1	225.0	331.1	32.0447
1996	111.1	338.7	449.8	24.69987

2001	115.0	518.9	633.9*	18.14166
2002	114.7	520.3	635*	18.06299
2003	114.9	605.9	720.8*	15.94062
2004	111.4	656.2	767.6*	14.51277
2005	113.3	779.4	892.7*	12.69183
2006	112.1	879.9	992*	11.3004
2007	107.8	1242.5	1350.3*	7.983411
2008	113.6	1313.6	1427.2*	7.959641
2009	117.6	1368.0	1485.6*	7.915994
2010	118.8	1408.3	1527.1*	7.779451
2011	130.6	1473.2	1603.8*	8.14316
2012 (P)	131.8	1544.7	1676.5*	7.861616

*-Includes omini-buses; P- Denotes Provisional

Source: 1. Offices of State Transport commissioners/ UT Administrations.

2. State Road Transport Undertakings.

The growth of the fleet strength of private buses and those of STUs during 1961 – 2012 is shown in the above table 3.10. From the table 3.10 it is clear that the share of STUs is steadily increasing from 31.69 percent during 1961 to 49.39 percent by 1976. Later on from 1981 till 2012, the table also shows that the percentage of public sector buses shows its graph decreasing to 7.86 percent by 2012 as against 42.98 percent in 1981, except a slight rise in percentage for the year 2011. The table 3.10 also indicates that the fleet strength was steadily growing from 56.8 to 1676.5 during 1961 – 2012. Therefore it is reasonable to assume that during the last 21 years, passenger's traffic may have migrated to private sector - buses, cabs, autos, lorries etc., because of public sector's failure to rise to the aspirations and needs of the people. The declining occupancy ratio caused by such migration leads to poor revenue realization which again restricts augmentation and it becomes a vicious circle.

Operational productivity Parameters

The following sections present some measures of physical productivity of SRTUs.

Table 3.11: Shows Fleet Utilization and Vehicle productivity of SRTUs during 2002-03 to 2012 -13.

Year	Fleet Utilization (%)	Productivity (Kms Per Vehicle held Per Day): Vehicle utilization
2002-03	92.1	296.2
2003-04	92.8	304.0
2004-05	92.3	306.0
2005-06	91.9	306.0
2006-07	92.2	314.0
2007-08	92.4	319.0
2008-09	92.3	321.0
2009-10	92.4	323.3
2010-11	90.5	311.5
2011-12	90.4	312.3
2012-13	91.7	312.9

Source: 1. Performance of STUs, CIRT, Pune, 2002-03 to 2012-13
2. Review of Performance of SRTUs 2009-10 to 2012-13, Ministry Roads & Highways – Annual Report
3. http://data.gov.in/catalog/physical-performance-srtus

Fleet Utilization:

Fleet utilization is defined as the ratio of the buses on road to the average fleet held by an undertaking. The average fleet utilization for all reporting SRTUs was marginally raise at 91.7 percent during the year 2012-13 compared to 90.4 percent during the previous year – as per the above table 3.11. There are several variations in inter – SRTU comparison of fleet utilization. (Ministry of Roads & Highways – Annual Report – 2012-13).

From the above table 3.11, it is clear that there has been an improvement of vehicle productivity of the reporting SRTUs over the years from 296.2 kms in 2002-03 to 312.9 kms in 2012-13. But there has been dwindle in vehicle productivity from 2010 – 11 to 2012-13 which may be attributed to the decreasing fleet size is due to non substitution of new buses to the condemned old buses of SRTUs. The improvement in quality of road network in recent years has been one of the contributing factors to the improvement in vehicle productivity during the review period.

Vehicle Productivity:

Vehicle productivity captures the average number of revenue earning kilometers performed by a bus per day. The below table 3.11 indicates the Fleet Utilization & Vehicle productivity in terms of Kms Per Vehicle held Per Day. The vehicle productivity in terms of average number of revenue earning kilometers was 296.2 during 2002 – 03 increased to 323.3 during 2009 – 10 and stands at 312.9 during 2012 – 13.

Table 3.12: Shows Man Power Productivity in STUs

Year	Staff / Bus Ratio	Kms/ Staff/ Day
2002-03	7.03	45.7
2003-04	5.9	51.4
2004-05	6.3	48.6
2005-06	5.8	52.8
2006-07	5.9	53.0
2007-08	5.9	53.9
2008-09	5.8	55.8
2009-10	5.6	57.5
2010-11	5.6	56.0
2011-12	5.5	56.5
2012-13	5.4	57.5

Source: 1. Performance of STUs, CIRT, Pune, 2002-03 to 2012-13
2. Review of Performance of SRTUs 2009-10 to 2012-13, Ministry Roads & Highways – Annual Report
3. http://data.gov.in/catalog/physical-performance-srtus

The table 3.12 shows that there has been some improvement in the use of man power indicated by declining staff per bus ratio, which improved from 7.3 persons in 2002-03 to 5.4 persons in 2012 - 13. This may be because of increase in the number of bus fleet during the reference period.

It is often pointed out that private operators operate their services with a lower staff ratio thereby minimizing man power cost. However, inadequate staff to operate buses can endanger safety by forcing the crew to work for long hours and without adequate man power being deployed on the maintenance of buses. The recent accident of Volvo bus of Jabber travels at Palem in Mahaboob Nagar district of Andhra Pradesh on 30th October, 2013 is an example for this, which 45 passengers were killed. The enquiry reports reveal that a single driver driving is the cause for this accident, since, it is mandatory to have two drivers during such long distances from Bangalore to Hyderabad.

The average revenue earning kilometers performed per worker per day could be considered as a parameter of staff productivity. The above table 3.12 shows that there has been improvement in man power productivity of STUs which increased from the average revenue earning kilometers performed per worker per day was 45.7 kms per staff per day during 2002 – 03 increased to 57.5 kms in 2012 – 13.

Table 3.13: Shows Capacity Utilization of Buses during 2002 – 03 to 2012 - 13

Year(s)	2001 - 02	2002- 03	2003- 04	2004- 05	2005- 06	2006- 07	2007- 08	2008- 09	2009- 10	2010-11	2011-12	2012- 13
Occupancy Ratio (OR) (%)	62.7	61.6	61.6	64.7	65.9	67.9	68.8	69.9	70.5	72.5	71.9	68.9
Avg. bus fleet held (No's)	-	98090	103302	109611	101273	107821	113649	117879	118768	130563	131824	133823
Staff Bus Ratio %	6.7	6.4	5.9	6.3	5.8	5.9	5.9	5.8	5.6	5.6	5.5	5.4

Source: 1. Performance of STUs, CIRT, Pune, 2002-03 to 2012-13

2. Review of Performance of SRTUs 2009-10 to 2012-13, Ministry Roads & Highways – Annual Report

3. http://data.gov.in/catalog/physical-performance-srtus

Capacity utilization of Buses:

Capacity utilization of a transport undertaking is the measure in terms of occupancy ratio (OR) representing the percentage of passengers' carried to seating capacity. Occupancy Ratio (OR) is the average percentage of seats in a bus taken by passengers vis – a – vis number of busses. Bus Staff ratio (BSR) compares the number of persons employed on the basis of bus – staff ratio which indicates the number of employees per bus on road.

Occupancy Ratio:

Occupancy Ratio relates the passenger Kilometers performed to passenger Kilometers offered. The table 3.13 shows occupancy ratio of SRTUs during 2012 – 13. It is observed from the table 3.13 that the OR has increased from 62.7 percent in 2001 – 02 to 72.5 in 2010-11 and stands at 68.9 percent in 2012 – 13. There was dwindled in percentage of OR during 2011-12 and 2012-13 may be because of competition from other modes of transport which have gained importance due to better quality buses, better amenities and services in recent times. It can be inferred that provision of better quality buses, infrastructure, amenities and better services push SRTUs to maximize public transport at desired level and get an edge over the other modes of transport.

The table 3.13 also throws light on bus staff ratio which was 6.7 in 2001 – 02 decreased to 5.4 percent in 2012– 13. There was a continuous decrease in bus staff ratio during the period of review except in 2004 – 05; it was 6.3 in that year. The staff bus ratio has dropped under the period of reference and it varies among SRTUs. The diving down of bus staff ratio denotes downsize in human resource. Reduction in bus staff ratio does not mean that employment opportunities in SRTUs are declining. It may be because of increase in fleet, which is more in proportion to that of staff, thereby causing decline in this ratio.

3.3.2.2. Financial Performance

The table 3.14 depicts the comparative analysis of top three profit making SRTUs as well as maximum three loss incurred SRTUs for the year 2011-12 and 2012-13.

Table 3.14: Shows Comparative Financial Performance of highest
Net Profit/ Loss making SRTUs during 2011-12 and 2012-13

| S.No. | Highest Profit Making SRTUs | | S.No. | Highest Loss Making SRTUs | |
	2011-12	2012-13		2011-12	2012-13
1.	Maharashtra SRTC (Rs.64.0 Crore)	Maharashtra SRTC (Rs.63.97 Crore)	1.	Delhi Transport Corporation (Rs. 2540.5Crore)	Delhi Transport Corporation (Rs. 2431.07Crore)
2.	Bangalore Metropolitan TC (Rs.25.0 Crore)	Bangalore Metropolitan TC (Rs.21.41 Crore)	2.	Andhra Pradesh SRTC (Rs. 528.7 Crore)	Andhra Pradesh SRTC (Rs. 545.30 Crore)
3.	Karnataka SRTC (Rs. 19.4 Crore)	Karnataka SRTC (Rs. 19.41 Crore)	3.	Gujarat SRTC (Rs. 402.3 Crore)	Kerala SRTC (Rs. 198.60 Crore)

Source: Compiled from Review of Performance of SRTUs 2011-12 to 2012-13, Ministry
Roads & Highways –Annual Report

Figure 3.9: Chart showing Profit making SRTUs during 2012 - 13

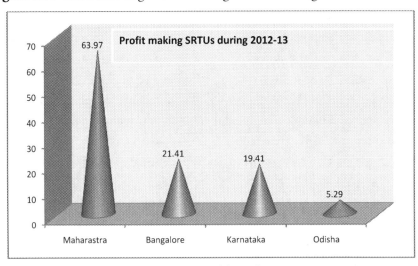

Source: Table 3.14

The table 3.14 reveals that Maharastra SRTU, Banglore Metropolitan TC and Karnataka SRTC stood as profit making SRTUs in 2011-12 with profit of Rs. 64 Crore, Rs. 25 Crore and Rs. 19.4 Crore respectively and maximum loss incurred SRTUs in 2011-12 were Delhi TC, APSRTC and Gujarat SRTUs were Delhi TC, APSRTC and Gujarat SRTC with Rs. 2540 Crore, Rs. 528.7 Crore and Rs. 402.3 Crore respectively. However, it is obvious from the table that the highest profit making SRTUs of 2012-13 were same as in 2011-12 with some slight change in their profits. But the highest loss making SRTUs in 2012-13 were delhi TC, APSRTC and Kerala SRTC with Rs. 2431.07 Crore, Rs. 545.30 Crore and Rs. 198.60 Crore respectively.

Table 3.15: Shows the Total Expenditure of STUs during 2002-03 to 2012-13 (in lakhs)

Year	Staff Cost	Fuel & Lubricant cost	Tyres & Tubes	Spare Parts	Interest	Depreciation	Taxes	Others	Total Costs	Total Revenues	Profit/Loss (in Crores)
2002-03	656520.12	470234.87	42794.45	51,417.60	61875.52	85195.63	151240.52	105668.35	1624981.65	1481714.11	-143267.54
2003-04	595728.19	444184.37	35612.08	38946.88	61004.95	76123.29	133000.21	114752.18	1499352.15	1340305.73	-159046.42
2004-05	803526.19	648917.04	48632.50	53225.45	93688.40	92772.78	172425.90	156918.08	2070106.34	1861779.21	-208327.13
2005-06	789955.00	703975.24	45782.80	52623.40	94032.58	86802.74	159773.42	134850.00	2068090.30	1853413.72	-214676.58
2006-07	884114.52	827995.09	62582.80	58242.45	110753.14	117016.45	176780.57	137798.54	2375283.67	2172165.10	-203118.57
2007-08	968891.99	865190.00	69889.68	62652.60	116472.51	138903.06	184687.91	153333.25	2560021.00	2361936.63	-198084.37
2008-09	1071072.19	956165.77	75504.91	69247.15	167659.60	166012.47	188550.94	146741.40	2840954.43	2520095.67	-320858.76
2009-10	1258718.45	950000.30	68443.26	72942.37	205319.53	181073.64	200498.51	170905.15	3107901.21	2634190.92	-473710.29
2010-11	1503998.78	1142298.86	87801.27	107114.45	256502.00	222835.42	248299.17	205554.15	3774404.10	3184337.69	-590066.41
2011-12	1686090.91	1283109.86	106169.27	123419.08	300337.05	228387.14	270084.29	265035.59	4262633.19	3592873.09	-669760.10
2012-13	1944964.32	1493520.87	114698.16	135332.35	363824.06	247175.02	272464.22	366750.11	4938131.85	4208937.40	-726966.84

Source: 1. Performance of STUs, CIRT, Pune, 2002-03 to 2012-13

2. Review of Performance of SRTUs 2009-10 to 2012-13, Ministry Roads & Highways – Annual Report

3. http://data.gov.in/catalog/financial-performance-srtus

The table 3.15 demonstrates that the total expenditure exceeded the total revenue of the reported STUs leading to losses during 2002 – 2003 to 2012 – 13. The expenditure in 2002 - 2003 is Rs. 1624981.65 lakh and revenue for the same year is Rs. 1481714.11 lakh. So the net loss during the year is Rs. 143267.54 lakh. In the year 2012 – 13, the total revenue increased by more than three times from Rs. 1481714.11 lakh in the year 2002 – 2003 to Rs. 4208937.40 lakh; the cost of STUs also increased about three times during the reference period from Rs. 1624981.65 lakh to Rs. 4938131.85 lakh. Therefore, the losses increased from Rs. 143267.54 lakh during 2002 – 2003 to Rs. 726966.84 lakh during 2012 – 2013.

It is also evident from the table 3.15, the staff cost increased from Rs. 656520.12 lakh to Rs. 1944964.32 lakh; fuel cost raised from Rs. 470234.87 lakh to Rs. 1493520.87 lakh; tyres and tubes from 42794.45 lakh to 114698.16 lakh; spare parts costs from Rs. 51417.60 lakh to 135332.35 lakh; interests from Rs. 61875.52 lakh to Rs. 363824.06 lakh; depreciation from Rs. 85195.63 lakh to Rs. 247175.02 lakh; taxes from Rs. 151240.52 lakh to Rs. 272464.22 lakh; other costs from Rs. 105668.35 lakh to Rs. 366750.11 lakh during the period under review - 2002 – 03 to 2012 - 13.

The table 3.15 gives us an understanding that due to the rising costs and inadequate support from the government, most of the STUs have been incurring losses resulting in a fall in their quality of service. On the other hand, there are STUs which have achieved a turnaround through innovative management strategies, and are incurring losses due to failure on the part of the state governments in arresting unethical and illegal private transport carriers.

Figure 3.10: Chart shows the Cost Structure of SRTUs for 2012 - 13

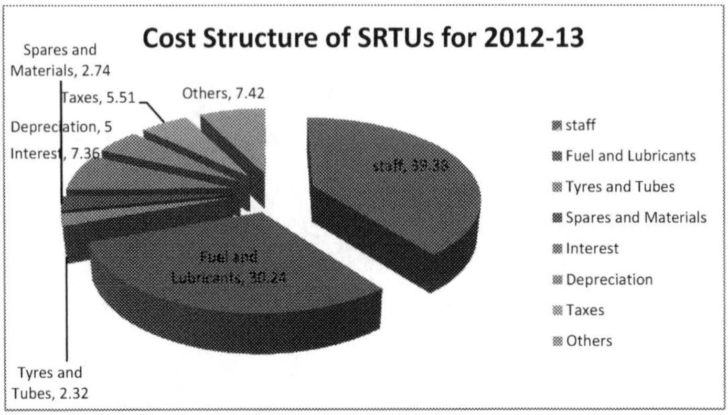

Source: Table 3.15

Table 3.16: Shows the Cost Structure and its Components
of all SRTUs during 2011-12 and 2012-13

S.No.	Cost Component	Year(s)	
	A. Operating Cost	2011-12	2012-13
1.	Staff	1686090.91 (39.55)	1944964.32 (39.38)
2.	Fuel and Lubricants	1283109.86 (30.10)	1493520.87 (30.24)
3.	Tyres and Tubes	106169.27 (2.49)	114698.16 (2.32)
4.	Spares and Materials	123419.08 (2.89)	135332.35 (2.74)
	B. Non - Operating Cost		
1.	Interest	300337.05 (7.04)	363824.06 (7.36)
2.	Depreciation	228387.14 (5.35)	247175.02 (5.00)
3.	Taxes	270084.29 (6.33)	272464.22 (5.51)
4.	Others	265035.59 (6.21)	366750.11 (7.42)

Note: Figures in the parenthesis denote percentage to the respective total.
Source: Review of Performance of SRTUs 2011-12 to 2012-13, Ministry Roads & Highways – Annual Report

The cost structure of reporting SRTUs for the years 2011-12 and 2012 – 13, from the above table 3.16 indicates that staff and fuel costs were the major elements of operating costs. These accounted for about 70 percent of the total costs, with staff costs and fuel cost constituting around 40 percent and 30 percent of the costs respectively. The performance of all the reporting SRTUs reflects that non – operating costs accounted for only 25.29 percent of the total costs during the year 2012- 13. Taxes accounted for 5.51 percent of total costs despite the fact that there were wide variations in the structure and rates of motor vehicle taxes among the states.

Figure 3.11: Shows operating cost components of reporting SRTUs during 2011-12 and 2012-13

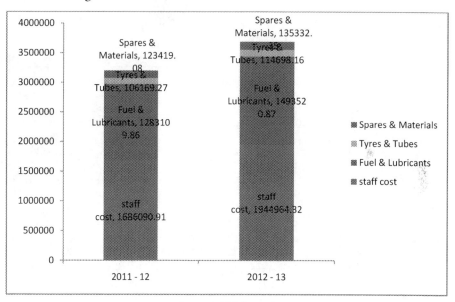

Source: Table 3.16

Figure 3.12: Shows Non - Operating cost components of reporting SRTUs during 2011-12 and 2012-13

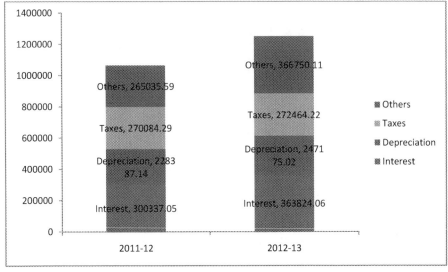

Source: Table 3.16

Table 3.17: Shows Income Vs Expenditure (In Crores)

Year	Total Revenue	Total Cost	Surplus(+) / Deficit(-)
2002-03	1481714.11	1624981.65	-143267.54
2003-04	1340305.73	1499352.15	-159046.42
2004-05	1861779.21	2070106.34	-208327.13
2005-06	1853413.72	2068090.30	-214676.58
2006-07	2172165.10	2375283.67	-203118.57
2007-08	2361936.63	2560021.00	-198084.37
2008-09	2520095.67	2840954.43	-320858.76
2009-10	2634190.92	3107901.21	-473710.29
2010-11	3184337.69	3774404.10	-59006.41
2011-12	3592873.09	4262633.19	-669760.10
2012-13	4208937.40	4938131.85	-729194.45

Source: 1. Performance of STUs, CIRT, Pune, 2002-03 to 2012-13

2. Review of Performance of SRTUs 2009-10 to 2012-13, Ministry Roads & Highways – Annual Report

3. http://data.gov.in/catalog/financial-performance-srtus

The State Transport Undertakings were set up with an objective of providing an efficient, adequate and economical and properly coordinately transport services. Due to rising costs and inadequate support from the government, most of the STUs have been incurring losses in their quality of service.

The facts about the table 3.17 were already analyzed in the table 3.15. To overcome the prevailing loses of the SRTUs, the government should take steps to prevent contract carriers operating as stage carriers which action enable STUs to raise their occupancy ratio and get profits.

Table 3.18: Shows Financial Performance of 38 reporting SRTUs during 2010-11 and 2011-12

S.No.	Financial Performance	All SRTUs		Percentage Change
		2011-12	2012-13	
1.	Number of reporting SRTUs	38	38	0
2.	Total Revenue (Rs Crores)	3592873.09	4208937.40	17.14
3.	Total Cost (Rs Crores)	4262633.19	4938131.85	15.84
a)	Operating Cost (Rs Crores)	3198789.19	3688515.7	15.30
b)	Non - Operating Cost (Rs Crores)	1063844.07	1250213.41	17.51
4	Net Profit/ Loss (Rs Crores)	-669760.10	-726966.84	8.54

Source: Review of Performance of SRTUs 2011-12 to 2012-13, Ministry Roads & Highways – Annual Report

The above table 3.18 shows that the net aggregate loss incurred by 38 SRTUs for which data on financial parameters has been received, increased by 8.54 percent from Rs. (–) 669760.10 Crore in 2011 – 12 to Rs. (–) 726966.84 in 2012 – 13.

During the year 2012 – 13, the performance of SRTUs reveals that 38 reporting SRTUs earned total revenue of 4208937.40 Crore and incurred a cost of Rs. 4938131.85 Crore which translated into a net loss of Rs. 726966.84 Crore during the year 2012 – 13. This contrasts with the net loss of Rs. 669760.10 Crore during 2011 – 12.

Figure 3.13: Chart shows Financial Performance of 38 reporting SRTUs during 2011-12 and 2012-13

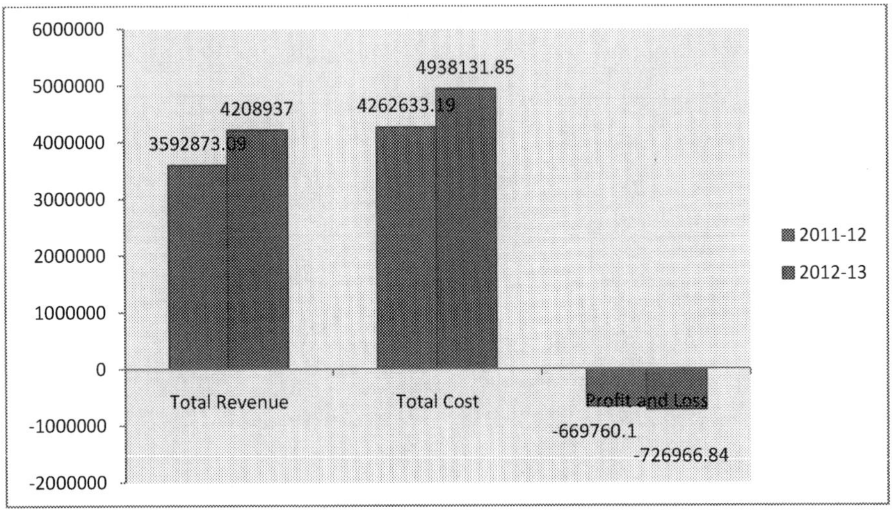

Source: Table 3.19

3.3. CONCLUSION

The main objective of State Transport Undertaking (SRTUs) was to provide an efficient, adequate, economical and properly coordinated transport service. But due to rising costs and inadequate support from the government, most of the SRTUs have been incurring losses resulting in a fall in their quality of service. In order to overcome the prevailing situation in SRTUs and to offset losses, the SRTUs need to be given financial support and greater functional autonomy from the government in order to achieve specified mile stones with respect to their performance parameters.

Chapter - IV

AP STATE ROAD TRANSPORT CORPORATION – AN OVERVIEW

The Present chapter "AP State Road Transport Corporation – An Overview" portrays the vision and mission of APSRTC. In this chapter, the researcher has endeavored to put forward the growth of APSRTC in the background of HRD Practices along with physical and financial aspects of the corporation. The chapter is presented in two sections – Section 'A' & 'B'. The profile, organization structure, physical and financial performance, impact of illegal private operators and impact agitations and state bifurcation were discusses in Section 'A'. The HRD practices in APSRCT – A study of its implication is discussed in Section 'B' covering practices like Training and Development, Performance Appraisal, Incentives etc.

SECTION A – PROFILE AND PERFORMANCE OF APSRTC

4.1. Backdrop of Andhra Pradesh

Figure 4.1: Andhra Pradesh Map

Andhra Pradesh is situated on the country's southeastern coast, was formed on 1st November, 1956. It lies between 12°41' and 22°N latitude and 77° and 84°40'E longitude, and is bordered by <u>Maharashtra</u>, <u>Chhattisgarh</u> and <u>Orissa</u> in the north, the <u>Bay of Bengal</u> in the east, <u>Tamil Nadu</u> to the south and <u>Karnataka</u> to the west. It is India's fourth largest state by area (2, 75,045 km²) and <u>fifth largest by population</u> (8, 46, 55,533)[214]. Andhra Pradesh occupies a land area of 2.75 Lakh Sq.km. Its capital and largest city is <u>Hyderabad</u>. The State, being predominantly an agriculture-oriented economy, depends on road transport for the movement of agricultural produce and raw and finished material. The <u>Andhra Pradesh State Road Transport Corporation</u> (APSRTC)

is the major public transport corporation owned by the government of Andhra Pradesh that connects all the cities and villages. A total of 146,954 km (91,313 mi) of roads are maintained by the State, of which <u>State Highways</u> comprise 42,511 km (26,415 mi), National Highways 2,949 km (1,832 mi), and District Roads 101,484 km (63,059 mi)[215].

4.2. Brief History of APSRTC

Before independence, passenger road transport operation was in the hands of private operators. The operation of bus transport by private agencies and individual proprietors, up to the nationalization of bus transport in India, has no doubt contributed to a rapid growth of the sector of Road Transport. However, the need for nationalization of bus transport was keenly felt, as the private operators could neither provide increased services to a growing extent as required by the people, nor could they improve the services to meet the demand of the users for better comfort and convenience of travel through introduction of new vehicles and modernized infrastructure. Road transport was something of a nightmare to passengers involving abnormal delays, overcrowding, fatigue and exhaustion. Amenities like bus stations, passenger shelters, canteens, retiring rooms etc. were beyond the contemplation of small private operators. The private operators also take the blame for an element of exploitation of the users through monopoly in operations. Such a situation gave rise to a demand for the policy of nationalizing passenger transport.

Shortly after independence, the nation embarked on a policy of nationalizing passenger transport. The objective of nationalization was to provide efficient economic and properly coordinated road transport with a view to accelerate the development in rural areas where 80 percent of the people were dwelling. In pursuance of the policy of the nation, parliament enacted the road transport corporation act in 1950. In the awake of this enactment various state governments enacted legislation for nationalization of bus transport since independence and began to implement it in a phased manner subject to financial, social and political considerations. Andhra Pradesh Road Transport Corporation was one among nationalized State Road Transport Corporations in India with 100 percent passenger bus transport nationalization as against to other states. In most of the states in India, nearly 50 to 75 percent of the passenger bus transport has been nationalized.

4.2.1 Formation of APSRTC

Andhra Pradesh Road Transport Corporation (APSRTC) was established on 11th January, 1958 under Road Transport Act, 1950. It is the major public transport in the country with its head quarters at Hyderabad. APSRTC serves a diverse customer base and is the largest provider of intercity bus transportation and also makes the buses to ply to link rural areas with towns and cities in A.P. The origin of APSRTC dates back to June 1932, when it was first established as Nizam State Rail and Road Transport Department (NSR-RTD) – a wing of Nizam State Railway in the erstwhile Hyderabad state, started with 27 buses and 166 employees. As a legal heir to its predecessor, Nizam State Rail and Road Transport Department, APSRTC has taken the responsibility to undertake the assets and liabilities. At the time of formation APSRTC in 1958, assets were valued at Rs. 2.25 crore[216].

The Nizam's guaranteed State Railway was a railway company in India and was owned by the dominion of Nizam or better known as the Hyderabad state during 1879 - 1950. Being one of the largest princely states of India, the Nizam of Hyderabad state wanted to build a railway line to connect Hyderabad with the rest of British India. The proposed line was to be built between Secunderabad railway stations – Wadi initially. It was built in 1879. Nizam bore all the expenses for the construction of the line. In 1883, a Management Company was formed to gradually take over these lines under the provision of a guarantee from the Nizam government of Hyderabad State. The Nizam guaranteed state railway – a railway which was under the British company until it was taken over by the Nizam government by squashing the contract in pursuance of the suggestion of Sir Akbar Haidari, the then Minister of Finance in Nizam government and established it as Nizam State Railways in 1932.

Nizam State Road was providing better and cheaper transport facility for long distance passengers. It could not provide short distance such as between country side and towns, towns and cities, towns and towns - vice versa. After getting down from rail the passengers have to face many difficulties to reach their destinations. This situation was an opportunity for private services to exploit the passengers and demand double the fares or more. Sir Akbar Haidari, the then Minister of Finance in Nizam government came to know the plight of the people in reaching their destinations after getting down in the railway station. To end the troubles of the passengers, Haidari initiated action with the approval of Nizam government to ply buses in between railway station and villages, villages and towns, towns and towns and between cities and towns. Henceforth the passenger transport came into existence with the benevolent efforts of the then Finance Minister of Government of Nizam, Sir Akbar Haidari and established it as Nizam State Rail and Road Transport Department (NSR-RTD) a part of Nizam State Railway in the former Hyderabad State in the year 1932.

The Nizam Government imported 27 Albion petrol buses from England with a capacity of 25 seats a bus. Out of 27 buses, 10 buses were allotted to Hyderabad, 10 buses to Narkedpalli and remaining 7 to Kazipet. The capital investment for these buses was Rs. 3.93 lakh[217]. Interviews were conducted to fill up the vacancies of drivers, conductors and mechanics by issuing press notification in Times of India. The first established depot was Kachiguda Depot. The first bus was operated between Kachiguda and Gulzar house in Hyderabad state. Road Transport was continued as a wing of Nizam State Railway until it emerged as full-fledged department of Government of Hyderabad State from 1st November, 1951 and carried till 1958 when Andhra Pradesh Road Transport Corporation (APSRTC) was born.

In the last 80 years, with the patronage of passengers APSRTC had grown to become the largest passenger bus fleet holding organization in the world with 22,507 buses (9,240 RTC buses plus 3,267 hired buses) and listed in Gunnies Book of World Records in 1986 for having largest fleet of vehicles and longest distance covered daily (80.77 Lakh Kms). APSRTC celebrated its platinum jubilee in the year 2006 – 2007; the celebrations were officially launched by the Honorable Chief Minister of A.P. Dr. Raja Shekar Reddy on 26th November, 2006. Mahatma Gandhi Bus Station (MGBS) in Hyderabad and Nehru Bus Stand in Vijayawada are among the largest Bus Stations in Asia – stands credit to the APSRTC[218]. There is a competition from the private operators to APSRTC who run number of buses connecting major towns and cities in A.P. as well inter-state luxury buses to neighbouring states. Private vehicles like cars, cabs, autos occupy major share of local transport – which in turn affects the revenue income of APSRTC and causes revenue losses to the corporation.

4.3. APSRTC - Profile

Andhra Pradesh State Road Transport Corporation registered a steady growth from 27 to 22,477 buses with 778 bus stations, 215 bus depots and 1,881 bus shelters. The Corporation buses cover 80.77 Lakh Kms a day and ferries almost about 154.63 Lakh passengers daily to their destinations. The Corporation with 1, 22,692 employees (male 1, 12,650 plus female 10,042) operating buses in 7,763 routes connecting 23 regions (Revenue Districts of A.P). It also connects 23,388 villages to all important towns and cities in A.P. which constitutes about 95 percent of road transport. APSRTC ply buses to cities and mofussil areas, places of business centers, historical places with religious importance and tourist attractive locations. The details of APSRTC operations are shown in the following table 4.1.

Table 4.1: Shows APSRTC Passenger Amenities

Particulars	Unit	2002-03	2003-04	2004-05	2005-06	2006-07	2007-08	2008-09	2009-10	2010-11	2011-12	2012-13
Depots	Nos	212	212	212	212	203	202	202	202	210	210	215
Bus Stations	Nos	756	758	763	766	766	765	767	767	773	776	778
Bus Shelters	Nos	1875	1879	1880	1880	1880	1880	1880	1880	1881	1881	1,881
Bus Fleet	Nos	19102	19108	19609	19407	19618	19987	20704	21606	21802	22170	22477
No. of Bus Routes	Nos	8217	8192	8132	7641	7363	7551	7701	7954	7983	8015	7,763
Avg. Seating Capacity	-	52.94	52.94	52.90	52.67	52.69	52.24	51.72	51.15	50.50	49.91	-
Avg Basic Fare	Ps	35.85	38.40	38.40	38.53	41.74	42.03	42.51	45.42	53.49	58.52	98.64

Source: 1. www.apsrtc.gov.in

2. www.apsrcinfo.com

4.3.1. Vision of A.P.S.R.T.C[219]

APSRTC is committed to provide consistently high quality of services and to continuously improve the services through a process of teamwork for the utmost satisfaction of the passengers and to attain a position of pre-eminence in the Bus Transport sector.

4.3.2. Corporate Philosophy[220]

> ➤ To provide safe, clean, comfortable, punctual and courteous commuter service at an economic fare.
> ➤ To provide employee satisfaction in financial and humanistic terms.
> ➤ To strive towards financial self-reliance in regard to performance and growth.
> ➤ To attain a position of reputation and respect in the society.

4.3.3. Guiding Principles of APSRTC[221]

> ➤ To provide efficient, effective, ethical management of the business.
> ➤ To assist the State administration in attaining good governance.
> ➤ To treat the customer, i.e. passenger, as a central concern of the Corporation's business and provide the best possible service.
> ➤ To explore and exploit technological, financial and managerial opportunities and developments and render the business cost effective at all times.
> ➤ To regularly and constantly improve the capabilities of employees for higher productivity.
> ➤ To focus on service conditions and welfare of the employees and their families consistent with their worth to the Corporation.
> ➤ To fulfill its obligation to the State and Central governments by optimizing return on investment.
> ➤ To emphasize environmental and community concerns in the form of reducing air and noise pollution.
> ➤ To consciously conform to the policy guidelines of the State in its business operations.
> ➤ To reach a position of pre-eminence in bus transport business.

4.3.4. Pioneer in Launching

Andhra Pradesh State Road Transport Corporation has been leading by an example. It has number of firsts to its credit among all other STU's (State Transport Undertakings) in India.

➤ APSRTC was first to nationalize passenger Road Transport Services in the country – 1932.

➤ First to introduce long distance night express services.

➤ First to initiate Single Deck Trailer Bus Services.

➤ First to set up Data Processing Machines.

➤ First to start out A/C Sleeper, Hi-tech, Metro Liner, Inter – City Services and Metro Express.

➤ First to introduce Depot computerization in 1986.

➤ First to appoint Safety Commissioner for improving the safety of passengers.

➤ First to computerize all the 211 depots in the State.

➤ First to start reservation of tickets on telephone and provide the service of tickets through door delivery.

➤ First to implement 33 percent reservation for women in filling the post in APSRTC – group 1, group 2, group 3, group 4 posts.

4.3.5. Laurels of Performance[222]

➤ 26 awards from Petroleum conservation Research Association (PCRA) on fuel conservation.

➤ Transport Minister's Trophy for lowest Accident Record in 2006-07 and 2010-11.

➤ APSRTC bagged Transport Minister's Trophy (Runners) and Cash Award from Govt. of India (Road Transport & Highways) for achieving lowest accident rate in Mofusil category among all other STUs in the country for the year 2007-08. Accordingly, an amount of Rs.50, 000/- along with Trophy was presented to VC & MD on 7.1.2011 at New Delhi.

> APSRTC bagged WINNER Award from ASRTU for Road Safety "Lowest Accident Records – in STUs Mofussil Services, Group -1" (having fleet strength above 10,000) for the year 2010-11.
> ASRTU Road Safety Award winner – highest KMPL in fuel efficiency – mofussil services Group-I STUs –2010-11
> Transport Minister's Trophy and Cash award of Rs. 2.50 lakh on road safety with lowest accident record under Mofussil's category 2010 – 11.
> At the latest, APSRTC achieved three National awards from ASRTU - one for better fuel consumption in mofussil services, second award for better fuel services in urban services and third award for Road safety award. This is the 39th time in 2014 APSRTC bagged the award for efficient fuel consumption[223].

4.4. Functional Setup

For any organization whether it is in public or in private sector the application of the "principle of de-centralization" is necessary to realize its objectives framed at the time of its inception. Andhra Pradesh State Road Transport Corporation – realized this fact of de - centralization principle and implemented it at all levels from corporate office to the level of depot manager at the depot level in letter and spirit to accomplish its goal. As a result, divisional setup came into existence in 1959 – 60. Consequently, first phase of nationalization of State Road Transport service covering Krishna, Guntur and West Godavari Districts was nationalized in between 1958 – 1961. RTC of Andhra Pradesh State introduced integrated depot setup appointing depot managers in depots in place of supervisor in-charge for the effective control of operations and to oversee administration in depot as the Head of the Department in 1965. Tirumala Tirupati Devastanam's buses were taken over by AP State Road Transport Corporation and constructed new Bus Stations and Shelters at Tirumala and Tirupati.

Andhra Pradesh State Road Transport Corporation was divided into 7 Zones with Head quarters at Hyderabad. The 7 zones are Vizianagaram, Vijayawada, Nellore, Cudapah, Karimnagar, Hyderabad and Greater Hyderabad. Executive Directors (EDs) have been posted to head these zones, each one covering 3 to 4 revenue districts. As Zonal Head, Executive Director is entrusted with vast powers to deal with any eventuality in operation of bus services and oversee the administration in his jurisdiction zone. In addition to the vast powers, the EDs were also made responsible for effecting cost controls in all key areas of expenditure besides taking steps to increase revenue.

For administrative convenience, A.P State Road Transport Corporation made each revenue district as a region headed by a Regional Manager in the rank of not less than the senior officer of APSRTC. There are at present 23 regions in A.P State Road Transport Corporation. The regional Manager is expected to exercise his powers in respect of operation of buses and administrative functions confined to the jurisdiction of revenue district – region.

4.4.1. Organization Structure of APSRTC

Urwick defined 'organization as determining activities that are necessary for a purpose (or plan) and arranging them in groups which may be assigned to individuals[224].' It is chiefly a designing process; without this it is inconceivable to appoint a person and pay him wages without an idea of the position he is likely to occupy. If jobs are not arranged properly, functional specialization is not possible and training people to occupy jobs falling vacant due to death or retirement becomes difficult. So that it is necessary for any commercial enterprise to create, develop and maintain organizational structure especially for State Road Transport Organizations like APSRTC to suit its own demands.

The AP State Road Transport Corporation, is organized into two dimensions-Horizontal and Vertical. The horizontal dimension refers to differentiation of the organizational job into different departments. As against to this, vertical dimension refers to hierarchy of the authority relationship with a number of levels from top to bottom. Authority flows downwards along these levels - from VC and Managing Director of APSRTC to Depot Managers of the corporation along Executive Directors of the zones and Regional Managers of revenue districts.

The organization structure of APSRTC has undergone several changes over the years. In this backdrop an attempt has been made to study the organizational structure and changes that have taken place since the inception of the public transport in Andhra Pradesh.

4.4.1.1. Organization Structure in the beginning

AP State Road Transport Corporation started as department of Nizam State Railway in June, 1932 and continued its status until Nizam State Railway was nationalized in 1951. With the nationalization of Railways, Road Transport came under the governance of Hyderabad State on 1st Nov, 1951 and functioned as Road Transport Department until taking the present corporation form in 1958. Superintendent was the in charge of Road Transport Department in the beginning and was responsible for supervising the departments of Mechanical Engineering (maintenance), Stores and Purchases. Superintendent at that time was assigned by the Deputy Road Transport superintendent who was in-charge of Traffic & Administration departments[225]. In 1957-58, a consultancy agency M/s IBCON PVT LTD., studied the organization structure and recommended to appoint a Chief Engineer to assist the Road Transport Superintendant in the matters of Mechanical Engineering, Civil Engineering, Stores and Purchases Department. These recommendations of the IBCON were accepted by the Road Transport department[226].

4.4.1.2. Organization Structure during 958-65

Figure 4.2: Shows organization structure of APSRTC during 1958-65

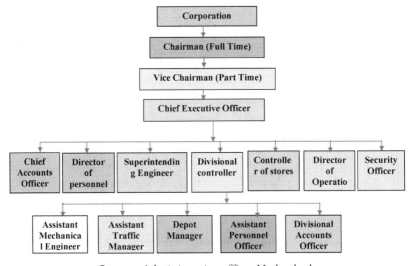

Source: Administrative office, Hyderabad.

The organization structure of APSRTC underwent several changes during this period as shown in the figure 4.2. During that time a full time, Chairman was appointed to coordinate and control the activities of the corporation; the Chairman of the corporation was assisted by the Vice-Chairman who was chief executive officer on part time basis. The chairman of the corporation was a public personality nominated by the Government of Andhra Pradesh. The Vice-Chairman was appointed either from state administration or from employee cadre of the corporation.

As exhibited in the Figure 4.2, the top management of the organization consists of Chief Accounts Officer, Director of personnel, Superintending engineer, Divisional Controller, controller of Stores, Security Officer and Director of Operations. The Chief Executive Officer was responsible for coordinating and controlling all the officers of top management. These officers in turn assist the Chief Executive officer in the matters of administration. The divisional controller takes care of depots in respect of Personnel, Operations, Maintenance and Accounts[227]. The Depot Mangers were representing the Depot operations and acting as supervisor in-charge to the divisional controller. There are other officials besides depot manager cadre - Assistant Mechanical Engineer, Assistant Traffic Manager, Assistant Personnel officer and Divisional Accounts Officer[228]. However with the inherent defects in the organizational setup combined with lack of integration and coordination at operational and divisional levels-resulted in organizational ineffectiveness.

With a view to offset the ineffectiveness of the organization, there were several committees appointed to study the operations of the corporation during that period and suggest steps to improve its efficiency and operational performance. Important committees among them were Sir Ananta Ramakrishnan Committee, appointed in 1960 and the National Productive Council in 1964. The National Productive Council submitted its report in 1965 stating that there was a need to restructure the corporation at operational level (depot level) as the policies of the corporation were put into action at this level[229]. The Corporation by accepting the NPC (National Productivity Council) recommendations had introduced radical changes at the operational level. As a consequence of the reforms of the organization, depot setup was first time established with depot manager as in-charge of the depot.[230]

4.4.1.3. Organization Structure during 965-78

Figure 4.3: Shows organization structure of APSRTC during 1965-78

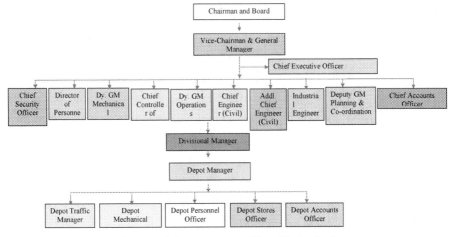

Source: Administrative office, Hyderabad

During this period 1965-78, Corporation adopted three-tier organizational setup-Head quarters, Division and a Depot as depicted in the table 4.3. The structure continued until 1978; in this setup the task of depot manager became more challenging with increase in the size of the depot as consequent to the expansion in operational area. Depot manager is empowered with operational flexibility for ensuring operational efficiency and assisted by supervisors in each functional area. Also the Divisional staffs were assisted by depot level staff as the division was a coordinating unit at middle level. Divisional Managers were supposed to act as liaison officers in between work shops and stores for making operations smoothly and effectively.

4.4.1.4 Organization Structure during 1978-94

Having realized the inherent defects under the existing system, the Corporation appointed a sub-committee with Nageswar Rao as Chairman to suggest measures for effective functioning of the organization[231]. The committee after careful study of various problems, with which the corporation was suffering, recommended a quadric tier administrative setup with head-quarters at apex level, zonal offices and Regional offices at the second and third levels respectively. The depots are at fourth level considered as the base of operations. The corporation after careful study of the recommendations of the Sub-committee accepted the proposals. As a result, the Regional setup was established from 16th Jan, 1978 with the main objective of autonomy and operational flexibility. The directions are flown from head office to regional level commensurate with delegation of power[232]. The head office is confined only to policy matters[233]. The regional managers were assigned with staffing role (coordination) as well plays liaison role with head quarters[234]. In this system, Depot level managers were vested with all necessary powers which are important for the effective functioning of operational units. In this setup divisional level is confined to staffing role - coordination of various regions.

Figure 4.4: Shows Organization Structure of APSRTC during 978-94

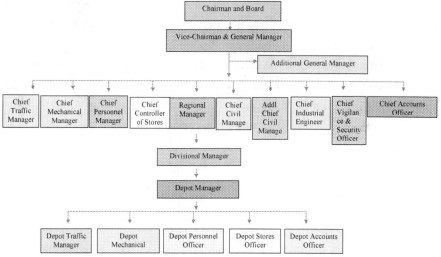

Source: Administrative office, Hyderabad

4.4.1.5. Contemporary organization structure from 1994 onwards

To further the concept of de-centralization, the Corporation initiated reorganization once again in the year May, 1994. Accordingly, the corporation was divided into 7 Zones, each Zone covering on an average 4 Revenue Districts headed by an Executive Director. Executive Director has been endowed with powers to coordinate the functions of work shop, Civil Engineering, Accounts, personnel and administration. The Zone formed at second level, where as Region and Depot at third and fourth level in this existing structure. The Region otherwise called as revenue district in the plan, is under the control of Regional Manager, whose main function was to streamline the inter-division and inter depot operations and had a close monitoring of man power utilization, financial performance, performance of Depots in several operations and mechanical engineering parameters. In the matters of discipline the RM has the reviewing power. At Operational level Depot Manager is responsible for the up keep of buses and their operations, maintaining passenger amenities to the level of passenger's satisfaction. He monitors the traffic, stores, accounts and personnel aspects of the depot. In this scheme of organization, there is a corporation board at the apex level consisting of eight Directors, apart from the Chairman and Vice Chairman of the board. Chairman and Vice - Chairman are also members in the board by virtue of their position. Generally the Vice-Chairman and Managing Director of the corporation are appointed from the IPS Cadre, whereas Chairman is a non official member. The corporation board is a well mix of both official and non official members. The term of office of the director is for three years. The board meetings are presided over by the Chairman of the corporation. All the policy decisions are taken by the board and implemented by the Vice - Chairman and Managing Director of the Corporation who was acting as chief executive officer. In addition to this important function, Vice-Chairman and Managing Director will attend to the day to day functions of the corporation and also try to resolve those problems which arise in the course of routine functions.

In this changed plan of organization structure, there are eight Directors in the corporate board. Chairman and Vice Chairman are ex-officio members in the board. Board members (directors) consisting of Principal Secretary to Govt. of AP., Transport Roads & Buildings Department. (dealing with APSRTC), Secretary to Govt. of AP., Finance (W & P) Department, FA & Chief Accounts Officer, South Central Railways, Secunderabad, Engineer-In-Chief (Roads), R & B Department, Joint Secretary (T), Dept. of R T & Highways, Ministry of Shipping, RT & Highways Government of India, New Delhi, Principal Secretary to Government of AP., LET & F Department,

Working President, APSRTC National Mazdoor Union, General Secretary, APSRTC National Mazdoor Union.

Figure 4.5: Shows Contemporary organization structure of APSRTC from 1994 onwards

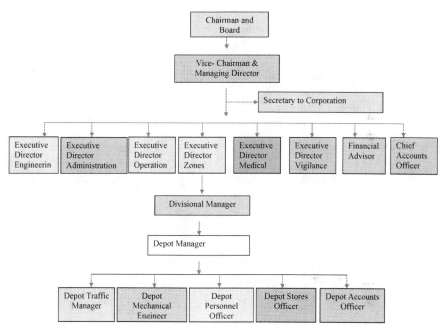

Source: Administrative office, Hyderabad

Figure 4.6: Shows Organization Structure of APSRTC - 2012

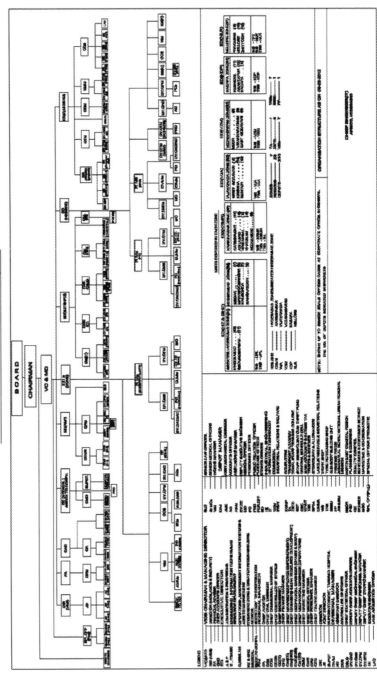

Source: www.apsrtc.gov.in

4.5. APSRTC: Physical Performance

To attain the assigned objectives and functions of APSRTC, management has designed certain performance parameters which are measurable and indicate the growth and achievement of objectives. The table 4.2 presents the operational backdrop of APSRTC from 2003-2013. The analyses of different parameters in different dimensions are also discussed to throw enough light on the state of corporation's affairs and operational status.

Table 4.2: Shows Operational Performance of APSRTC during 2003- 04 to 2012 - 13

	Particulars	Unit	2003-04	2004-05	2005-06	2006-07	2007-08	2008-09	2009-10	2010-11	2011-12	2012-13
1	No. of Scheduled Bus on Road	Nos	18970	19495	19250	19485	19873	20605	21515	21701	21411	22402
2	Avg. No. of vehicles held	Nos	19108	19609	19407	19618	19987	20704	21606	21802	22,170	22477
3	Kms. Operated	Crore (For 12 months)	226.65	232.50	238.08	244.73	253.47	267.49	277.16	289.58	287.15	297.83
		AVG/ Day	62.09	63.69	65.22	67.04	69.44	73.28	75.93	79.33	78.67	81.59
4	Taffic Earning	Rs / Crore (For 12 months)	2786.44	2949.48	3198.97	3667.10	3891.41	4251.25	4427.44	5208.10	5716.69	6527.74
		AVG/ Day	763.40	808.07	876.43	1004.68	1066.13	1164.72	12.99	1426.87	1566.21	1788.42
5	Traffic EPK	Ps	1229	1269	1344	1498	1535	1589	1598	1799	1991	2192
6	OR	%	60	62	65	68	70	72	69	67	68	69
7	Traffic EPB	Rs/Bus	4004	4207	4495	5192	5407	5716	5707	6545	7045	7957
8	HSD KMPL	Kms/Ltr	5.37	5.29	5.27	5.26	5.24	5.25	5.28	5.17	5.13	5.15
9	Avg. Tyre Life	Kms / Lakh	1.66	1.78	1.85	1.82	1.77	1.68	1.69	1.68	1.70	1.71
10	SBR (on Held)	Nos	6.53	6.31	6.31	6.16	6.13	6.04	6.01	6.04	6.01	5.94
11	Profit/ Loss	Rs/ lakhs	-42.02	-224.84	-42.78	-111.82	+135.67	+110.79	-514.82	-317.38	-585.31	-291.73*

Source: 1. http://data.gov.in/catalog/physical-performance-srtus

2. APSRTC Annual Reports

3. Annual Performance review of SRTUs - Ministry of Road Transport and Highways 2009-10 to 2012-13

The operational scenario of the A.P. State Road Transport Corporation and its analysis by different parameters in different dimensions throws more light on the state of affairs and operational status. The table 4.2 presents the detailed operational scenario of the APSRTC during 2003-04 to 2012-13. The table reveals that the number of scheduled buses on road was increased from 18970 during 2003 - 04 to 21286 during 2011 – 12 and stood at 22402 in 2012 – 13. The average number of fleet held during 2003 – 04 was 19108 which increased to 22477 during 2012 – 13. It is evident from the table that the APSRTC operated 62.09 lakh Kms a day during 2003 – 04, which rose to 81.59 lakh Kms a day during 2012 -13. During the period of review the average Kms operated per day shows a continuous increase except during 2011 – 12. The reason for the drop in Kms operated per day was due to Sakala Janula Sammya for separate Telangana state. Coming to the traffic earnings, the table depicts continuous increase during the reference period. It was increased from 763.40 lakhs during 2003 – 04 to 1788.42 lakhs during 2012 – 13. The Occupancy Ratio (OR) which is an index of bus productivity. The table gives us an understanding about the Occupancy Ratio (OR) was 60 percent during 2003 – 04 raised to 72 percent during 2008 – 09 and stands at 69 percent during 2012 – 13. The OR drop from 2009 – 10 to 2012 – 13 can be attributed to Telangana and Andhra Agitations in the state. It is evident from the table that Earnings per Km (EPK) in APSRTC were 12.29 paise during 2003 – 04 and increased to 2192 paise during 2012 – 13. In the entire period of review, the EPK shows that increase may be due to the raise in operation of Kms by AP State Road Transport Corporation during the review period.

The remaining parameters of the table 4.2 – Traffic EPB, HSD KMPL, Average Tyre life, Staff Bus Ratio (SBR) held are discussed in table 4.5.

Table: 4.3: Shows Quality Performance of APSRTC 2003-04 to 2012-13

	Particulars	Unit	2003-04	2004-05	2005-06	2006-07	2007-08	2008-09	2009-10	2010-11	2011-12	2012-13
1	Total Cancellation	%	2.05	2.01	3.04	1.76	2.18	1.76	3.99	2.54	5.21	1.89
2	Rate of Accidents / One Lakh Kms	Nos	0.10	0.10	0.11	0.12	0.12	0.11	0.10	0.11	0.09	0.09
3	Breakdown (BD) Rate / 10,000 Kms	No/ 10,000 Kms	0.13	0.12	0.13	0.13	0.12	0.09	0.08	0.10	0.08	0.07

Source: 1. http://data.gov.in/catalog/physical-performance-srtus

2. APSRTC Annual Reports

3. Annual Performance review of SRTUs – Ministry of Road Transport and Highways 2009 – 10 to 2012-13

The table 4.3 discusses the quality performance of different parameters of APSRTC – Total Cancellation, Rate of Accidents / One Lakh Kms, Breakdown (BD) Rate / 10,000 Kms during 2003 – 04 to 2012 – 13. As per the table, the Total Cancellation of bus services was from 2.5 percent during 2003 – 04 and dropped to 1.89 percent during 2012 – 13. Fluctuation in the percentage of cancellation of bus services during the review period indicates the lapse of administration at the depot level.

Road accidents cause great concern not only to the travelling public but also to the APSRTC because Transport Corporation has to pay heavy compensation to the accident victims. The table depicts that the average rate of accidents per lakh effective Kms was 0.10 during 2003 – 04 increased to 0.12 during 2007 – 08 and stood at 0.09 during 2012-13 the table also speaks about the number of break downs per 10,000 Kms was from 0.13 during 2003 – 04 was dropped to 0.07 during 2012 – 13. The average number of breakdowns per 10,000 Kms during the period under review ranged between 0.13 (2003 – 04) to 0.07 (2012 – 13).

The decrease in bus breakdowns and accident rate by 2012 – 13 was due to introduction of new and improved quality of buses like Volvo, Mercedes Benz on the road in view of the competition from private operators. Customer orientation was also another cause for the corporation to introduce new and modern technology buses.

Table: 4.4: shows Cost Performance of APSRTC 2003-04 to 2012-13

	Particulars	Unit	2003-04	2004-05	2005-06	2006-07	2007-08	2008-09	2009-10	2010-11	2011-12	2012-13
1	HSD KMPL	Kms/ Ltr	5.37	5.29	5.27	5.26	5.24	5.25	5.28	5.17	5.13	5.15
2	Avg. Tyre Life	Kms / Lakh	1.66	1.78	1.85	1.82	1.77	1.68	1.69	1.68	1.70	1.71

Source: 1. http://data.gov.in/catalog/physical-performance-srtus

2. APSRTC Annual Reports

3. Annual Performance review of SRTUs – Ministry of Road Transport and Highways 2009 – 10 to 2012-13

The table discusses different parameters of cost performance and throws light on merits and demerits of the functioning of APSRTC during 2003 – 04 to 2012 – 13. The table depicts that the Kms run per litre of diesel was 5.37 during 2003 – 04 and decreased to 5.15 during 2012 – 13. The Km per litre diesel ranges between 5.13 (2011 – 12) to 5.37 (2003 – 04) during the review period.

The table analyses the Average Tyre Life per one lakh Kms which was 1.66 during 2003 – 04 and increased to 1.71 during 2012 – 13 with some deviations in the Average Tyre Life in between the review period. It ranged between 1.66 (2003 – 04) to 1.82 (2006 – 07).

Table 4.5: Shows Productivity Performance of APSRTC 2003-04 to 2012-13

	Particulars	Unit	2003-04	2004-05	2005-06	2006-07	2007-08	2008-09	2009-10	2010-11	2011-12	2012-13
1	Crew Utilization	Kms	142	149	152	157	160	165	161	160	157	162
2	Employee Productivity	Kms	50	51	53	55	57	59	59	60	58	60
3	Fleet Utilization	%	99.27	99.41	99.19	99.32	99.42	99.52	99.57	99.53	96.57	99.66
4	SBR (on Held)	Nos	6.53	6.31	6.31	6.16	6.13	6.04	6.01	6.04	6.01	5.94

Source: 1. http://data.gov.in/catalog/physical-performance-srtus

2. APSRTC Annual Reports

3. Annual Performance review of SRTUs-Ministry of Road Transport and Highways 2009-10 to 2012-13

Productivity performance of different parameters – Crew Utilization, Employee Productivity, Percentage of Fleet Utilization, Staff Bus Ratio-of APSRTC during 2003 – 04 to 2012 – 13 are discussed in this table. The table depicts the Crew Utilization as 142 Kms during 2003 – 04 which increased to 149 Kms of crew utilization during 2004 – 05 and stood at 162 Kms of crew utilization during 2012 – 13. The crew utilization ranged between 142 Kms during 2003 – 04 to 165 Kms during 2008 – 09 under the review period.

The table depicts the average effective Kms staff achieved per day which was from 50 Kms during 2003- 04 increased to 60 Kms during 2012 – 13. There was a continuous increase of staff productivity – achievement in Kms during the review period except dwindle down of few Kms during 2011 – 12. The table gives us an understanding that the average number of staff per bus on road was 6.53 during 2003 – 04 dropped to 5.94 during 2012 – 13. The diving down of bus staff ratio denotes the downsizing in human resources. It was evident from the table, that there was a continuous decrease in staff per bus ratio during the reference period except a small step up in staff bus ratio during 2010 – 11. Reduction in bus staff ratio doesn't mean that employment opportunities in APSRTC are declining. The table gives an understanding that the reduction in staff bus ratio is not detrimental to the achievement of staff productivity in average effective Kms during the period under review. It implies that because of increase in bus fleet, which is more in proportion to that of bus staff, a decline occurred in this ratio. Higher the ratio, the more is the number of avenues in public sector bus transport system compared to that of private operators.

Fleet utilization is the proportion of buses put on road to the buses held. It increased from 99.28 percent during 2003 – 04 to 99.66 percent during 2012 – 13. It is evident from the table that the percentage of fleet utilization stood high ranging between 96.57 (2011 -12) percent and 99.66 percent (2012 – 13) during the period under review. It is a positive signal for physical performance of APSRTC.

Table 4.6: Shows Vehicle Utilization Parameter in APSRTC during 2002-03 to 2012-13

	Parameter	Unit	2002-03	2003-04	2004-05	2005-06	2006-07	2007-08	2008-09	2009-10	2010-11	2011-12	2012-13
						Vehicle Utilization Parameter							
1	Avg. No. of vehicles held	Nos	19102	19108	19609	19407	19618	19987	20704	21606	21802	22170	22477
2	Avg. No. of Vehicles on Road	Nos	18957	18970	19495	19250	19485	19873	20605	21515	21701	21411	22402
3	Percentage of Utilization of vehicles	%	99.24	99.27	99.41	99.19	99.32	99.42	99.52	99.57	99.53	96.6	99.7
4	No. of Employees	Nos	122358	119219	117400	115946	115529	113340	113370	115898	120566	123615	1,23,615

Source: 1. http://data.gov.in/catalog/physical-performance-srtus

2. APSRTC Annual Reports

3. Annual Performance review of SRTUs-Ministry of Road Transport and Highways 2009-10 to 2012-13

The above table 4.6 focuses on the vehicle utilization parameters in APSRTC during 2002 – 03 to 2012 – 13. It is evident from the table that the average number of vehicles held by the corporation was 19102 during 2002 – 03 increased to 22477 during 2012 – 13. As per the table, the average number of vehicles on road of the APSRTC was 18957 during 2002 – 03 increased to 19495 during 2004 – 05 and stood at 22402 during 2012 – 13. Thus over the study period the percentage of utilization of vehicles by the APSRTC ranged between 96.6 percent (2011 – 12) to 99.7 percent (2012 – 13). The table shows steady increase in percentage of vehicle utilization during the period of study.

The table speaks that number of employees in APSRTC during 2002 – 03 was 122358 and the same increased to 123615 employees during 2012 – 13. In between there was a decrease in employees' number in the corporation in the reference period. This is because of the slowdown in recruitment and downsizing of human resources.

4.5.1. Growth of APSRTC since Inception

Table 4.7: Shows growth of APSRTC since Inception

Parameter	1932-33	1958-59	2009-10	2010-11	2011-12	2012-13	Percentage Change during 2011-12 & 2012-13
Buses	27	679	21606	22265	22170	22477	1.38
Employees	166	5081	115878	120566	123045	1,23,615	0.46
Kms / Day(Lakhs)	0.03	0.88	75.93	79.34	78.67	81.68	2.93
Income (Rs. Crs)	0.28	2.66	4427.44	5208.10	5716.69	5983.05	4.65

Source: 1. *www.siamonline.in/SAFE-AC..../Raj%20Shekhar%20-%20APSRTC.pdf*
2. Annual Performance review of SRTUs-Ministry of Road Transport and Highways 2009-10 to 2012-13

It is evident from the table 4.7 that the total buses were 27 during 1932 – 33, which increased to 22477 buses during 2012 – 13. It is raised by 1.38 percent from 22170 buses in 2011 – 12 to 22477 in 2012 – 13.

Figure 4.7: Shows the graphical representation of APSRTC growth since Inception

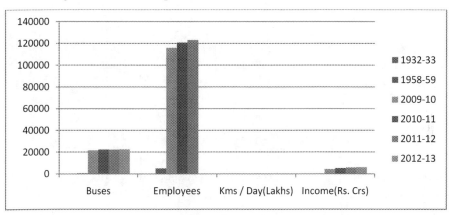

Source: Table 4.9

According to the table 4.7, employees increased to 123045 during 2011 – 12 from 166 employees during 1932 - 33. In contrast, there was a raised of 0.46 percent from 123045 employees in 2011 – 12 to 1, 23,615 employees during 2012 – 13. The increase in employees' percent can be inferred as due to the increase in number of buses in 2012 – 13. It is evident from the table that the 0.03 lakh Kms which the corporation buses operated per day during 1932 – 33, increased to 81.68 lakh Kms in 2012 – 13. The table speaks of continuous increase in income in the period of review from Rs. 0.28 Crore during 1932 – 33 to Rs. 5983.05 Crore in 2012 - 13. Income increased by 4.65 percent from Rs. 5716.69 Crore during 2011 – 12 to Rs. 5983.05 Crore during 2012 – 13.

Table 4.8: Shows Total number of vehicles during
2004-05 to 2012-13 (In Crores)

Years	Number of vehicles held		
	APSRTC	Hired	Total
2004-05	17920 (91.38)	1689 (8.61)	19609 (100)
2005-06	17705 (90.79)	1794 (9.20)	19499 (100)
2006-07	17770 (91.83)	1580 (8.16)	19350 (100)
2007-08	17944 (91.25)	1719 (8.74)	19663 (100)
2008-09	17096 (83.90)	3279 (16.09)	20375 (100)
2009-10	17288 (81.33)	3967 (18.66)	21255 (100)
2010-11	17896 (82.08)	3906 (17.91)	21802 (100)
2011-12	18297 (82.17)	3992 (17.92)	22265 (100)
2012-13	18997 (84.41)	3507(15.58)	22504 (100)

Note: Figures in the parenthesis denote percentage to the respective total.
Source: 1. Statistical Abstract, Directorate of economics and Statistics, Government of A.P, Hyderabad, Table 11.5, P. 298 A.P, 2011.
2. APSRTC Administrative reports;
3. www.apsrtcinfo.com

It can be understood from the table that the percentage of APSRTC buses were 91.38 percent during 2004 – 05, decreased to 84.41 percent in 2013 – 13. In coincidence the hired buses increased from 8.61 percent during 2004 – 05 to 15.58 percent during 2012 – 13. It can be deduced that APSRTC strategically resorted to hire buses to meet the demand of the public and as policy to restrict illegal operation of buses by private operators.

The table also shows that total buses of RTC (including hired buses) were raised from 19609 during 2004 – 05 to 22504 during 2012 – 13 with some dwindle in number of buses during 2005 – 06 and 2006 – 07. In that period, it can be understood that there was no enough replacement of new buses to the condemned old buses. The percentage of increase of the total buses in the review period is 14.76 percent.

4.6. APSRTC: Financial Performance

AP State Road Corporation is one of the largest state Road Corporations in India with 215 Depots and more than 123000 employees. RTC bus was famous as red bus (Erra bus) in the earlier period and earned the name as Prajala bus in providing transportation services to people, about 150000 a day, to make them reach safely to their destinations as compared to Railways in the state. Railways transport about one lakh people a day in Andhra Pradesh[235]. APSRTC was also recognized as a symbol of Andhra Pradesh development. However, that was history. The present position of RTC seems to be different to the researcher. It may be on account of the policies of State Government, combined with State Road Transport Corporation's own operational defects.

At present, AP State Road Transport Corporation is simmering with neck deep debts. It has existing debts of Rs. 4,200 Crore which piled up over the years[236]. To the existing burden of the corporation, Seemandhra strike for 'United Andhra Pradesh' agitation added another Rs. 700 Crore to the loss, on an average it was estimated as Rs. 18 Crore a day[237]. Another bitter pill for the corporation is that it has Rs. 290 Crore annual liability in the form of payment of interest[238]. Adding fuel to the fire, in view of the recent steep hike of diesel price, corporation will have to shell out an additional burden of Rs. 715 Crore a year. It may be working out to be Rs. 2 Crore a day during 2012-13. In the financial year 2011-12 it incurred losses of about Rs. 585.31 Crore. Complete picture of zone-wise losses of APSRTC during 2011-12 was given in table 4.9[239].

Table 4.9: Shows Zone-wise losses of APSRTC

Zone	Loss in Crores
Vizianagaram	53.97
Kadapa	117.02
Vijayawada	54.65
Nellore	75.73
Hyderabad	64.96
Karimnagar	73.98
Greater Hyderabad	144.03
Total	585.31

Source: The Hindu Daily News Paper, 'Krungina pragathi chakralu', P. 4, 30th April, 2013

It is only 15 depots that earned profit out of 213, in Andhra Pradesh State for the financial year 2011-12. Remaining 198 Depots were running in losses of about Rs. 585.31 Crore as stated in the above table 4.9. The situation of losses continued in the following financial year 2012-13[240].

Given the situation combined with Seemandhra agitation, there is a threat to payment of salaries to its employees in the month of October, 2013[241]. There was already a burden of Rs. 2000 Crore Loans that the Corporation borrowed from different financial institutions combined with cumulative losses of over Rs. 4000 Crore accrued over the years[242]. For critics, the corporation has become insolvent and is not in a position to purchase diesel and even pay salaries to its employees. As a result, critics argue that financial institutions that helped earlier are reluctant at present, to come forward and give fresh loans to the Corporation[243].

Table 4.10: Shows Financial Performance of APSRTC
during 2010-11 and 2012-13.

(In Lakhs)

S.No.	Financial Performance	All APSRTC		Percentage Change
		2011-12	2012-13	
1.	Total Revenue (Rs Lakhs)	667740.33	763918.99	12.59%
2.	Total Cost (Rs Lakhs)	726271.29	771990.05	2.03%
a)	Operating Cost (Rs Lakhs)	511083.56	353752.30	30.78%
b)	Non – Operating Cost (Rs Lakhs)	215187.73	207545.75	3.55%
3.	Net Profit/ Loss (Rs Lakhs)	-58530.96	-80710.60	27.48%

Source: Performance of STUS 2012-13, Ministry of Road Transport and Highways, Annual reports.

Figure 4.8: Exhibits Financial Performance of APSRTC during 2010-11 and 2012-13.

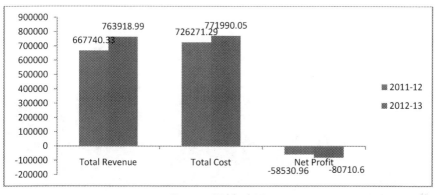

From the above table 4.10 it is clear that the total revenue of the APSRTC for which data on financial parameters was received - increased by 12.59 percent, rose from Rs. 667740.33 lakh in 2011 – 12 to Rs. 763918.99 lakh in 2012 – 13. However, due to 2.03 percent increase in the total cost over the same period, the AP State Road Transport Corporation incurred a net aggregate loss. The total loss increased by 27.48 percent, rose from Rs. (-) 58530.96 lakh in 2011 – 12 to Rs. (–) 80710.60 lakh in 2012 – 13.

4.6.1 Mortgaging

"We do mortgage our properties on regular basis for regular needs. This apart, we are also holding payments to our suppliers to ensure sufficient money with us to pay salaries at the end of the month" said the senior official of the corporation who doesn't want to be identified[244].

The above two arguments generally give the impression that RTC is in financial crisis and debt ridden. For the sound existence of the organization, together with safety and welfare of its large number of employees, RTC unions demanding the state government to come into the rescue of the Road Transport Corporation by giving sufficient financial help or come forward and hand over the APSRTC by recognizing it as government department[245]. They are also requesting the government to treat them as government employees and give salaries on par with the salaries of government employees.

In this backdrop the researcher wants to study the actual financial position of the A.P Road Transport Corporation and submit suggestions to leverage it from debt burden.

Table 4.11: Shows Traffic Revenue and Non Traffic Revenue of APSRTC during the years 2003-04 to 2012-13 (In Crores)

Years	Traffic Revenue	Reimbursement from Government/ Subsidy	Non – Traffic Revenue	Total Revenue
2003-04	2773.19 (88.85)	152.73 (4.86)	348.01 (11.14)	3121.20 (100.00)
2004-05	2937.42 (91.34)	170.69 (05.30)	278.38 (0.08)	3215.80 (100.00)
2005-06	3192.60 (86.84)	368.50 (10.02)	115.27 (03.13)	3676.37 (100.00)
2006-07	3658.19 (87.36)	405.35 (09.68)	123.85 (02.95)	4187.39 (100.00)
2007-08	3879.14 (87.02)	433.96 0(9.73)	144.45 (03.24)	4457.55 (100.00)
2008-09	4237.70 (84.08)	469.37 (09.31)	332.76 (06.60)	5039.53 (100.00)
2009-10	4398.55 (84.48)	540.79 (10.38)	266.92 (05.12)	5206.26 (100.00)
2010-11	4398.54 (84.34)	540.79 (10.37)	143.93 (02.76)	5214.85 (100.00)
2011-12	5705.92 (85.45)	747.51 (11.19)	166.37 (02.49)	6677.40 (100.00)
2012-13	-	-	-	7639.18 (100.00)

Note: Figures in the parenthesis denote percentage to the respective total.

Source: 1. http://data.gov.in/catalog/financial-performance-srtus

    2. www.apsrtcinfo.com

    3. Performance of STUS-2009-10 to 2012-13, Ministry of Road Transport and Highways, Annual reports.

    4. APSRTC Annual Accounts Reports 2009-10 to 2011-12.

The table 4.11 presents the break – up of the total revenue of APSRTC during 2003 – 04 to 2012 – 13. Out of the total revenue the traffic revenue is the dominant component, where as non traffic revenue assumes a minor share. It is as evident from the fact that over the years under review, proportion of the traffic revenue of the corporation's total revenue was ranged between 85.45 percent (2011 – 12) to 88.85 percent (2003 – 04). The traffic revenue is collected through sales of tickets, contract services, postal services and from hired vehicles.

Corporation provides different types of services to passengers with subsidy/ with concession rates based on the direction of the Government of Andhra Pradesh.

Non Traffic revenue: the table depicts that the Non-Traffic revenue contains different sources like subsidy concessions, rents, sale of scrap vehicles, sale of scrap material, clinical service charges, advertising fees etc.

Total Revenue: The table explains the total revenue of the Corporation was Rs. 3121.20 crore during 2003 – 04 and increased to Rs. 7639.18 crore during 2012 – 13.

Table 4.12: Shows T(In Crores)

Years	Personnel Cost	Material Cost - Fuel	Other Material Cost	M.V. Taxes	Interest on Borrowings	Payment to Hire Buses	Depreciation on Buses	Miscellaneous and others	Total Cost	Profit/ Loss
2003-04	1313.91 (41.89)	838.00 (26.49)	202.64 (06.40)	339.27 (10.72)	105.22 (03.32)	233.50 (07.38)	110.85 (03.50)	19.83 (00.62)	3163.22 (100.00)	-42.02
2004-05	1359.20 (39.50)	1015.01 (29.50)	203.02 (05.90)	361.89 (10.51)	102.90 (02.99)	262.28 (07.62)	115.79 (03.36)	20.55 (00.59)	3440.64 (100.00)	-224.84
2005-06	1417.28 (38.10)	1258.86 (33.84)	232.38 (06.24)	248.96 (06.69)	86.49 (02.32)	275.22 (7.40)	142.87 (03.84)	87.09 (02.34)	3719.15 (100.00)	-42.78
2006-07	1744.77 (40.58)	1428.04 (33.21)	296.67 (06.90)	260.28 (06.05)	76.13 (01.77)	206.75 (04.80)	167.90 (03.90)	118.67 (02.76)	4299.21 (100.00)	-111.82
2007-08	1585.92 (36.69)	1440.17 (33.32)	317.34 (07.34)	257.82 (05.96)	91.25 (02.11)	322.61 (07.46)	176.24 (04.07)	130.53 (03.02)	4321.89 (100.00)	135.66
2008-09	1658.61 (33.89)	1548.89 (31.65)	318.15 (06.50)	263.24 (05.38)	116.87 (02.38)	691.84 (14.14)	190.96 (03.90)	104.17 (02.12)	1928.74 (100.00)	110.79
2009-10	2206.95 (38.57)	1501.09 (26.23)	320.69 (05.60)	279.43 (04.88)	114.64 (02.00)	306.19 (05.35)	224.91 (03.93)	166.89 (02.91)	5720.81 (100.00)	-514.55
2010-11	2369.27 (43.20)	1885.18 (34.37)	337.85 (06.16)	326.91 (05.96)	145.80 (02.65)	-	250.14 (04.56)	168.47 (03.07)	5483.66 (100.00)	-268.81
2011-12	2683.33 (36.95)	2018.56 (27.79)	408.93 (05.63)	432.08 (05.94)	271.84 (03.74)	-	306.21 (04.21)	1141.73 (15.72)	7262.71 (100.00)	-585.30
2012-13	2871.64 (37.19)	2341.02 (30.32)	431.77 (05.59)	144.75 (01.87)	368.61 (04.77)	554.81 (07.18)	427.34 (05.53)	1134.73 (14.69)	7719.90 (100.00)	-8071.06

Note: Figures in the parenthesis denote percentage to the respective total.

Source: 1. http://data.gov.in/catalog/financial-performance-srtus

2. Performance of STUS-2009-10 to 2012-13, Ministry of Road Transport and Highways, Annual reports.

The table 4.12 explains that out of the total expenditure of APSRTC, personnel cost during 2003 – 04 was Rs. 1313.91 crore (41.89 percent) which increased to Rs. 2871.64 crore (37.19 percent) during 2012 – 13. In this review period the personnel cost was dwindled down during 2007 – 08 and 2008 – 09. It may be because of a large number of retirements of the employees of APSRTC and no proportionate fresh recruitments made during that dwindled down period. The increase in personnel cost during the period under reference was Rs. 1557.73 crore.

The personnel cost includes salaries and allowances for staff, provident fund, gratuity, cleaning and sweeping charges and clerical charges etc.

Material cost: In RTC, material cost includes fuel/ power, lubricants, reconditioned items cost. The material cost (fuel) in APSRTC was Rs. 838 crore during 2003 – 04 increased to Rs. 2341.02 crore during 2012 – 13. Material cost (fuel) contains 30.32 percent of the total cost during 2012 – 13. Material cost including the cost of other materials (total material cost) was Rs. 1040.64 crore increased to Rs. 2772.79 crore during 2012 – 13. The percentage of total material cost contains 35.91 percent of the total cost during 2012 – 13.

M.V. Tax: As per the table, the total M.V. Tax paid by the corporation to the government was Rs. 339.27 crore during 2003 – 04 and decreased to Rs. 144.75 crore during 2012 – 13. It is 1.87 percent of the total cost in the period of reference. In 2005, the government reduced the M.V. Tax and 10 percent to 5 percent on city services and 12.50 percent to 7 percent on district services[246].

Interest on Borrowings: One of the important expenditure of APSRTC was paying interest on borrowings from various financial institutions. The interest cost of such borrowings to the corporation was Rs. 105.22 crore during 2003 – 04 and increased to Rs. 368.61 crore (4.77 percent) of the total cost during 2012 – 13. The fluctuations in interest cost during the period under review were due to the difference in borrowings.

Payment to Hire Buses: The table explains that the payment cost of APSRTC towards hire buses was Rs. 233.50 crore during 2003 – 04 and increased to Rs. 554.81 crore during 2012 – 13. Payment to hire buses in the corporation was increasing every year throughout the period under review. The share of payment to hire buses was 7.18 percent of the total expenditure of the corporation in 2012 – 13.

Depreciation on Buses: The Depreciation cost of APSRTC on buses was Rs. 110.85 crore during 2003 – 03 increased to Rs. 427.34 crore during

2012 – 13. It contains 5.53 percent of the total cost in that year. It was observed that Depreciation cost was increasing every year under the period of reference.

Miscellaneous: According to the table 4.12, it was Rs. 19.83 crore during 2003 – 04 and increased to Rs. 1134.73 crore during 2012 – 13. It contains 14.69 percent of the total cost.

Total Cost: As evident from the table 4.12, the total expenditure of APSRTC was Rs. 3163.22 crore during 2003 – 04 increased to Rs. 7719.90 crore during 2012 – 13. The expenditure was increasing every year during the review period. The increase in expenditure for the period of review was Rs. 4556.68 crore.

From the table 4.12, it is clear that corporation made profits in 2007-08 and 2008-09, in the other years it was put to losses. It may be assumed that the profits in 2007-08 and 2008-09, that the corporation gained because of reduced motor vehicle Tax.

Based on the analysis of capital structure and revenue & expenditure parameters, the financial performance of APSRTC is not satisfactory.

Table 4.13: Shows Total Assets and Liabilities of
APSRTC during 2003 – 04 to 2011 – 12

(In Crores)

Years	APSRTC Total Assets	APSRTC Total Liabilities	APSRTC's Credit Worthiness
2003-04	3303.10	3303.10	0
2004-05	3800.75	3800.75	0
2005-06	3744.89	3744.89	0
2006-07	4288.72	4288.72	0
2007-08	4520.66	4520.66	0
2008-09	4866.48	4866.48	0
2009-10	4104.38	4104.38	0
2010-11	5195.89	5195.89	0
2011-12	6994.59	6994.59	0

Source: 1. Srinivas Rao Chilumuri, "Financial Performance Evaluation of APSRTC", International Journal of Management and Business Studies, Vol. 3, Issue 1, January – March – 2013.
2. APSRTC Annual Accounts Reports 2009-10 to 2011-12.

This result may be because most of the RTC's assets including the bus stations have been pledged to raise loans from different financial institutions.

Tables 4.14: Shows Total Revenue and Expenditure of
APSRTC during 2003-04 to 2012-13

(In Crores)

Years	APSRTC Total Revenue	APSRTC Total – Cost/ Expenditure	Profit/ Loss
2003-04	3121.20	3163.22	-42.02
2004-05	3215.80	3440.64	-224.84
2005-06	3676.80	3719.15	-42.35
2006-07	4187.39	4299.21	-111.82
2007-08	4457.55	4321.89	135.66
2008-09	5039.53	4928.74	110.79
2009-10	5206.26	5720.81	-514.55
2010 - 11	5214.85	5483.66	-268.81
2011 - 12	6677.40	7262.71	-528.70
2012 - 13	7639.18	7719.90	-80.71

Source: 1. http://data.gov.in/catalog/financial-performance-srtus
2. Performance of STUS-2009-10 to 2012-13, Ministry of Road Transport and Highways, Annual reports.

As evident from the table 4.14, the total revenue of the corporation was Rs. 3121.20 crore during 2003 – 04 and increased to Rs. 7639.18 crore during 2012 – 13. The table shows that every year there is a continuous increase in the revenue during the reference period. It is clear from the table that the expenditure of APSRTC was Rs. 3163.22 crore and increased to Rs. 5720.81 crore during 2009 – 10 and stood at Rs. 7719.90 crore during 2012 – 13. The drop in expenditure to the corporation during 2010 – 11 can be attributed to the Telangana Agitation.

The table recorded profit to the corporation during 2007 – 08 and 2008 – 09 as Rs. 135.66 crore and Rs. 110.79 crore respectively. The profits to the corporation in that particular period were mainly because of reduction of motor vehicle tax (M.V. Tax) by the Government. Based on the analysis of revenue and expenditure parameters, the financial performance of the corporation is not up to the mark.

Table 4.15: Shows Total EPK Vs CPK = PPK

Financial Year	Total EPK (In Paise)	Total CPK (In Paise)	PPK (in Paise)
2002-03	1288	1369	-81
2003-04	1377	1396	-19
2004-05	1383	1480	-97
2005-06	1544	1562	-18
2006-07	1711	1757	-46
2007-08	1759	1705	+54
2008-09	1884	1843	+41
2009-10	1878	2064	-186
2010-11	2122	2232	-110
2011-12	2324	2528	-204
2012-13	2564	2592	-28
	EPK- Earnings per KM	CPK-Cost per KM	PPK-Profit/ Loss per KM

Source: 1. http://data.gov.in/catalog/financial-performance-srtus
2. Performance of STUS-2009-10 to 2012-13, Ministry of Road Transport and Highways, Annual reports.

It is evident from the table 4.15 that the EPK in APSRTC was 1288 paise during 2002 – 03, increased to 2564 paise during 2012 – 13. In the same way the CPK in APSRTC was 1369 paise during 2002 – 03 increased to 2592 paise during 2012 – 13. In the review period, it was observed that the expenditure is over riding the income of APSRTC. According to the table, during the last financial year, APSRTC could recover overall costs up to 98.95 percent leaving 1.05 percent of the total cost uncovered resulting in a net loss of 28 paise per km. From the table, it is seen that APSRTC had to get surplus to the tune of 54 paise during 2007 – 08 and 41 paise during 2008 – 09. It can be noted that during this period, the total number of buses has been considerably increased.

It can be inferred that the losses to APSRTC, in the reference period were due to uncontrolled illegal private buses operated by the private operators. The private operators illegally operate their travels as stage carriers on contract carrier permit. Cabs, autos and Lorries are also affecting the income of the corporation added to the private operators.

4.7. Safety & Maintenance Standards of APSRTC

Andhra Pradesh State Road Transport Corporation (APSRTC) to keep impeccable safety standards maintains high turnover of buses given the operating conditions of fitness to travel. It is necessary to replace about 12 to 15 percent of their rolling stock every year to ensure that the over aged vehicles are phased out from their fleet. To this purpose VEMA's – Vehicle Maintenance Computerized System is useful for the corporation to identify the performance of the vehicle periodically. As per policy norms of APSRTC Motor Vehicle inspectors of transport department yearly examine and certify the fitness of the bus, age of the bus, engine condition and fitness to transport passengers to their destinations.

According to A. Koteswar Rao, Executive Director of Greater Hyderabad Zone, "The current fleet of APSRTC stands at 19,320 and at least 15 percent of them are being decommissioned every year. In 2012, APSRTC decommissioned over 1500 old buses from Hyderabad and other major cities in the state[247]".

G. Jai Rao, Executive Director (Engg & IT) stated that of the RTC's fleet strength of 19240, an estimated 4500 buses had crossed the upper limit of 12 Lakh Kms of operation, while about 5,500 of them have run over 10 Lakh Kms. According to Executive Director, G. Jai Rao, "On an average we need to replace about 2000 vehicles every year. Despite of our financial status, being what it is we have managed to do a good job replacing 1450 buses through JNNURM (Jawaharlal Nehru National Urban Renewal Mission) in the year 2012 and 1000 in this year - 2013[248]".

Table 4.16: Shows Buses added during the past 10 years

Year	Addition	Replacement	Total
2002-03	-	668	668
2003-04	14	1333	1347
2004-05	238	1732	1970
2005-06	204	244	448

2006-07	359	765	1124
2007-08	293	1573	1866
2008-09	822	1000	1822
2009-10	1279	897	2176
2010-11	653	937	1590
2011-12	987	3149	4136
2012-13	-	1450	-
2013*	-	1000*	-

Source: The Hindu Daily News Paper

APSRTC has an enormous in-house facility for maintenance and engineering. In respect of this, it follows two-tire maintenance i.e. preventive maintenance of buses at depots and majors repairs / over hauls at work shops. To serve this purpose, corporation has constructed 7 retreading shops and 7 work-shops. The bus body building unit at Miyapur, Hyderabad, builds more than 600 bodies every year. Modern and updated technologies have also been introduced. Buses are fabricated with latest fabrications. For bus cleaning in minimum possible time, 28 automatic washing machines were installed at major bus stations and depots at district head quarters with a cost of 28 millions. Each machine washes about 250 buses a day effectively.

To meet the requirement of power for electric trolley bus project, a 10MW wind energy project was commissioned at Ramagiri in Anantapur District in the month of October 1995. The cost of the project is Rs. 400 Million. Until such time the electric trolley bus system is grounded, the generated power from the wind farm is being utilized for all zonal work – shops, all zonal retreading shops, major bus stations, bus body building works and head office units – in total 23 high tension (HT) units. The average generation of power from the energy project is 12 Million KWH per annum[249].

Tyres, spare parts – the major items of consumption are purchased from the manufacturers and their recognized original equipment manufacturers under the purchase policy. The scrap materials like Tyres, spare parts and condemned buses are sold through open auction.

4.8. Services

AP State Road Transport Corporation established during late fifties and first phase of nationalization of bus transport was completed covering Krishna, Guntur and West Godavari districts during 1958 – 61. It is the state owned corporation first to nationalize passenger service in India during Nizam Government ruling in 1932. It entered the Guinness book of record for owning largest fleet in the Country.

In parallel to APSRTC, private transport operators concern for profits in their services. They eye on the profitable routes at the cost of rules and regulations. Rising to the situation, APSRTC also in competition with private operators, ply luxury buses like Garuda, Garuda plus, Indra, Meghadhoot and Vennela buses to important towns and cities in the neighbouring states of Tamilnadu, Puducherry, Karnataka, Maharastra, Orissa, Chattisgarh and Goa. A service like Mayuri, a sleeper service, operated on few routes most notably between Hyderabad and Shridi by the Corporation. It also runs nonstop buses between important towns and cities. APSRTC at present operates 1,201 buses on 475 inter-state routes. After the introduction of Volvo and Multi axle Mercedes Benz buses which provided comfort and convenience to travel to long distance places – it is observed that the demand for the luxury buses is increasing.

Pallevelugu buses to villages, Metro liners as city services, Sapthagiri buses in the holy town of Tirumala Tirupathi are also operated by the corporation.

Table 4.17: Shows APSRTC inter-state buses - Vizianagaram zone

S.No.	Service No.	Service No.	Service Name	Type	Depot
1.	3477	3478	VSP – Bangalore	Garuda Plus A/C	VSP
2.	3487	3488	VSP – Bangalore	Garuda A/C	VSP
3.	3475	3476	VSP - Chennai	Garuda A/C	VSP
4.	2635	2636	KKD – Bangalore	Garuda A/C	KKD
5.	2637	2638	KKD - Bangalore	Garuda A/C	KKD

Source: APSRTC official pamphlet.

4.9. Significance of 'z' on APSRTC Bus Number Plate

Before the last Nizam Osman Ali Khan Bahadur handed over the RTC to Indian government, he put a condition in the agreement with government of India that every bus number plate should posses the letter 'Z'. AP9Z 9423 is an example. The letter 'Z' stands for Zahra Begum Nawab Mir Osman Ali Khan Niza - seventh mother.

4.10. Corporation's Social Responsibility – A focus

APSRTC is at present giving concessions in fares to different categories of commuters who travel in RTC buses – as per the policy of the state government. The concessions are estimated to Rs. 750 Crore[250]. This burden of amount as expenditure as social responsibility by APSRTC will be reimbursed by the state government as agreed every year. But in actual practice the state government is not keeping its promise of repaying the subsidy amount to the Corporation. However, the RTC continuing to issue monthly season tickets (MSTs). To general commuters traveling up to maximum distance of 100 Kms every day. The rate of this ticket is fixed on the basis of 20 days – up and down – fare allowing the holder to perform travel on all days of the month including Sundays and public holidays etc. Concession is extended to the following categories of beneficiaries is shown in table 4.18.

Up to the Month of May 2013, the State Government gave 90 percent concession on student bus passes, the remaining 10 percent were borne by the student. From June 2013 onwards the policy of government on student passes changed. As per the new policy the government is giving concession on bus tickets to students is 66.7 percent only. The rest of the 33.3 percent are to be borne by the student. It may seem the difference on concessional rise on student passes - 23.3 percent in actual practice in some routes the hike appears to be 100 percent. For example, until now students are paying Rs.175 only on below 22 Kms category of bus passes. At present for the same category of bus pass, students have to pay Rs. 780. This shows extra burden of Rs. 605 on every student. This rise on student bus passes may affect the education of the students and result in the raise in drop – out percentage in educational institutions.

Table 4.18: Shows Type of pass and Extent of concession allowed

S.No	Type of pass	Extent of concession allowed on certain conditions
1.	Student below 12 years	100%
2.	Girl Student studying up to 10th class	100%
3.	School/ College/ Technical institutions	Slab rated bus passes City-100% Rural-35%
4.	Physically Disabled	City-100% Rural-50% Escort-50%
5.	Free Bus Passes to M.L.A's, M.L.C's, M.P's and their spouses	100%
6.	Freedom Fighters 65 years of age and above	100%
7.	Accredited Journalists	City-100% Rural-66.6%

AP State Road Transport Corporation has allowed concessional benefits to certain targeted groups. For this APSRTC is providing provisions such as Vanitha (2 years validity for five family members with 10 percent concession), Navya Card, Travel As You Like, Students Exclusive Bus Passes Monthly Season Ticket/ Monthly Route Passes, GBT (Monthly General Bus), BARAT (Bus Advanced Reservation Any Time), TREATS (Travel Regularly and Earn Additional Free Trip Scheme), GIFT (Gain Instant Free Travel Scheme), CAT (Concessional Annual Travel with 10 percent concession), NGO- Bus Passes, Vihari (50 percent concession for 7 days except AC buses), Greater Hyderabad Darshan (Twin Cities), Krishnaveni Darshan – in Vijayawada and Vishakadarshan for Visakhapatnam.

Table 4.19: Shows the details of Hike in Bus Passes

Route Passes in Towns and Cities for 3 Months (in Rupees)			
Pass Type (Kms)	Charges before Hike	Charges after Hike	Burden on student
0-4	85	315	230
0-8	105	420	315
0-12	130	520	390
0-18	150	680	530
0-22	175	780	605
District High School and College Students Passes for 3 Months			
0-5	155	260	105
0-10	215	315	100
0-15	255	470	215
0-20	340	575	235
0-25	430	730	300
0-30	470	885	415
0-35	515	1040	525
District High School and College Students Month Passes			
0-5	55	90	35
0-10	75	105	30
0-15	90	160	70
0-20	120	195	75
0-25	150	245	95
0-30	165	295	130
0-35	180	350	170

4.11. I.T Initiatives of APSRTC

APSRTC has been working on the implementation of I.T in Andhra Pradesh. Implementation and effective use of IT has helped APSRTC in:-

1. Providing better Services to Passengers
2. Reduction of passengers' waiting time at the time of ticketing & issue of bus passes.
3. Effective Managerial Controls.
4. Reduction in waiting time of conductors at the counters.
5. Effective Maintenance Management of Vehicles.
6. Faster communication of information.

7. Better inventory control.
8. Standardization and simplification.
9. Effective Transfer Pricing and better Inter-Unit transactions.
10. Better Service to the Employees in Welfare schemes.

4.11.1. Major Areas of IT Applications are:

Operations:

Ticket Issuing Machines (TIMs): The main aim of introducing TIMs is to issue tickets even after completion of ground booking and to pick up more no. of passengers en-route. TIM's were introduced in APSRTC in May 2000[251].

Pass Automation & Accountal System (PAAS): This system was being implemented at Vijayawada, Visakhapatnam and Twin Cities. Under this system, citizens can take pass at any center in Hyderabad and can renew at any center. Between 8 A.M to 8 P.M expect on Sundays. On Sundays it works between 9 A.M to 3 P.M[252].

Online Passenger Reservation System (OPRS): The system facilitates ticket issue on 'Any-where to Any-where basis. This Booking facility through web interface is implemented at 117 Bus Stations throughout the Corporation with about 6000 services.

OLIMS - Online Inventory Management System.

PMS - Personnel Management System

Maintenance: VEMAS - Vehicle Maintenance & Testing system.

Inventory Management System:

STOINS -Stores Inventory System.

OLIMS - Online Inventory Management System.

Computer Aided Design Systems:

CIVIL- CAD Work Stations.

MIS - Management Information Systems.

Computer Training: All the 6 Zonal Staff Training Colleges and the Training Academy are provided with full fledged computer systems for imparting training to System supervisors on application software and system administration of operating systems.

- Regional/ Zonal core group supervisors are trained on latest developments and software maintenance.
- Assistant Depot clerks of the depots are trained on the day to day activities to be carried out on the application software and operating system.

For advanced courses, all the categories that are using computers are trained at reputed Training Institutes.

4.11.2. Future Plans of A.P.S.R.T.C.

A wide area network is being planned to connect all the Bus Stations in A.P. and adjoining states, to provide facility to passengers know the reservation status of the services from any Bus Station. This network will be connected to the existing network which covers Corporate Office, MGBS, JBS, Zonal and Regional Offices and Depots.

Tracking System

In addition to the above plans, APSRTC is contemplating to soon introduce Intelligence Transport System (ITS) to improve the punctuality of buses and there by provide better services to their passengers'. This tracking system would be introduced on pilot basis on 3,500 buses in Hyderabad on the Hyderabad - Nellore, Hyderabad – Vijayawada and Hyderabad Karimnagar routes. It also plans to extend to other routes based on the success of the project[253].

Advantages of Tracking System

The Vehicle tracking system would not only improve punctuality but also inculcate discipline among the employees of the corporation. This apart, electronic display boards and real time passenger information system would be put up at bus stations to enable passengers to know the arrival time of their bus and use the waiting time effectively[254].

Online Ticket booking

Hereafter RTC would introduce online booking system in its 213 depots in place of manual booking and see that Cheepurupalli like incidents will not happen in future. In Cheepurupalli Depot, Vizianagaram District – online ticket fraud – took place because of multi location access by ATB (Authorized Ticket Booking) agents followed a policy of frequent change of passwords[255]. The Corporation to prevent such malpractices in future, is planning to initiate online credit top-up is compulsory, for the on-line passenger reservation system. RTC would incur expenditure of Rs. 49 crore for implementing information technology in all its departments including online ticket booking by providing a unique password to its agents all over the State and make an agreement with Tata Consultancy Services (TCS) for this purpose.

RFID Readers in TIMs

This is proposed to provide RFID reader in TIMs to obtain the following advantages.

1. Verification of authority and validity of bus passes.
2. Online renewal of bus passes which enables the pass holder to renew the bus passes without going to any counter.

4.12. Impact of Globalization on the performance of APSRTC

Under the GATT Agreement, the Government of India resorted to integrate raw material distribution of National Petroleum products into the international economy in the year 2010[256]. In pursuance of the policy of market economy, the government of India appointed several Committees to suggest methodology for pricing of diesel and cooking fuel. One such important committee is Kiritparikh Pannel. The panel suggested to the Petroleum and Natural Gas Ministry to making the Price of Diesel as market determined and take steps to pass on the impact of rise in prices of diesel to the consumers[257]. With this policy of Union Government, the prices of petrol and diesel are rising time and again. As a result the maintenance burden of the A.P. State Road Transport Corporation is proliferating in unexpected terms. The government and private partnership is the part of the strategy in the concept of LPG. But in India, in reality it is the understanding partnership between politician and industrialists. This unethical partnership between politicians in power and businessmen paved the way to loot the people and resources of the country which ultimately led the state to bankruptcy. This is other-wise called as 'crony capitalism'. No political party is exception in this unethical practice. In Andhra Pradesh, Political leaders are involved in Bus Transport business and travel agencies are running on their surnames. Diwakar Travel and Kesineni Travels are some of the examples in this regard[258]. Diwakar Travels belong to J. C. Diwakar Reddy a former Congress Minister in the State. About 300 buses are in Kesineni Travels which belong to Kesineni Srinivas a prominent Telugudesam leader in the State. Private bus operators because of their political clout are not observing transport rules and regulations. They often violate the rules by not having proper bus permits, fitness certificates, etc. In contrary to the transport rules the bus agencies run the buses in 5 or 6 routes at the same time on single registration number[259]. This all happen in the name of Public private partnership as a consequence of LPG. They don't even pay taxes to Government. As per transport rules, for every three months private agencies have to pay for each seat Rs. 3675 for national permit, Rs. 2625 for state permit and for tourist permit Rs. 900[260]. But in actual practice, private operators ply their buses on tourist permit to distinct places in competition with APSRTC as stage carriers. Everyday about 250 buses from Vijayawada ply to distinct places viz., Hyderabad, Banglore, Chennai, Visakhapatnam etc[261]. As a result, they are causing huge loss to APSRTC as well as State Government. The recent accident occurred in Palem, Mahaboobnagar District on Banglore – Hyderabad express highway revealed the above astonished malpractices of private operators. In that accident 45 passengers charred to death because of the lapses in observing road transport rules by the private operators.

The implications of market – economy is not limited to private bus agencies only. It extended to international airports express highways so on and so forth. Similarly express highway construction companies are extracting toll gate charges more than required. This is a kind of nationalized loot continuing in express highways in the name of toll gate. For example, a bus from Hyderabad to Bangalore has to spend about Rs. 1000 to various toll gates on the express highway. Even RTC is not an exception from toll gate burden. All this add to the corporation's losses.

To offset the losses, APSRTC instead of increasing number of bus services, occupancy rate, operational efficiency and by avoiding unnecessary expenditure, corporation resorting to the common practice of rising ticket charges. As it is not enough, in addition to the existing 3200 lease buses, RTC management wanted some more lease buses against to the wishes of RTC unions[262]. RTC unions argue that private agencies monopoly may increase in that routes and in future they may demand for much profit earning routes at the cost of RTC interest[263]. Unions fear that if this practice of increasing the number of lease buses continues, the private operator's domination on RTC will strengthen and gradually lead Corporation into the hands of private operators as a strategy of LPG.

4.13. FOCUS ON PRIVATE TRAVELS ILLEGAL OPERATIONS

Since from its inception, APSRTC has to face a challenge from the private operators. As per one estimate there are 1500 buses in Andhra Pradesh which are operating illegally by the private agencies. Private operators to get profit earning routes, every month on an average bribe the politicians and transport authorities with an amount of Rs. 18 Crore and Rs. 4.5 Crore respectively. For this purpose each bus is collecting an amount of Rs. 5000 per day[264]. Out of the total loss, Rs. 1600 crore was from illegal operations of private operators and another Rs. 400 crore by illegal transport through private buses[265]. According to APSRTC unions, the illegal operations by private operators resulted in loss to APSRTC on an average of Rs. 2000 Crore a year[266]. Critics argue that the Private travels seem to run a parallel Government in the State by dictating terms to the transport ministry and government of Andhra Pradesh in allotting profit earning routes to the private operators. In this process all the transport rules were kept in cold storage.

The Volvo bus belonging to J.C. Uma Reddy which was leased to Jabber travels met with an accident on 30th October, 2013 at Palem when coming from Banglore to Hyderabad in Mahaboob Nagar district, Andhra Pradesh. In that mishap, 45 passengers were charred to death and 5 persons including the driver providentially escaped from the accident. Also there is another incident of Volvo bus under private travels, which met with an accident near Hospeta while coming from Nellore to Bangalore. The accident killed 5 passengers including 24 years old pregnant women and six year old boy and along with 28 passengers' was injured[267]. But Palem accident has become prominent because there was a wide spread agitation against the Government of Andhra Pradesh and Ministry of Transport. Palem accident has exposed many loop holes in issuing permits to the private operators in their illegal operations with no proper records. Private operators run buses as stage carriers on tourist permit. On single permit, private travels are running more than two buses to distinct places against to the transport rules. Private Travels instead of appointing two drivers, illegally manage with a single driver in transporting the passengers to their destinations. In addition to this, private operators are not maintaining the proper record of the passenger which is mandatory as per law – on the particular date of journey. Over speed and allowing extra passengers into the bus are commonly seen in private bus operations. Private operators are also maintaining online reservation which action of the private travels was not accepted by the rules. The Palem accident has paved the way to public debate over the excesses of the private operators. As a consequence, with public and media pressure, the transport department cracked whip on private travels which resulted in increase in the income to the APSRTC with an amount of Rs. 3 Crore per day 2013 – 14[268].

At least this is the time for the Government of Andhra Pradesh to look into the malpractices of Private travel agencies and match fixings between transport officials and private operators and take all essential measures like strengthening of Transport rules by amending Transport Act, cancellation of the provision of online ticket booking by private operators, taking criminal action on private operators those who violate and bypass the transport rules and also cancel their bus permits for the existence of RTC in its healthy continuation in discharging its services. At the same time the government also has to think whether there is a possibility of merging private travels in RTC and treat their employees as RTC employees.

4.14. IMPACT OF SAMAIKYA ANDHRA AGITATION ON THE PERFORMANCE OF APSRTC

4.14.1. Backdrop

The State of Andhra Pradesh was formed on 1st November, 1956 with the recommendations of 1st State Re-organization Commission (SRC) under the Chairmanship of Fajul Ali. On the basis of gentlemen agreement, the two regions of Telugu speaking people - Telangana (a part of erstwhile Hyderabad State) and Andhra state were merged to form as the State of Andhra Pradesh on linguistic ground, with Hyderabad as its State Capital.

Since the first day of formation of the Andhra Pradesh State there are some allegations from Telangana leaders that the Seemandhra leaders are violating the gentlemen agreement norms, as a consequence we are putting into losses in respect of employment opportunities, Education and Resources. In course of time the Telangana leaders and intelligentsia nursed grudge over the Seemandhra businessmen and politicians saying that these people are exploiting their resources at the cost of the welfare of the Telangana region. As a result there were agitations of 'Jai Telengana' and counter 'Jai Andhra' movements for separate statehood in 1969 and 72 respectively. In a step to insulate the interests of Andhra people from the affects of Mulki rules the Union Government by taking Constitutional Amendment-32 inserted Article 371D in Indian Constitution and Presidential order was issued to that effect in 1973. As a result the Zonal system was established in State to appease the people of Andhra region in the field of Education and Employment. However, the attitude of Telangana leaders did not change. In course of time the Telangana leaders developed Telangana sentiment to their political gains, rather than to the interest of Telegana region. With a view to pacify the Telangana agitation, the Union Government appointed a Committee headed by Justice B. N. Srikrishna to study and recommend the feasibility for the formation of Telangana State. The Committee submitted its report on 30th December 2010, a day before its term was to expire. Before the Srikrishna Committee, the Union Government appointed Pranab Mukarjee Committee Rosaiah Committee, A. K. Anthony Committee, and Group of Ministers (GOM) Committee for the same Telangana issue.

4.14.2. Seemandhra Movement

As it is a bolt from the blue, agitation erupted in Coastal Andhra and Rayalaseema regions together with protests, a day after the United Progressive Alliance (UPA) agreed to the division of A.P and formation of separate Telangana State. APSRTC employees of Seemandhra region joined to the issue with the Seemandhra APNGO's by demanded the center to withdraw the proposal of bifurcation of Andhra Pradesh. RTC strike started on 13th August, 2013 and continued till the call off date i.e. 13th October, 2013[269]. During the 61 days strike period, RTC buses of Seemandhra region go off the road. RTC employees had withdrawn their strike after reaching an agreement between State Government and Seemandhra RTC unions on certain demands. Their important demand was to merge RTC with the State Government and insulate the Corporation from financial crisis[270].

4.14.3. Seemandhra RTC Employees Drive towards Agitation - Causes[271]

- ➤ The average revenue generated per bus and earnings per KM is higher in Telangana than in Seemandhra region.
- ➤ When it comes to sharing of losses, Telangana would get a lesser share than that of Seemandhra region.
- ➤ Most of the assets and infrastructure lie in Telangana while there are hardly any such facilities in Seemandhra region.
- ➤ Most of the Corporations' assets including Bus Stations have been pledged to raise loans.
- ➤ Incidentally the Corporation's only bus body building unit is in Miyapur (Hyderabad)[272].
- ➤ Training academy is at Hakimpet (Hyderabad)[273].
- ➤ RTC Super Specialty hospital is at Taranaka (Hyderabad)[274].
- ➤ Printing Press is at Miyapur (Hyderabad) and RTC Kala Bhavan is at Bagh Lingampally[275].

4.14.4. Debt Ridden – APSRTC

APSRTC, in adition to the existing credit debt of Rs. 4200 Crore, the recent hit of Seemandhra RTC employees strike has added some more losses of about Rs. 650 Crore. In addition to these, another bitter pill for the Corporation was annual liability of Rs. 290 for the debt in the form of payment of interest[276]. As a consequence to the agitation, 1500 buses were put to break down due to lack of fitness certificate, on an average 100 buses in every district. It is because of Motor Vehicle inspectors who are still continuing in the agitation and not available to issue fitness certificates, causing further lose to RTC.[277]

The Seemandhra agitation has affected the Transport Corporation at the time of the Corporation has high potential to earn revenue in view Brahmotsavams in Tirupati and Dasara festival. In the festival seasons, the APSRTC makes additional revenue by running special services every year. Meanwhile the private operators are making hey to make a quick buck or charging double the fare in the absence of Public Transport during the strike period[278].

Given the situation, there was a threat to the payment of salaries to its employees (RTC) in the month of October, 2013 unless, the State Government extended some financial help[279].

"We do mortgage our properties on regular basis for regular needs. This apart, we are also holding payments to our suppliers to ensure sufficient money with us to pay salary at the end of the month" said the senior official who doesn't want to be identified[280].

4.14.5. Sakala Janula Samme of Telangana Agitation

There was a Sakala Janula Samme in Telangana region for separate Telangana state in the past. This agitation continued unabatedly for 27 days; as a consequence of the agitation APSRTC lost revenue of about Rs. 250 Crore[281]. In any agitation whether it is Telangana or Seemandhra, it is the APSRTC buses that have been bearing the brunt of public ire, resulting in losses of Crores of rupees to the public exchequer[282]. Over the past 8 years as many as 1538 RTC buses have been destroyed in agitations and riots[283]. Most of the buses were destroyed during the year 2009-10 when anti social elements damaged nearly 872 transport buses while another 301 buses were destroyed during 2004-05[284]. The destruction of buses meant that hundreds of bus days are lost each year. As a result it could not operate about 980.07 Lakh Kms besides suffering a loss of 22.74 Crore passengers and wastage of 2.71 Lakh vehicle days[285]. The State had to spend Rs. 10.54 Crore on repairing buses which were partially damaged[286].

4.14.6 Action Plan of APSRTC to Shore-up Lost Revenues in Telangana Agitation[287]

- ➤ The thrust is on increasing the occupancy level by additional 1percent.
- ➤ Plans to operate 2000 additional Kms extra per day from each region.
- ➤ STAR-Strategic Tools for Augmentation of Revenues, the Corporation has decided to pay allowances to drivers and conductors involved in extra operation.
- ➤ SAVE APSRTC-A fort night drive would be observed from 1st November, 2011 to 15th November, 2011 across all the depots of the Corporation.
- ➤ Plans to hold gate meetings to bring about attitudinal change among the staff.

4.14.7. Impact of State Bifurcation as Telangana and Residuary A.P on A.P State Transport Corporation: A Focus

Table 4.20: Shows average Day-wise income of APSRTC from past 11 months

Month & Year	Average Day wise income in the Month (In Crores)	Growth Rate (In Crores)
April 2013	17.84	
May 2013	21.53	+ 3.69
June 2013	20.35	- 0.18
July 2013	18.11	- 2.24
August 2013	10.90	- 7.21
September 2013	7.76	-3.14
October 2013	14.00	+ 6.24
November 2013	19.26	+ 5.26
December 2013	18.87	- 0.39
January 2013	19.47	+ 0.60
February 2013	21.17	+ 1.7

Source: Andhra Bhoomi Daily news paper, "RTC Adayam pina samme ata", p. 2, 4th March, 2014.

The table 4.20 depicts that day wise income during April 2013 to February 2014 is not encouraging. Though Officers Association of APSRTC claims that from January 2014 to February 2014, the growth of RTC revenue income in one month is Rs. 1.7 crore, due to employee's commitment to shore up lost revenues. Against to the claim of the officers association of APSRTC, it is evident from the table that the picture is gloomy during the period of review as presented in the table 4.24. If any positive signs about growth in revenue appeared in October and November months of year 2013, is because of Seemandhra agitation; in the agitation period, personnel cost of the corporation was saved due to the policy of the government – "no work no pay". Diesel cost also added to the corporation's savings, which resulted in hike of average day wise income during the months of October 2013 and November 2013.

4.14.8. A.P State Bifurcation Blues on A.P.S.R.T.C.

Comparative with other STUs in India, APSRTC has the reputation that it holds better standards in maintaining bus services in A.P. However over the years, APSRTC was running in losses; at present its losses reached to the extent of more than Rs. 4800 Crore. To insulate RTC from losses, IIM Bangalore submitted its report to the state government suggesting some measures to offset losses to the corporation. But reasons best known to the State Government, that the report was put on the back burner.

4.14.8.1. APSRTC on Sticky Wicket

Adding to the present fiscal crisis, the state bifurcation into Telengana and residuary Andhra Pradesh state brought some more problems to the Corporation particular to its properties partition in Andhra Pradesh. All the valuable fixed assets belonging to APSRTC viz., famous Bus Bhavan, Office of the Managing Director, Office of the Staff Retired Benefits Scheme (SRBS), CC Office, Officers Training Center, Super Specialty Hospital, Kalyana Mandapam etc Crores of rupees properties are located in Hyderabad, which invariably belong to Telengana State[288]. Buses which are operating in Telengana belong to the Corporation, where as in 13 Seemandhra districts, majority bus routes belong to private operators[289]. In Seemandhra districts there are no enough fixed assets to APSRTC; if there are any assets to the corporation in Seemandhra, they are not developed to get revenues[290]. Some assets belong to APSRTC in the region were in BOT (Build Operate Transfer) Mode. The properties of the Corporation at present in Vizag are in BOT. Most of the RTC's fixed assets in Seemandhra region are either on pledges to financial institutions or leased out to some private individuals or institutions[291]. With the division of State, out of 2000 buses belong to Seemandhra will go to Telengana resulting to about 10000 workers of the corporation remain with no work in Seemandhra region. Source from the employees unions reveal that bifurcation blues are more on Seemandhra region than its counterpart in Telangana.

To overcome this present crisis in APSRTC, ensuing State and Central Governments after elections must come forward to Corporation's rescue and see that the APSRTC get out of its crisis in the state by making financial assistance in the form of grants particularly to the residuary Andhra Pradesh State Road Transport Corporation. At present AP State Road Transport Corporation is operating with 213 depots, 22000 buses and 123000 employees.

SECTION B - HRD PRACTICES IN APSRTC: A STUDY OF ITS IMPLEMENTATION

4.15. HRD PRACTICES IN APSRTC

It is evident that HRD Practices is a systematic acquisition of attitudes, concepts, knowledge, roles and skills that result in improved performance at their respective works. It is a planned learning Experience designed to bring about a permanent change in an individual's knowledge, attitudes and skills. The fundamental purpose of these HRD Practices is to help the person to develop skills and abilities, which when applied at work, will enhance their average job performance. To meet the above challenges, APSRTC is implementing the under mentioned HRD Practices.

❖ **RECRUITMENT**

In order to calculate the requirement of staff in each category, APSRTC has fixed separate norms for all the categories. Based on those norms the requirement for each depot is calculated and sanction of the competent authority is obtained. In the case where specific norms are not laid down, industrial engineering department will offer its recommendations for those posts. The total manpower position of APSRTC during 2002-03 to 2012-13 was depicted in table 4.21.

Table 4.21: Shows the Total manpower position of APSRTC during 2002-03 to 2012-13

Year	No. of Employees
2002-03	122358
2003-04	119219
2004- 05	117400
2005- 06	115946
2006- 07	115529
2007- 08	113340
2008- 09	113370
2009- 10	115898
2010- 11	120566
2011- 12	123615
2012- 13	1,23,871

Source: APSRTC Annual Reports

Recruitment Practices: In APSRTC, vacancy occurred has to be filled up as per the directions of the Ministry of Road Transport and Roads and Buildings Department and principal secretary transport. Class - I officers are filled by HRD department but the final decision is taken by VC & MD, Class - II employees i.e. Assistant Managers (supervisors) are filled by the head of the department.

The recruitment in Maintenance side is done in 1:1 ratio i.e. 1 percent is for direct recruitment and 1 percent is for promotion, Traffic side it is 2:3 i.e. 2 percent for Direct Recruitment and 3 percent for promotions, whereas for Personnel and Accounts side it is 12:18 ratio i.e. 12 percent for promotions and 18 percent for direct recruitment giving preference to internal reference and some ratio is filled by HRD Department. Class - III and Class - IV employees are filled by the individual department with the help of personnel Department at Zonal and regional level (conductors and Drivers) from internal as well as external sources.

The Corporation advertises its recruitment notification in the daily newspapers, APSRTC website and in the employment exchange. Direct recruitment posts in all classes of services both technical and non-technical shall be filled up as per the reservations. The persons, who are already in the service of the corporation and has been appointed regularly is permitted to apply for a post filled by direct recruitment; in such case his period of service up to a maximum of 10 years shall be deducted from his age for the purpose of maximum age limit, provided that this age concession shall be allowed where the maximum age limit prescribed for the post is 40 years or above. Further, the employees belonging to scheduled castes, scheduled Tribes and Backward class communities, who are already in service of the corporation and have been appointed regularly are permitted to apply for the post to be filled by direct recruitment shall be allowed to deduct their entire service from the age for the purpose of maximum age prescribed for the post, subject to the condition that after allowing such concession the age of the employees should not exceed 45 years and an additional 5 years shall be allowed in respect of the candidates belonging to scheduled castes/ scheduled tribes. When a limited recruitment is conducted under regulation 12 (2) (f) (i), subject to the condition that after allowing such age concession of 10 years for the physically handicapped persons, an age concession not exceeding 3 years in respect of defense service personnel of the Indian union, concession shall be allowed in addition to the length of service rendered in defense services for any post to be filled by direct recruitment. An age concession depending on the extent of service rendered shall be allowed in respect of emergency commissioned officers for the purpose of appointment in the corporation.

The requirement of personnel is worked out based on schedules as per the approved norms provided for the staff. Recruitment activity is a decentralized function in Andhra Pradesh State Road Transport Corporation and is taken up at 3 levels i.e. Apex level (Corporate Office), Zonal office and regional based three tire system of seniority.

Corporate: Officers including Medical officers & Accounts Officers, Assistant Engineer, Traffic Supervisor (Trainee) Mechanical Supervisor (Trainee),

Paramedical Staff and Foreman (Printing), Charge Man (Printing) Section Officer (Civil), Deputy Section Officer (Civil)

Zonal Office: Categories like Stenographers, Junior Assistants and equivalent cadres, telephone Operator, Dy. Superintendent (Material/ Purchase), Jr. Assistant (Mat/Pur) conducted by the Middle Officers.

Regional Office: The bulk of recruitment is conducted for Drivers, Conductors, Mechanics, Cleaners and Artisans (R.M)

Generally in APSRTC, any vacancy occurred has to be filled up as per directions of the Ministry of Transport. There are various departments like Accounts, Personnel, Civil, Mechanical, and Canteen in APSRTC. Positions in the APSRTC are divided into four cadres or classes where in the recruitment process adopted could be centralized or decentralized. For Class-I, Class-II cadre employees the process is centralized and for Class-III and Class-IV cadre the process is decentralized. Recruitment for various posts in these cadres takes place with respect to particular qualifications as stated against each post.

Any vacancy arise in the corporation is informed through media, newspaper and employment exchanges; based on the class of the post the publicity is given in States or regional or Zonal wise, the advertisement consists of all details pertaining to the post viz., qualification, age, reservations, pay scales, method of recruitment and other details. Initially applications are invited for the particular post, then a written test and/ or interview follows; for some posts only interview is conducted. For some special posts like typist or driver skill test is also conducted apart from written test and interview.

Type of Recruitment: According to APSRTC Employees Recruitment Regulations Act-1996, appointments to various posts are made by direct recruitment, by promotion and by transfer on deputation of an official already in the service of the department of Central or State Government or State Transport Undertaking.

The direct recruitment at corporate level is communicated by the chief Personnel Manager of various posts on an annual basis, based on which the recruitment is taken up.

Main Sources of recruitment:

a) External/ Direct Recruitment
b) Internal Recruitment

External / Direct Recruitment: In Direct recruitment the candidate should be appointed directly to some post in the organization other than by promotion or transfer from any post in the service of the corporation.

The appointment to any post in APSRTC by direct recruitment is done if the person is satisfied with the following eligibility:

a) Who has sound health, possess active habits and is free from bodily defects.
b) Whose character and antecedents are such as to qualify for such service; and
c) Who has completed the age of 18 years.

Direct recruitment to all the State level seniority posts are being taken up at apex level (Corporate level). At present there is a ban on recruitment to all posts to control bus staff ratio/ personnel cost. However at Corporate level, recruitment is conducted and continued regularly for certain essential posts.

Advertising in the Newspapers: The Corporation will advertise the job openings in all leading daily newspapers inviting applications from the general public who fulfill the conditions laid down by the corporation for recruitment. Generally speaking, most of the corporation's recruitment is done through advertising method only.

Employment Exchanges: The organization informs the employment exchanges about manpower requirements. The exchanges send messages to the suitable candidates to apply for such posts.

These exchanges match both the demand and supply of the labour force. The candidates should receive the information from the employment exchanges and if they are willing to apply, they can submit application form by disclosing their full bio-data.

Generally vacancy arises in any posts in various classes either because of retirement of the employees, death of the employees, to increase in the employees or to increase in the number of schedules.

Internal source of recruitment: It is the process of filling up the job vacancies from and within the corporation by giving promotions or transfers is known as the internal source of recruitment.

Recruitment and selection policy in APSRTC:

1) The Recruitments made by APSRTC are governed by its Regulations called Employee Recruitment Regulations approved by Government.

2) These regulations shall apply to all classes of service under the corporation except to the extent otherwise expressed by or under these regulations.

3) The appointment of an employee hold additional charge of another post or discharge the current duties connected there to, doesn't amount to appoint to the latter post.

4) Approved candidate means a candidate whose name appears in an authoritative list of candidate approved for appointment to any service, class or category.

5) **Appointment and Qualifications**: Appoints to the posts in the corporation shall be made (a) by direct recruitment (b) indirect recruitment i.e. by promotion, (c) by transfer or deputation of an official already in the service of department of Central or State Government or State Transport Undertaking.

6) **Approved Candidates**: All the direct recruitment shall be made from the list of approved candidates. Such list is prepared to generally by the special orders of the corporation to the selection committee appointed in this behalf. Where the candidates in such list are arranged in an order of preference, appointments to the services shall be made in such order. The inclusion of the candidates name in a list of approved candidates for any post shall not confer on him any right to appointment to such post otherwise than in accordance with these regulations.

7) **Application Fees:** Every candidate for appointment by direct recruitment to a post in the service shall remit the fee prescribed by the corporation in the prescribed manner with his application. Provided

that, candidates who are already in service and those belong to SC, ST, BC and Physically Handicapped persons and candidates who have rendered "WAR SERVICE" and apply for appoint to a post filled in by direct recruitment shall not be required to pay the fees prescribed.

❖ SELECTION PROCEDURE

Application Form: APSRTC has evolved an application form for Class - III categories (Junior Assistant's, Drivers, Conductors, Shramics) and Class IV categories (Cleaners/ Khalasi). Zone wise recruitment process mainly personal back ground 1) Information 2) Education attainments 3) work experience 4) personnel details. However, Class - I Services categories is by online filling.

Evaluation of application form: Class - I and Class - II applications are screened by concerned Departments'. Zonal wise ineligible applications are removed from the application blank only and only eligible candidates are called for written test/ Interview.

Employment tests: APSRTC follows different employment tests in order to find out suitable employees in line with the job requirement. Trade tests are conducted for technical vacancies and in case of non-technical vacancies, aptitude test may be conducted by individual departments with coordination of HRD department.

Interview: After the declaration of the written examination the corporation calls the merit list of the candidates for an interview. At the same time they verify all original certificates at the time of interview whatever the candidate submitted in photo copies along with application. In the interview three members of the concerned heads of the department, conducting officers verify the above all certificates, and then they give the marks to the candidates.

Appointment Order: In APSRTC, after the final decision, concern authority has to intimate the decision to the successful candidates. APSRTC sends the appointment orders to the successful candidates within 15 days.

Medical Examination: In APSRTC every candidate appointed in the organization is required to undergo a medical examination by its Medical Officer at the time of appointment and produce a physical fitness certificate.

Induction: In APSRTC, the induction programme is entrusted to the concerned head of the department. The induction programme talks about the history of the organization, and short discussion with an officer in personnel department who will describe the organization benefit plans, the new comer will be introduced to other workers by senior employee of the concerned departments. It may be noted that the induction program is not organized systematically in APSRTC.

Placement: In APSRTC, the fresh candidate on joining the organization will be placed as probation officer for two years. The candidate will be trained during the probation - Traffic Supervisor, Mechanical Supervisor, for one year, junior clerk for one year and mechanics, Drivers, conductors 6 to 8 weeks.

❖ TRAINING AND DEVELOPMENT

Andhra Pradesh State Road Transport Corporation is the largest passenger road transport corporation in the world. It is the only State Transport Undertaking which got the place in 'Guinness book of world records' in 1999 for having largest fleet. As per the vision and mission of the organization, it has the responsibility to create a work environment which helps to remove barriers that limit the ability of staff to act in empowered ways. The advantage of employee empowerment is that "it encourages employees to gain the skills and knowledge that will allow them to overcome obstacles in work environment and in life and help them to develop within themselves".

Training is imparted only to newly recruited employees like OUTs (Officer Under Trainees), A.Os (Accounts Officers), M.Os (Medical Officers), M.S.Ts (Mechanical Supervisor Trainee), T.S.Ts (Traffic Supervisor Trainee), in service employees, Contract Conductors and Contract Drivers etc., both through external agencies and In – house Training Institutions and also by outside organizations/ Departments.

Induction Training Courses: Induction Training is imparted by the AP State Road Transport Corporation to the candidates selected to the skilled jobs for which they are recruited. First aid training is imparted by the doctor attached to the regions and driving instructors are entrusted with the job of imparting practical training, etc. In addition to the above, the Trainees are also impressed on aspects like, attending duty with proper uniform, to attend and study accident spots to analyze causes leading to the accident under the personal supervision of the training officer looking after maintenance and cleanliness of vehicles and precautions that are taken for avoiding damages to the buses.

Conductors: Since 1986, uniform syllabus is adopted for imparting induction training to all the persons selected for the post of Conductors. Besides job training an emphasis is laid on aspects like organizing queue systems for the passengers boarding buses, guiding the passengers in bus stations, helping the disabled, aged and lady passengers in boarding the buses.

Drivers: Heavy vehicle drivers are recruited based on educational qualification, medical examination and on practical driving test. After recruitment, the new appointed drivers are imparted with both theory and practical training for a period of 12 weeks. In the course of training to the drivers the emphasis on the aspects of courtesy and present behaviour with passengers, co – workers and other road users, acquaintance with various types of road conditions, accident spots and precautions to be taken to avoid accidents, good driving habits with a view to avoid damages, simultaneously achieving fuel and tyre economy, cleanliness and maintenance of vehicles, attending to minor breakdowns etc.

Traffic Apprentice/ Deputy Traffic Superintendent: The Training period of Deputy Traffic Superintendents is for a period of 72 weeks which include both theoretical (23 weeks) and practical training (49 weeks) covering the aspects of general management rules and regulations of APSRTC.

In – House Training and Training through Outside Agencies: In-House training is conducted at the corporate level in Transport Academy, Hakimpet, Hyderabad and at Zonal level in Zonal staff training colleges situated at Hyderabad, Warangal, Kurnool, Nellore, Gannavaram and Vizianagaram.

While Transport Academy imparts training to officers and frontline Supervisors, the zonal staff training colleges imparts training to lower level Supervisors, Medical Staff, Artisans, Ministerial Staff and the Crew. Regular training programmes are also conducted at depot level for the crew and Mechanical Staff.

The officers, senior supervisors and staff are deputed for management development programmes and computer related programmes conducted by reputed institutions in the country like CIRT governed by Association of State Road Transport Undertakings(ASRTU) New Delhi, Administrative Staff College of India(ASCI), Hyderabad, Centre for Organizational Development Hyderabad, Engineering Staff College of India, Hyderabad; Indian Institution of Industrial Engineering, Navy Mumbai; Federation of A.P. Chambers of Commerce & Industry (FAPCC & I), Andhra Pradesh Productivity Council, Hyderabad (APPC), Quality Circle forum of India, Hyderabad; Hyderabad Management Association(HMA) and Indian Roads & Transport Development Association (IRTDA), Bombay etc. Besides the above, they will be deputed to premier institutions, 'B' Schools, National Productivity Council (NPC) branches, Ramakrishna Mutt, Brahma Kumaries etc.,

Apprentice Training: As statutory requirement, the corporation imparts regular stipendiary apprenticeship training to ITI holders, diploma holders, engineering graduates, intermediate (vocational) certificate holders and sandwich apprenticeship program to polytechnic students which make them eligible appoint for appointment.

The training modules at all training institutions have been drawn up with proper blend of theoretical and practical inputs, in order to update knowledge, skills and attitudes at all levels. The focus of the training program is to develop organizational commitment, courteous attitude and to promote provision of safe, reliable, regular, punctual and cost effective operations to improve customer satisfaction.

Instructors set up in APSRTC for T & D: The human resource development wing in APSRTC was formed during 1990 - 91. It provides training to front line supervisors and officers of the corporation. The chief manager, human resource development conducts the activity of training and development of human resource in APSRTC at corporate level. It also imparts training to new recruits in the cadre of officers, traffic and mechanical supervisors, apart from conducting apprenticeship for graduate engineering apprentice.

The APSRTC is divided into seven zones, in each zone there is one training college which is headed by a principal of the rank of senior manager who is assisted by front line supervisors of different departments of the corporation. They also serve as a faculty to the training college. In addition to the training colleges at zonal level, there is one Transport Academy at corporate level and another training institute - Central Institute of Road Transport (CIRT), Pune.

From depot manager to deputy superintendent - all the front line officers are given training by training academy. The employees of the next level like senior clerks, drivers and conductors, controllers, mechanics, will be provided training at zonal colleges.

The Automobile Research and Transport Academy at Gannavaram is headed by a director, who is supported by a senior manager acting as principal, Deputy Managers of personnel, finance, operational and Mechanical departments. They also serve as faculty. In this academy research is done on automobiles, which wing is supervised by senior engineer, Mechanical.

Preparatory sources of short term duration are conducted at regional training colleges, for the personnel from finance, operational, maintenance and material departments. Training is also given to the supervisors on computers as detailed below:

1) Personnel Department Supervisors - PINS (Personnel Information Systems)

2) Finance Department Supervisors - FACTS (Finance Accounting Systems)

3) Traffic Department Supervisors - OLTAS (Online Ticket Accounting Systems)

4) Stores Department Supervisors - STOINS (Stores Information Systems)

5) Mechanical Department Supervisors - VEMAS - (Vehicle Maintenance Systems)

The Central Institute of Road Transport (CIRT) was established in 1967 on the joint initiative of the Association of State Transport Undertakings

(ASTU) and the then Ministry of Shipping and Transport. The objective of CIRT is to improve the efficiency and productivity of the transport sector, with particular emphasis on State Transport Undertakings. CIRT has strength of 240 employees of whom 70 are professional staff.

CIRT offers over 50 management development programmes in a year covering general management, transport operations and maintenance engineering. The programmes are meant for practicing managers in STUs and other organizations operating transport services. All programmes are residential and their duration ranges from one week to three weeks.

CIRT has been awarded the ISO 9001 Certificate by Bayern of Munich, Germany for the design and execution of training, research, consultancy and testing services. The Training programmes in APSRTC for Class - I and Class - II services are in the following:

1) Refresher Programmes
2) Management Development Programmes (MDP) and
3) Supervisory Development Programmes (SDPP)

The total training programmes conducted by APSRTC and employees trained during the last six years has been given in table 4.22. It is observed from the table that about 392 programmes were conducted to officers and supervisors during 2005 - 06 to 2010 - 11. In the period of reference, 1542 officers and 8212 supervisors were given training in their respective areas. Besides this 63 other staff members were also given training in the above said period. The table reveals the highest expenditure incurred towards officers training during 2009 - 10 was Rs. 94.94 Lakh. Expenditure incurred towards supervisor's training in the same year was Rs. 37.16 Lakh.

Table 4.22: Statement showing training programmes and details of employees trained during the period – 2005-06 to 2010-11.

(P) - Denotes provincial

Period	No. of Programmes conducted	No. of officers trained	No. of supervisors trained	No. of Staff trained	Total number trained	Total Expenditure (In Lakhs)
2005 – 06	08	194	--	--	194	9.70
2005 – 06	45	--	1541	--	1541	2.43
2006 – 07	11	227	--	--	227	1.17
2006 – 07	51	--	1518	--	1518	2.59
2007 – 08	13	445	--	--	445	3.16
2007 – 08	60	--	1190	--	1190	2.57
2008 – 09	06	143	--	--	143	0.23
2008 – 09	48	--	1181	--	1181	2.61
2009 – 10	13	246	--	--	246	94.94
2009 – 10	59	--	1372	--	1372	37.16
2009 – 10	02	--	--	63	63	0.02
2010 – 11	16	287	--	--	287	5.9
2010 – 11	60	--	1410	--	1410	0.91
2011 – 12	--	--	--	--	--	--
2012 – 13	04	514	--	--	514	--
2013 – 14(p)	04	--	--	233	233	--
2013 – 14(p)	--	--	93	--	93	--
2013 - 14(p)	02	40	--	--	40	--
Total	400	2096	8305	296	10697	162.58

Source: APSRTC Annual Administrative Reports

❖ PERFORMANCE APPRAISAL IN APSRTC

Performance Appraisal or merit rating is a systematic evaluation of an individual with respect to his performance on the job and his potential for development. An accepted system of performance appraisal is a great asset in the development of human factor in an organization; it helps to assess its managerial strengths and weaknesses. Such a system should also be made an effective tool for the growth of an individual as well contributes to an increasing recognition of identity between the organization and the people working in it. Thus Performance Appraisal system has evolved as an imperative in an organization.

In APSRTC, the performance Appraisal is carried through the merit rating report. Merit rating reports help to identify the key performance areas of the employees that are needed to improve their efficiency and effectiveness. These Merit Rating reports are very objective i.e., the Appraiser doesn't rate an employee on his personal like or dislike, but judge by his work during the whole time he has been under his control.

Every year the merit rating reports are rated by the authority concerned or the concerned Head of the department where the employees are working and this rating report has to be counter signed by their immediate supervisory officer. They are confidential reports which determine the future promotion of an employee. The objective of Performance Appraisal system is to attain value to the corporation, to cater the need for further training, transfer on promotion, to counsel the employees appropriately regarding the employee strengths and weaknesses and assist in developing them to realize their full potential in time with the organizational objectives and goals.

There are 13 categories of employees in APSRTC, but the rating begins from class - III employees onwards who are designated differently in various departments. After appointment of an employee, the concerned authority observes him for three months. After three months, the employee will be informed where he stands in his job. If required he is guided and counseled accordingly. The employee performance is reviewed again after six months. If he stands good, he is appreciated suitably; otherwise a memo is issued to highlight his week points. This procedure is followed to provide a chance to the employee to correct himself and get acquainted with the office rules and regulations within three months of time. After nine months from the date of appointment, the employee is again counseled with a particular reference to the advice already given after six months. If he stands good, it can be presumed that he is improving or else his explanation is called for to find out whether there are any difficulties by which he is unable to do his job satisfactorily. Under the present practice in vogue, for calculation of marks for merit rating report, the marks allotted will be added to the columns. The total allotment of marks is 190. If the officer gets below 40 percent of marks, it is considered as adverse report. In such cases the custodian officer will communicate to the concerned officer to improve his performance.

Evaluation of Merit Rating Report: If the performance of the employee is outstanding, he will be graded as "A"; and the total marks allotted will be 10. If the performance of the employee is Good, he will be graded as "B", and the total marks will be 7. If the performance of the employee is Above Average, he will be graded as "C", and the total marks allotted will be 6. If the performance of the employee is Average, he will be graded as "D", and the total marks allotted will be 5. If the performance of the employee is Poor, he will be graded as "E", and the total marks allotted will be 4. The employee who stands for periodical counseling will be graded as explained in the above is shown in the below table:

Excellent (A)	Good (B)	Average (C	Below Average (D)	Poor (E)

After the completion of Appraisal process, the managers whose performance is an average and below are advised to improve their performance in those areas where they are found to be lagging behind; In case, if a manager feels that his performance is not properly evaluated and the appraising officer has shown some bias, he may lodge a complaint with a Managing Director of APSRTC. If the Managing Director is satisfied that the appraisal is not properly done, he will appoint another officer to evaluate the performance of the aggrieved manager.

❖ PROMOTIONS

Promotion in service to a selection grade/ selection category shall be made on the grounds of merit; Seniority being considered only where merit is approximately equal. A member of service may be required to get himself relieved and join in the higher post within 30 days from the date of receipt of the order of promotion.

Promotions of Officer Under Training: In this category of officers, first they are appointed as junior scale officers and their promotions will be as in the following:

EXECUTIVE DIRECTOR

↑

HEAD OF THE DEPARTMENT

↑

SENIOR SCALE OFFICER

↑

JUNIOR SCALE OFFICER

Drivers Promotions: On successful completion of all the formalities as casual driver - on payment of Rs. 141 a day, the drivers are recruited on promotion at Grade - II level. The selection officers will give promotion to Grade - II drivers on successful completion of required experience and seniority as Grade - I drivers. After successful completion of experience as Grade - I driver for about 20 or 25 years, his services may be considered to a post at depot level.

Conductors Promotion: On successful completion of all the formalities as casual conductors - on payment of Rs. 141 a day, the conductors are recruited on promotion at Grade - II level. The selection officers will give promotion to Grade - II conductors on successful completion of required experience and seniority as Grade - I conductor. After successful completion of experience as Grade - I driver for about 20 or 25 years, his services may be considered to a post at depot level.

Class - I Services Promotion/ Super Scale Services/ Executive Director: A minimum of 15 years service in the corporation with responsible position in managerial capacity - as Depot Manager/ Divisional Manager/ Regional Manager - is necessary for promotion from class - I services as Executive Directors. Out of which at least six years should be in the category of regional manager/ Head of the Department (which are interchangeable with RM's).

Transfers: In an organization like APSRTC - activities are dispersed over a large number of geographically separated centers; therefore, transfers from one place to another place at reasonable intervals are inevitable. There is no rule in RTC which guarantees a life time employment at the same place. It is considered reasonable to fix the normal tenure as 7-8 years for an employee at a place engaged in direct work or responsibility; 5-6 years in respect of supervisors and 3-4 years in respect of officers. However the above conditions may not prevent the management from transferring an employee before the completion of such tenure on administrative reasons - such as inefficiency or misbehavior or administrative convenience.

Conditions for Transfer: An employee may be transferred from one post to another in the Corporation. However, the administration can't transfer the employees of the corporation in normal way in the following circumstances.

1) Where he is holding the post of additional charge.
2) Officiate in a post carrying less pay on lien than the pay of the permanent post on which he holds.
3) Would hold a liaison had his liaison not been suspended under 15 of the Rules and Regulations of the Corporation.

A Convention has been developed over the years in AP State Road Transport Corporation by which the employees of the Corporation request for their transfers to be considered on the basis of their application date. On experience it was proved that this is not a sound convention because, as it works to the advantage of the more alert and scheming employees. On the other hand, it would be better if such requests are considered on the basis of assessment and the need of the employee. Example, an employee 'A' has spent most part of his service of over 20 years in a place far away from Hyderabad. Now the need has arisen for him to seek a posting in Hyderabad as his son is admitted in the local Medical College. Employee 'B' had spent over 15 years of service in Hyderabad and was transferred to Karimnagar four years ago. The day he assumed charge at Karimnagar, he had submitted an application for re-transfer to Hyderabad on the ground that he has to build a house and to look after their old sick parents. Medical reasons are another ground on which he may seek transfer and posting of his choice by enclosing medical reports. In such a case any sensitive and fair management would give preference to employee 'A' over Employee 'B'. There is another convention has also been prevailing in APSRTC, by which service seniority will be considered for transfer. This practice is not just on the interest of the organization. Again this doesn't stand the test of equity and fair play. Suppose if the junior employee on promotion had come to place 'A' after long years of service, outside areas and a senior employee might have spent all his service at place 'A' in such a situation fair play demands that a junior employee on promotion should be given priority and post him at place 'A' by transferring Senior Officer. In case both wife and husband are employees, the corporation management will consider either of the spouse's requests for place while affecting their transfers.

❖ INCENTIVE SCHEMES

Depot Incentive Scheme: The Depot incentive scheme was introduced in all the depots of the Corporation from 1st March, 1980. The scheme was scientifically designed and developed as a performance oriented scheme. The aim of scheme was to improve the performance of key parameters through motivation by way of incentives and simultaneously to create cost consciousness among employees of the corporation. All the staff working at Depot Manager is eligible for incentive payments. Separate schemes are designed for District/ City/ Town services, based on their operational status.

Incentive payment to system In-charge of Depots: System supervisor in Depot, Core group supervisors of the Regions will receive incentives under certain conditions.

Incentive for Administrative and Accounts Staff and others at Depots: The Accounts personnel and the staff categorized in depots are eligible to receive Incentive amount, equal to the sum of 25 percent of individual Traffic Supervisor Incentive, and 25 percent of individual Mechanical Staff (Class - III) incentive and exclusively incentive eligible on appreciating parameters.

Incentive for Depot Manager: The Depot Manager is eligible to receive the sum total of the incentives paid to individual mechanical and traffic supervisors. In Addition, the Depot Manager is eligible to receive the sum total of incentive, on achieving the percentage of service targets and contributing to improvement in HSD KMPL. He is also eligible to receive incentive amount earned on appreciating parameters such as breakdown rate and percentage of mechanical cancellations.

Conditions for payment of incentive: All employees not less than 23 days of minimum attendance in a month, except February - are eligible for incentive in APSRTC. For February month, minimum attendance for eligibility is 22 days. In case of Depot Manager and office staff, when the working days happens to be less than 23 days in a month, they are eligible for incentive if they attend to their duties on all working days during that month.

Incentive to Conductors/ Drivers under conditions: Drivers and conductors will receive incentives under certain conditions. They are not eligible to receive incentive amount payable to them at the end of the month, when they are facing public complaints viz., misbehavior with the passengers, complaint against stoppage at stages, non display of destination boards and any other complaint.

Depot Pool Amount: All the employees of the depot are eligible for incentive from the depot pool amount. The depot pool amount shall be equivalent to 1.33 times of the amount earned by the drivers of the depot on reaching the base target. The amount payable to drivers on crossing the base target will not be reckoned for the purpose of arriving at the depot pool amount.

Distribution of Depot Pool Amount: Out of the Depot Pool amount, 20 percent of the amount should be transferred to maintenance pool. The remaining 80 percent of the Depot Pool amount is payable, as per the sharing of percentage of cancellation parameter, attained by the depot at the end of the month. The amount thus earned should be distributed as under:
- Conductors - 25%
- Drivers - 25%
- General Staff - 50%

Maintenance Pool: The amount earned by the maintenance staff from Depot pool, savings on HSD oil & tyres parameter, forms maintenance pool. 70 percent of the above pool amount is payable directly, 20 percent of the amount payable is linked to the cancellation parameter as per the eligible slabs and 10 percent of the pool amount payable is linked to the failure rate as per the eligibility slabs.

Maintenance Incentive payable (ceiling limit): The incentive payable to conductors is Rs. 300/- per month and drivers is Rs. 300/- per month. In case, the driver exceeds individually higher HSD base KMPL target, the maximum incentive will be Rs. 375/- per month. General staff Rs. 300/- per month, maintenance staff Rs. 300/- per month. In case the maintenance staff exceeds higher HSD oil base KMPL target, the maximum incentive payable in Rs. 375/- per month, security staff Rs. 300/- per month.

Incentive Allowance: There is a special allowance given to the maintenance staff apart from incentives. This is given for their performance in maintenance of the Depot.
- ➤ Depot Manager - Rs. 60/-
- ➤ C.I/ M.F/A.M/ (M/P/F) - Rs. 35/- STI/ AMF/ SSS - Rs. 30/-
- ➤ I-III/ LH/ DC - Rs. 20/-

The attending clause for eligibility is 21 days for all employees.

4.16. SWOT ANALYSIS OF HRD PRACTICES IN APSRTC

A SWOT analysis (alternatively SWOT Matrix) is a structured planning method used to evaluate the strengths, weaknesses, opportunities, and threats involved in a project or in a business venture. It can be carried out for a product, place, industry or person. It involves specifying the objective of the business venture or project and identifying the internal and external factors that are favorable and unfavorable to achieving that objective[292].

In this direction an attempt has been made to develop the strengths, weaknesses, opportunities and threats (SWOT) analysis of HRD Practices in APSRTC. Fig 5.3 presents SWOT of HRD Practices in APSRTC.

Figure 4.9: Exhibits the SWOT Analysis of HRD Practices in APSRTC

	Helpful To achieve the objectives	Harmful To achieve the objectives
Internal — Contribution of the organization	**STRENGTHES** ➢ Consist experienced Employees to design HRD Programmes ➢ Improves efficiency of employees ➢ Quality of Services ➢ Skilled Human Resources ➢ Possibility of innovative Services	**WEAKNESSES** ➢ Heavy work load ➢ Large No. of employees with different classes ➢ Sensitive towards change in Technology ➢ Lack of follow up from top management after the execution of training. ➢ Appraisal of one employee may de-motivate the other ➢ Zone wise HRD practices are not practiced fine tune to the Organizational structure and climate of the organization.
External — Contribution of the organization	**OPPORTUNITIES** ➢ Can reach to the needs of the organization by implementing HRD Practices ➢ Expanding training facilities for Senior Scale Officers at Zonal level ➢ Improves production and performance of the employees ➢ Develops Team Work ➢ Aims at providing positive working environment ➢ Better performance of the employees can be identified and utilized	**THREATS** ➢ Functioning in a Competitive business environment ➢ HRD Practices are Expensive to implement ➢ Financial worries of the organization to invest in HRD Programmes ➢ Technological Advancement ➢ External Competition from its private counterparts

On the *strengths* side, the corporation employs 1.23 lakh employees with a good combination of experienced employees to design well suitable HRD programmes to the employees of the organization to reach both individual and organizational goals. The HRD practices implemented in letter and spirit improves the efficiency of the employees. HRD practices help the workforce to render qualitative services in reaching the goals of the organization. Many HRD Practices like performance appraisal, counseling, and training and development practices to the employees increase the skills and capabilities of the employees and provide an opportunity to execute their tasks innovatively.

On the *weaknesses* side, implementation of HRD is neglected with heavy work load of the employees. So awareness about fruits of HRD practices must be conveyed to the employees to make them seriously involve in their HRD Practices. Employees can be given proper counseling to overcome the pressure of heavy workloads. The corporation consists of large number of different classes of employees, so that HRD must be designed with utmost care to meet the required job needs of the employees. HRD programmes must be reviewed periodically and required changes in technology should be taken for consideration in designing the HRD programmes. Once the HRD programme is implemented, proper follow up from top management is necessary and output of the employees after training and counseling must be measured and conveyed. Due care must be taken while appraising the employees. It is because appraisal of one employee may de-motivate the other employee performance. To achieve organizational goals, implementation of HRD practices should be fine tune the organizational structure and climate of the organization at zonal level.

On the *opportunities* side, HRD practices to the employees help them in directing towards the needs of the organization. HRD Practices ensure training facilities for senior scale officers and provide opportunity to expand the training facilities for all classes of employees at zonal level. HRD practices facilitate employees to improve their performance and production by undergoing the HRD practices offered by the organization. These practices develop teamwork amongst the employees. HRD Practices aims at providing positive working environment, organization structure and HRD climate for its employees. On the other hand, Better performance employees can be identified and utilized for organizational need.

On the *threats* side, APSRTC is facing many challenges for its survival in the competitive business environment. HRD Practices are expensive to be implemented. The corporation in the wake of financial constraints neglecting to implement HRD practices to its full extent. APSRTC with the fear of investing huge amount towards HRD Practices, it is practicing the age old training methods that are designed at the time of inception. In this context, corporation couldn't afford to train its employees with latest methods. Thus, the rapid advancement in technology is another bane for the corporation to implement innovative training techniques. In addition, APSRTC has lot of external competition from its private counterparts like illegal private bus operations as stage carriers, cars, jeeps, autos etc.

The SWOT analysis of HRD practices in APSRTC clearly gives an idea that unless some changes are brought in to the need of the time, in terms of technology, administration, structural and financial wise, the corporation may not be able to achieve its goals. So it is suggested that HRD has to be recognized as an important function and proper care should be taken in providing good working environment and positive organization structure that suit the needs of the employees and the organization.

4.17. CONCLUSION

A part from extending financial support from the Government and reducing the impact of certain liabilities, the APSRTC has to be given greater functional autonomy than is available in the Andhra Pradesh State. Strategic and operational freedom along with HRD practices particularly at the zonal level is essential to improve the performance of the employees of the organization. In order to achieve organizational goals, implementation of HRD practices should be fine tune the organizational structure and climate of the organization at zonal level.

Chapter – V

ANALYSIS OF THE DATA

In this chapter the researcher attempts to give dimension-wise analysis of HRD practices of APSRTC. The main objectives of this chapter are to assess the extent of HRD Practices prevailing in APSRTC at zonal level. For this, a case study of Vizianagaram zone has been chosen by the researcher. The analysis was made by giving item wise mean scores and corresponding percentage scores were calculated and MLR test and ANOVA test was applied to verify the validity of the obtained results. Further, the researcher also seeks to interpret the results of the survey.

INTRODUCTION

Any organization can be dynamic and survive in the competitive world by proper selection of its employees and nurture their competencies to meet the present and future job challenges. For this purpose, effective managers do not manage all people in the same way, except for some basic rules. They manage each person according to individualistic requirements and what motivates the employees to do their best. It is accomplished by proper implementation of HRD Practices to the employees in the organization. HRD Practices are widely recognized as a significant vehicle for improving the performance and productivity of employees and organization. This can be complicated but is essential for success.

In the present chapter, attempt has been made to analyze the manager's perception towards HRD Practices in APSRTC with reference to Vizianagaram zone. Since the researcher intends to inspect the impact of HRD Practices at zonal level, a case study of Vizianagaram zone has been chosen depending on the performance and contribution of Vizianagaram zone with respect to various other existing zones in Andhra Pradesh. All the statements of each dimension have been separately exhibited with the help of tables, followed by their respective interpretations. To elicit the information from the respondents, questionnaire which was framed on 7 most important practices of HRD as variables on a five point Likert Scale, with 1 for "Not at all true", 2 for "Not so true", 3 for "Partly true", 4 for "True" and 5 for "Very much true". The questionnaire was divided into three sections. Section A was designed to obtain demographic information of the respondents. It covers qualification, age, gender, present designation, department, monthly salary, length of service, marital status and nature of work. Section B measures the seven most important dimensions of HRD practices. The HRD dimensions taken up for the study are Training and Development, Organizational structure and culture, HRD Knowledge and Skills, HRD climate, Performance Appraisal, Counseling, and Career planning and Development. Section C estimates the overall satisfaction of the respondents towards HRD practices in the organization. In Section C various aspects of HRD practices are measured on a five point Likert Scale, with 1 for "Highly Dissatisfied", 2 for "Dissatisfied", 3 for "Neutral", 4 for "Satisfied" and 5 for "Highly Satisfied". On the basis of these three sections in the questionnaire, the HRD practices have been judged in APSRTC and analysis has been made.

To evaluate the prevailing Human Resource Development practices' dimensions, mean scores have been calculated, in which mean score 5 indicates – very much true, mean score 4 indicates – true, mean score 3 indicates – partly true, mean score 2 indicates – not so true, mean score 1 indicates – not at all true. Mean score 4 indicates that employees in APSRTC agree that good HRD Practices are prevailing in the organization. It indicates that HRD Practices are at a desirable level, whereas mean score 3 indicates that HRD practices prevailing in APSRTC are average and mean score 2 indicates poor HRD Practices on each dimension. In the present study, in order to make the interpretations easy the mean scores have been converted into percentage scores by using the formula, Percentage score = (Mean Score – 1) X 25. As per this measure the score 1 represents – 0 Percent, 2 represents – 25 Percent, 3 represents – 50 Percent, 4 represents – 75 Percent and

5 represents – 100 Percent. The percent Score indicates the degree to which a particular dimension exists in that organization out of the ideal 100. Hence, it is desirable for APSRTC to have percentage scores above 50 on each and overall on all items. For evaluating the results of the survey, the item-wise mean score and corresponding percentage scores are calculated. Standard deviation formula is applied to know the nature of the distribution. On the basis of overall mean score, different ranks have been assigned to different attributes in each dimension. The highest – rated attribute has been ranked one, the second highest rated rank two and so on until the lowest rank. The mean score of all items in each dimension gives the dimension score of that practice in APSRTC.

In the present study, multiple linear regression (MLR) analysis is used to find out the association of HRD Practices with that of the demographic factors (qualification, age, gender, designation, department, monthly salary, length of service, marital status and nature of work) of the employees in APSRTC, Vizianagaram zone is significant at 5 percent level. Further, ANOVA test is conducted to test the significant difference between two mean scores among the variables of HRD practices with that of Demographic variables of the employees at 10 percent level of significance is considered. Also ANOVA test is conducted to find the significant difference in the mean score among the respondents of various designations (SSO, JSO & LLM) for the overall opinion of the respondents to the HRD practices in APSRTC.

HYPOTHESIS OF THE PRESENT STUDY

A hypothesis can be defined as an assertion or conjecture about the parameter or parameters of a population, for example the mean or the variance of a normal population. They may also concern the type, nature or probability distribution of the population. It is categorized in two types that are as follows:

- ➢ Null Hypothesis (H_0)
- ➢ Alternative Hypothesis (H_1/ Hα)

Null Hypothesis (H_0)

The Null Hypothesis typically corresponds to a general or default position. For example, the null hypothesis might be that there is no relationship between two measured phenomena or that a potential treatment has no effect. It is important to understand that the null hypothesis can never be proven. A set of data can only reject a null hypothesis or fail to reject it. It only means that there is no enough evidence to reject the null hypothesis. A null hypothesis is denoted as H_0.

Alternative Hypothesis (H_1/ $H\alpha$)

In hypothesis testing, a proposition that is accepted if the null hypothesis is rejected is known as an Alternative Hypothesis. In other words, alternative hypothesis is the "hypothesis that the restriction or set of restrictions to be tested does not hold". It is often denoted as H_1 or $H\alpha$.

Level of Significance

The significant level is usually denoted by the Greek symbol α (lowercase alpha). Popular levels of significance are 10 percent (0.1), 5 percent (0.05), 1 percent (0.01), 0.5 percent (0.005) and 0.1 percent (0.001). If test of significance gives p-value lower than the significant level α, the null hypothesis is rejected. Such results are informally referred to as 'statistically significant'. The Confidence Interval (CI) chosen for the present study is 90 and 95 percent for which level of significance is 0.1 and 0.05 percent[293] (www.wikipedia.com).

The seven most important dimensions of HRD Practices on which the questionnaire has been divided is the base for developing the hypothesis for the study. The following hypothesis emerges out of the variables selected for conducting research at managerial level in APSRTC.

H_{01}: Training and Development doesn't have significant impact on the employee's performance.

H_{02}: Organizational structure & culture doesn't have significant impact on the employee's performance.

H_{03}: HRD knowledge & Skills doesn't have significant impact on the employee's performance.

H_{04}: HRD Climate doesn't have significant impact on the employee's performance.

H_{05}: Performance Appraisal doesn't have significant impact on the employee's performance.

H_{06}: Counseling doesn't have significant impact on the employee's performance.

H_{07}: Career Planning & Development doesn't have significant impact on the employee's performance.

H_{08}: Overall level of satisfaction on HRD Practices doesn't have significant impact on the employee's performance.

H_{09}: HRD practices don't have significant impact on the designation i.e. level of management.

SAMPLE SIZE AND METHOD

The sample size constitutes of 132 employees at managerial level in APSRTC at Vizianagaram zone. The managerial level employees include three levels of manager's viz., Senior Scale officers (SSO), Junior Scale officers (JSO) and Low Level Managers (LLM). Since the total number of respondents at managerial level is less, the researcher has decided to employ census survey method.

Table 5.1: Shows Sample Size of the Thesis

Designation	Frequency	Percent
Senior Scale Officer	27	20.5
Junior Scale Officer	37	28.0
Low level Manager	68	51.5
Total	**132**	**100.0**

Source: Primary Data Survey

Section-wise perception of Managerial Employees
towards the HRD Practices in APSRTC

Section – A: Analysis of Responded Employees Demographical variables

Educational Qualification:

Education has a determining effect on the mind, quality or corporeal aptitude of an individual. As such, the upper the academic qualification, the better will be the amount of maturity that can be expected in human beings. As the educational background of people has some effect on their perceptions about various aspects of work culture and lifestyle, their academic details are accorded due weight age in the present study. Further, certain academic and technical qualifications are mandatory to be eligible to certain posts in the organization.

Table 5.2: Shows the distribution of Educational Qualification among the respondents

Qualification	Frequency	Percent
P.G	59	44.7
Diploma	43	32.6
Below graduation	22	16.7
Any other (Ph.D)	8	6.1
Total	**132**	**100.0**

Source: Field Survey

The table 5.2 designates the distribution of qualification of the respondents of the sample. For the convenience of analysis, the researcher has sorted the respondents into four categories according to their qualification viz., below graduation, Diploma, P.G and Others, which includes Ph.D. Out of the total sample of 132, it is observed from the data that a majority of respondents' qualification 44.7 percent is Post graduation, while 32.6 per cent respondents are Diploma holders. Similarly, 16.7 per cent respondents are below graduation followed by 6.1 per cent respondents are other categories of educational qualification.

From the above analysis it is understood that more than 50 percent of the respondents who are selected for the study have P.G and Ph.D with either technical or Non- technical skills. The graphical representation of these details is presented in figure 5.1.

Figure 5.1: Exhibits distribution of educational qualification among the respondents

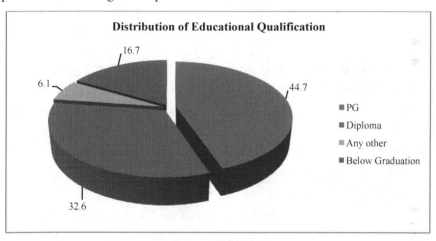

Source: Table 5.2

AGE:

Age is the time of life when a person becomes capable to assume certain civil and legal duties. And the prime of youth is crucial for achieving the goals when it is coupled with experienced people. Age influences the perceptions of people. One can find a marked difference in the opinions of younger and older generations. The young want everything to be rapid and efficient whereas the old and the experienced prefer the slow and stable. In order to record the perceptions of the respondents according to their age, the collected data are sorted into feasible age-groups as presented in Table 5.3

Table 5.3: Shows the Age distribution of the respondents

Age	Frequency	Percent
25 - 30	18	13.6
31 - 35	13	9.8
36 - 40	10	7.6
41 - 45	27	20.5
46 - 50	37	28.0
Above 50	27	20.5
Total	**132**	**100.0**

Source: Field Survey

Table 5.3 exemplifies the Age-wise distribution of the respondents. Out of the total sample of 132, it is evident from the above data that a majority of respondents 28 per cent, are in the age group of 46-50 years while equal distribution of about 20.5 per cent of the respondents fall in between 41-45 years and above 50 years of age group followed by 13.6 percent of the respondents are below 30years of age. Whereas 9.8 percent respondents are in the age group of 31-35 years, the least percentage i.e.7.6 per cent respondents' age is in between 36-40 years.

The survey results reveal that the corporation maintains a good ratio of all age groups of employees. It can also be analyzed that proportionate number of managerial staff of age between 25-35 years and above 50 years are employed in APSRTC. So this can be considered as a positive sign in the organization to design and implement HRD Practices with right proportion of young and experienced minds. The graphical representation of these details is presented in figure 5.2.

Figure 5.2: Exhibits Age distribution of the respondents

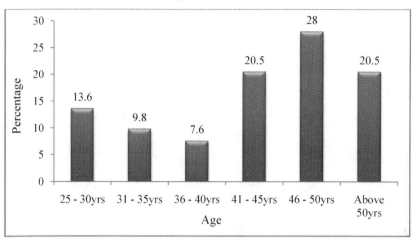

Source: Table: 5.3

Gender

According to Shakespeare, 'beauty lies in the eyes of the beholder'. However, the view of a person is influenced to some extent by various factors such education, age, gender etc. As for instance, men and women because of their differences in culture, creed, social position and other reasons, hold different views on most of the issues.

Believing that the gender of the respondents plays a role in their perception of HRD practices in APSRTC, the researcher has gathered the relevant data and arranged them accordingly in Table 5.4.

Table 5.4: Shows the Gender distribution among the respondents

Gender	Frequency	Percent
Male	110	83.3
Female	22	16.7
Total	**132**	**100.0**

Source: Field Survey

Earlier women used to attend only house hold activities, but today they are well educated and seeking employment on par with men. Traditionally, married men have been assigned a social role of earning money at work, whereas married women have been assigned a social role of fulfilling responsibilities at home (Eagly, 1987). Table 5.4 reveals that a vast majority of the respondents 83.3 per cent are men while the remaining 16.7 per cent are women are employed at managerial level in APSRTC.

The investigation reveals that female managerial staffs are lower when compared to male staff. So to enhance the prevailing female managerial staff, the organization must give some percentage of priority for women in promotions in addition to the existing women reservation exercised in recruitments. The graphical representation is shown in figure 5.3 as a doughnut diagram.

Figure 5.3: Exhibits Gender distribution of the respondents

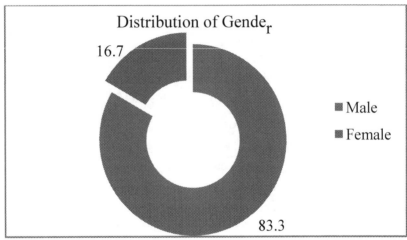

Source: Table 5.4

Designation:

Table 5.5: Shows the Designation distribution among the respondents

Designation	Frequency	Percent
Senior Scale Officer	27	20.5
Junior Scale Officer	37	28.0
Low level Manager	68	51.5
Total	**132**	**100.0**

Source: Field Survey

Designation means-the act of putting a person into a non-elective position. The position in the hierarchy of the organization for any employee is a symbol of status and gives recognition in the organization as well as in the society. The above table indicates the distribution of designation of the respondents. For the convenience of analysis the researcher has taken three categories of designations i.e., senior scale officer, junior scale officer and low level managers. Out of the total sample 132, a majority of 51.5 percent are Low level managers, 28 percent respondents are junior scale officers followed by senior scale officers of 20.5 percent.

From the above analysis, it can be inferred that most of the respondents in APSRTC entered the organization at lower positions and have grown to higher positions depending on the length of service and educational qualifications. Only few respondents were appointed directly in executive cadre. The Table further reveals that APSRTC managerial staff comprises of three levels of managerial officers viz., SSO, JSO, LLM. The diagrammatic representation is shown as a Pie Chart in figure 5.4.

Figure 5.4: Exhibits the designation distribution of the respondents

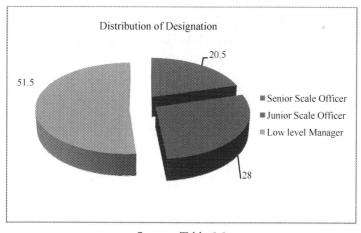

Source: Table 5.5

Department:

Table 5.6: Shows the Department distribution among the respondents

Department	Frequency	Percent
Technical	45	34.1
Non-Technical	58	43.9
Both	29	22.0
Total	**132**	**100.0**

Source: Field Survey

Department is a specialized <u>functional area</u> within an <u>organization</u> or a <u>division</u>, such as <u>accounting</u>, <u>marketing</u>, <u>planning</u> etc. Generally every department has its own <u>manager</u> and <u>chain of command</u>[294]. For the purpose of analysis the researcher has categorized the department in APSRTC into three categories i.e., technical, non-technical and both technical and non-technical. Out of total of 132 respondents 58 respondents are non-technical which yields the percentage of 43.9 percent, 34.1 percent respondents are from technical and the remaining 22 percent respondents come under both the departments.

It can be observed from the analysis that majority of the managerial staff in APSRTC belong to non-technical department. However, corporation consists of both technical and non-technical departments; it has to maintain good balance of technical and non-technical managerial staff. The study also reveals that the corporation needs more technical staff to perform better on par with their counterparts. The graphical representation of these details is presented in figure 5.5.

Figure 5.5: Exhibits distribution of Department of the respondents

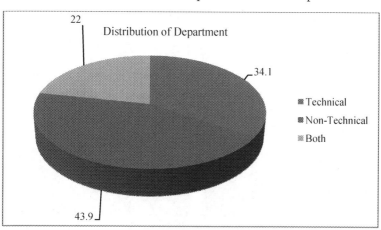

Source: Table 5.6

Annual Income:

Among the different aspects that exert some sort of influence on the perceptions of people, income occupies a prominent place. Normally, the earnings of individuals keep them in various economic strata e.g. rich, upper middle-class, middle class and poor. And accordingly, they develop a mindset that is typical of the economic category that they belong.

In a bid to elicit the different perception levels of the respondents based on their annual income, the researcher collected the relevant data and divided the respondents into five feasible income-groups viz.,

a) Respondents earning less than Rs. 15,000

b) Those who earn from Rs. 15000-25000

c) Respondents whose annual earnings are between Rs. 25000 -35000

d) Respondents whose annual earnings are between Rs. 35000 -45000

e) e) Respondents with more than Rs. 45000 of income per month.

The income-wise details of the respondents are presented in Table 5.7.

Table 5.7: Shows the Monthly Income distribution among the respondents

Monthly Income	Frequency	Percent
Below 15000	14	10.6
15000-25000	27	20.5
25000-35000	44	33.3
35000-45000	15	11.4
Above 45000	32	24.2
Total	132	100.0

Source: Field Survey

Salaries in organizations, for that matter, at any work place, are generally in proportion to the qualification and experience of the employees. Further, one should bear in mind the fact that annual income of a person encompasses his salary, incentives, bonus, increments, rewards etc.

A large number of respondents did not disclose their monthly salaries correctly. It is due to either they did not have proper idea regarding their monthly salaries or may be due to some personal reasons.

The table 5.7 illustrates that the highest income-group i.e. more than 45000 per month constitutes 24.2 per cent of the total sample, while the least income group i.e. less than Rs. 15000 per month records 10.6 per cent of the sample. Similarly, respondents whose annual income is in the range of Rs. 15000-25000 are found to be 20.5 per cent in the entire sample followed by 33.3 percent respondents fall in between 25000-35000 as against to the 11.4 per cent respondents that are earning Rs. 35000-45000 per month. The graphical representation of these details is presented in figure 5.6.

Figure 5.6: Exhibits the monthly income of the respondents

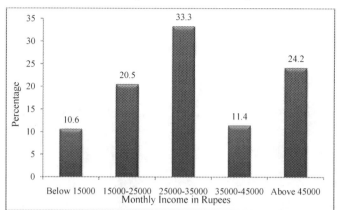

Source: Table 5.7

Length of service:

Table 5.8: Shows the length of the service of the respondents

Length of service	Frequency	Percent
0 – 10	31	23.5
11 – 15	5	3.8
16 – 20	15	11.4
21 – 25	49	37.1
26 – 30	22	16.7
Above 30	10	7.6
Total	**132**	**100.0**

Source: Field Survey

Experience comprises knowledge of or skill of something or some event gained through involvement in or exposure to that thing or event. The researcher has divided length of service into six categories. The table 5.8 reveals that majority of 37.1 percentage of the respondents are having 21-25 years of experience followed by below 10 years of experience, whereas 16.7 percent of the respondents are having 26-30 years of experience, 11.4 percent respondents are having 16-20 years of experience 7.6 percent of the respondents are having above 30 years of experience and the remaining 3.8 percent respondents are having 11-15 years of experience.

As the organization under study is an age old organization, it is expected to have more experienced managerial staff. But the survey reveals that a good composition of youth and experienced managerial staff were placed and employed at managerial level in APSRTC. The graphical representation of these details is presented figure 5.7.

Figure 5.7: Exhibits the Length of the Service of the respondents

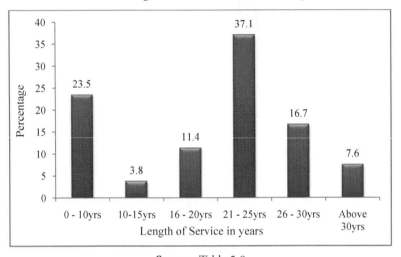

Source: Table 5.8

Marital Status:

Table 5.9: Shows the Matrital Status of the respondents

Marital status	Frequency	Percent
Married	117	88.6
Unmarried	14	10.6
Widowed	1	8
Total	**132**	**100.0**

Source: Field Survey

Marriage is universal. In traditional societies, it acts as a status device. It enlarges the social responsibility and role obligations arising out of kinship and social network. Marriage creates certain responsibilities on the part of the employee towards the family and influences significantly his/ her commitment towards their work.

Here in table 5.9, **marital status** indicates whether the person is <u>married</u>. Out of the total respondents of 132, a vast majority of 88.6 percent respondents are married, 10.6 percent respondents are unmarried and only 1 percent respondents are widowed. It means a majority of employees in the corporation are married. A study reveals that parental status don't affect men (Correl, Benard & paik, 2007). Recent research has found that even mothers show definitive evidence that they are highly competent and committed to their jobs (Benard & Correl, 2010). So it can be concluded that marriage is not a barrier for employees to perform better. The pictographic representation is shown in figure 5.8.

Figure 5.8: Exhibits distribution of Marital Status among the respondents

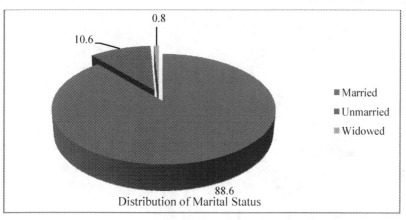

Source: Table 5.9

Nature of work:

Table 5.10: Shows distribution of nature of work among the respondents

Nature of work	Frequency	Percent
Technical	61	46.2
Non technical	57	43.2
both	14	10.6
Total	**132**	**100.0**

Source: Field Survey

The table 5.10 depicts the distribution of the nature of work of the respondents. Out of the total 132 respondents, 46.2 percent 'respondents' nature of duty is completely technical, 43.2 percent respondents duty is Non-technical, whereas the remaining 10.6 percent respondents' duties are both technical and non-technical in nature.

From the above analysis it is observed that majority of the employees were engaged in non technical work. Nature of work depends on employees' educational qualification. For an employee to perform well, they should be placed in job that suit their educational qualification and skills. Hence, for an employee to work efficiently educational qualification should match the nature of work performed in the organization. The diagrammatic representation is shown as a pie chart in figure 5.9.

Figure 5.9: Exhibits distribution of Nature of Work among the employees

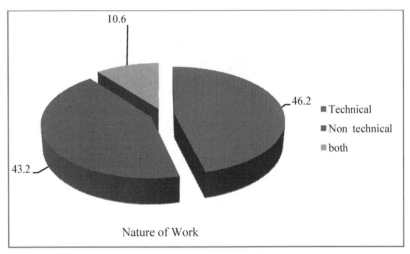

Source: Table 5.10

Section B: HRD Practices

Dimension 1: Training and Development

Table 5.11: Shows the percentage analysis of employees perception on Training and Development

Sl. No.	Statements on Training and Development	Very much true	True	Partly true	Not so true	Not at all true
1.	Employees perception towards training is satisfactory	6.6	71.7	19.7	1.3	0.7
2.	Managers are sponsored to training programs on the basis of carefully identified training needs	11.8	55.9	24.3	5.9	2
3.	Management recognizes performers and creates facilities for non performers to improve	10.5	49.3	25.7	13.2	1.3
4.	Organizations training programs are evaluated and improved upon every year	10.5	52	33.6	3.3	0.7
5.	Significant improvement is observed in performance of the managers after training	11.4	21.2	29.5	21.2	16.7
6.	Job rotation is practiced widely to help people develop their potential in new areas	10.5	47.4	27	12.5	2.6
7.	Change in the output of the employees returning from training is measured and utilized	7.6	21.2	36.4	18.2	16.7
	Average Percentage	**9.84**	**45.52**	**28.02**	**10.80**	**5.81**

Source: Compiled and Computed from Primary Data

Training and Development activity plays a significant role in the service organizations like APSRTC. Organization designs training program for its employees for acquiring the required competencies to meet the current and future job roles. APSRTC, in the wake of greater financial deregulation and peer competition, and the challenges to survive and develop in this global economic scenario, could not afford to ignore the Training and Development practices. According to Cole (2004), human resources are the most dynamic of all the organizations resources. They need considerable attention from the organizations management. Each employer who invests in the area of Training and Development will reap the benefits of an enriched working environment with higher levels of staff retention as well as increased productivity and performance.

In the present study, the table 5.11 reveals that the overall average opinions of the employees in the table reveal that maximum 45.52 percent of the employees felt that the statements on training and development are true and only 5.81 percent employees opined as not at all true. Where as nearly 28.02 percentage of employees opined as partly true, 9.84 percent employees felt as very much true and about 10.80 percent employees felt that training and development practices are not so true.

The table 5.11 reveals that an equal of 16.7 percent employees express as not at all true for the statements - significant improvement is observed in performance of the managers after training and change in the output of the employees returning from training is measured and utilized. Whereas only 0.7 percent employees jointly opined as not at all true for the statements that employees perception towards training is satisfactory and Organizations training programs are evaluated and improved upon every year.

Further, majority of 71.7 percent employees opined as true for the statement that the employees 21.2 percent perception towards training is satisfactory and an equal number of employees jointly share the opinion as true for the statements - significant improvement is observed in performance of the managers after training and change in the output of the employees returning from training is measured and utilized. From the analysis it can be interpreted that the managerial staff follow up toward trained employees is neglected, and not measured or utilized properly. So it is necessary for the management of APSRTC to measure the impact of training and information can be used in drafting future programmes.

Training and Development for new breed of employees is crucial while managing human factor. From the above results it can be inferred that APSRTC is spending huge amount in providing training to their employees. But unfortunately the course content of the training program is not framed in consonance with the duties and responsibilities discharged by them as well as to the organizational goals. It is observed that training programmes adopted in APSRTC by specialized agencies are not properly designed to the needs of the organization. So the management of APSRTC must implement proper training programmes after careful identification of traing needs of the employees and corporation as a whole. It was identified the same by Kondayya (2003) in his study on 'HRD in APSRTC – A Study with reference to managerial personnel'. It was more than a decade ago that Kondayya identified that training and development practices in APSRTC were not properly planned and executed. Regrettably, APSRTC was not able to fill the gap in this course of time. To the present prevailing loses, management of the Corporation has to take due care in providing training to the employees, in line to the objectives of the organization.

It is suggested that training and development program needs should be identified periodically by taking latest developmental aspects into consideration. It is identified from the analysis that some interventions are necessary in sketching the training and development programmes to enhance managerial, technical and non technical skills of the employees.

Figure 5.10: Exhibits the Overall employees opinion on
Training and Development

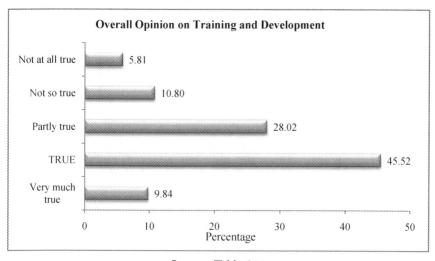

Source: Table 5.11

Friedman's Mean Rank Test:

Table 5.12: Shows the mean score of the statements
on Training and Development

Sl. No.	Statements on Training and development	MEAN	S.D	PERCENTAGE
1.	Employees perception towards training is satisfactory	3.7955	.60201	69.8875
2.	Managers are sponsored to training programs on the basis of carefully identified training needs	3.7424	.82537	68.56
3.	Management recognizes performers and creates facilities for non performers to improve	3.5455	.89412	63.6375
4.	Organizations training programs are evaluated and improved upon every year	3.6894	.73238	67.235
5.	Significant improvement is observed in performance of the managers after training	3.6136	.83481	65.34
6.	Job rotation is practiced widely to help people develop their potential in new areas	3.5455	.92764	63.6375
7.	Change in the output of the employees returning from training is measured and utilized	3.3712	.94429	59.28
	Overall Mean Score	**3.614**	**0.822**	**65.368**

Source: Compiled and Computed from Primary Data

Friedman's Mean Rank Test identifies the Training and Development variables which have significant influence on the employee's productivity. "Employee perception towards training is satisfactory is the most significant factor", with mean score 3.79 attained first rank, followed by "managers are sponsored to training programs on the basis of carefully identified training needs" (3.74) and "organizations training programs are evaluated and improved upon every year (3.68)". These two ranked the second and third influences. The fourth rank attribute focuses on the attribute that significant improvement is observed in performance of the managers after training (3.61). Some of the respondents prefer that the management recognizes performers and creates facilities for non performers to improve, while similar number of respondents opined job rotation is practiced widely to help people develop their potential in new areas (3.54). These two attributes jointly shared the fifth priority as per Friedman's mean rank coefficient. The statement, "change in the output of the employees returning from training is measured and utilized" occupies the last. That is sixth place. It can be concluded that the respondents do not have equal level of agreement for all the Training and Development strategies adopted by the corporation.

Regression Analysis: Training & Development *versus* Demographic factors of the responded employees

H_{01}: Training and Development doesn't have significant impact on the employee's performance.

Table 5.13: Shows the regression analysis between demographic factors and Training and Development

Predictor	Coefficient	SE Coefficient	T-Value	P-Value
Constant	3.0688	0.6351	4.83	0.000
Qualification	0.04791	0.05191	0.92	0.358
Age	-0.03957	0.05722	-0.69	0.491
Gender	*0.3087*	*0.1554*	*1.99*	*0.049*
Designation	-0.0270	0.1418	-0.19	0.849
Department	0.07762	0.09150	0.85	0.398
Monthly Income	0.00000102	0.00000710	0.14	0.886
Length of service	0.04666	0.05731	0.81	0.417
Marital status	-0.1232	0.1667	-0.74	0.461
Nature of work	-0.1195	0.1025	-1.17	0.246

Source: Compiled and Computed from Primary Data

R-Sq = 5.8% P-value: 0.586

MLR analysis was carried out to study and establish the relationship between the demographic factors of respondents and Training and Development being adopted in an organization. The R-square value 5.8 percent reveals that there is a 5.8 percent variation due to the independent variables on the dependent variable training and development. It considers the regression equation in the model and examines the strength of the independent variables in predicting the dependent variable. It was assumed that there is no significant linear relationship between the demographic factors extracted above and their probability of association with various HRD Practices is studied. A regression analysis was conducted with the dependent variable Training & Development and the independent variables such as qualification, age, Gender, Designation, Department, Monthly Income, Length of Service, Marital status and Nature of work. Only one variable (Gender) out of nine contributed significantly to the equation at 5 percent level of significance. For this variable further T-test is conducted as follows.

Table 5.14: Shows ANOVA analysis of Gender factor
with Training and Development

Gender	n	Mean	S.D	T- value	P-value	Decision
Male	110	3.2675	.59992	-1.788	0.076	Not significant
Female	22	3.5130	.52101			

Source: Compiled and Computed from Primary Data

The average opinion score of female respondents is 3.5130, greater than male respondents and it is not statistically significant at 5 percent level as per the t-test value and its corresponding P-value is 0.076 for the dimension 'Training and Development". The same is mentioned as an Individual value plot, the blue color circled plus indicates the Average value, and the male respondents' variation is more when compared with female respondents. But the gender categories are significant at 10 percent level of significance for its corresponding dimension Training and Development. This indicates that the null hypothesis (H_{01}) that Training and Development doesn't have significant impact on the employee's performance is accepted.

Figure 5.11: Exhibits individual value plot showing opinion of the respondents on Training and Development by Gender

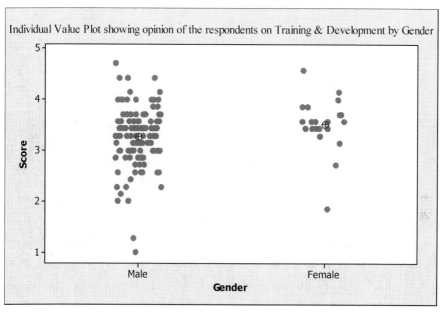

Source: Table 5.14

Dimension II: Organizational structure and climate

Table 5.15: Shows the percentage analysis of employees perception on Organizational Structure and Climate

Sl. No.	Statements on Organizational structure and climate	Very much true	True	Partly true	Not so true	Not at all true
1.	De-centralization of authority is satisfactory	6.6	63.8	21.7	7.2	0.7
2.	Management philosophy of the organization helps to utilize human resource effectively	19.7	54.6	18.4	7.2	Nil
3.	Employees are encouraged to participate in decision-making and formulation of organizational goals	7.6	17.4	27.3	25	22.7

4.	Encourages the practice of self motivation and commitment	9.8	12.9	25	24.2	28
5.	Allows open and free flow of communication	11.2	48	29.6	9.9	1.3
6.	Team spirit is high in the organization	20.4	43.4	25	9.9	1.3
7.	Officers maintain good human relations with their employees	12.5	43.4	34.9	7.9	1.3
	Average Percentage	**12.55**	**40.51**	**25.99**	**13.05**	**7.90**

Source: Compiled and Computed from Primary Data

Organizational Climate is influenced by factors such as organizational context, organizational structure, organizational process, physical environment, and system value and norms. Organization structure and climate increases employee performance. Organization that resembles structurally had a more facilitative climate. Administrative support and autonomy were high in the structurally resembling organization and work pressure and control were also high in structurally resembling organization[295].

A peep into the average opinions of the respondents on organizational structure and climate in table 5.15 demostrates that maximum of employees, 40.51 percent opined as true and minimum of employees, 7.90 percent opined as not at all true. However, 25.99 percent employees expressed as partly true, 13.05 percent employees felt not so true and about 12.55 percent employees expressed as very much true. The same is diagramatically represented in figure 5.12.

The table 5.15 dipicts that maximum of employees, 63.8 percent felt as true for the statement that "decentralization is satisfactory" and minimum of employees, 12.9 percent felt that "organizational structure" and climate encourages the practice of self motivation and commitment is true. Whereas, 22.7 percent employees opined as not at all true for the statement that Employees are encouraged to participate in decision-making and formulation of organizational goals and none of the respondents' agreed with the statement that management philosophy of the organization helps to utilize human resource effectively. It can be deduced from the analysis that the corporation fails to encourage the practice of self motivation and commitment. It is suggested that corporation must promote employees to try out new methods in accomplishing their tasks.

From the above survey results, it is observed that APSRTC has positive organizational structure and climate for their employees. At the same time it is observed that the corporation has failed in some aspects like providing freedom to the employees in fulfilling their entrusted tasks and welcoming new ideas from the employees of the organization in the process of decision – making. APSRTC, by giving grandness to these aspects can enhance the confidence and create belongingness of the employees to the corporation. Management of APSRTC should create favourable atmosphere for their employees to exhibit their full potential in accomplishing their tasks. By observing the results of the survey, it is understood that APSRTC has failed to provide freedom and independence to their employees in fulfilling their entrusted jobs. The reaction of the employees and the degree to which they welcome and accept managements' philosophy as a basis to utilize human resource effectively is crucial to the development of favourable organizational climate. So it is suggested that the Corporation should understand the importance of creating favourable atmosphere and practice of selfmotivation and commitment must be encouraged amongst the employees for extracting higher productivity.

Figure 5.12: Exhibits the Overall employees opinion on Organizational structure and climate

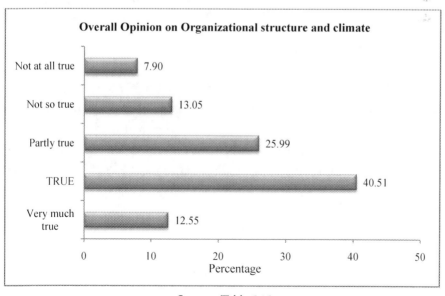

Source: Table 5.15

Friedman's Mean Rank Test:

Table 5.16: Shows the mean score of the statements on
Organizational structure and climate

Sl. No.	Statements on Organizational structure and climate	MEAN	S.D	PERCENTAGE
1.	De-centralization of authority is satisfactory	3.6742	.74645	66.855
2.	Management philosophy of the organization helps to utilize human resource effectively	3.8636	.81749	71.59
3.	Employees are encouraged to participate in decision-making and formulation of organizational goals	3.5909	.81918	64.7725
4.	Encourages the practice of self motivation and commitment	3.6894	.81149	67.235
5.	Allows open and free flow of communication	3.5758	.85713	64.395
6.	Team spirit is high in the organization	3.6894	.94208	67.235
7.	Officers maintain good human relations with their employees	3.5909	.86452	64.7725
	Overall Mean Score	**3.667**	**0.836**	**66.693**

Source: Compiled and Computed from Primary Data

Friedman's Test assesses the level of preference for the statements on Organizational Structure and Climate of APSRTC. The first rated attribute is management philosophy of the organization helps to utilize human resource effectively (3.86). "Encourages the practice of self motivation and commitment (3.68) along with team spirit is high in the organization (3.68)" are the second preferred attribute. "De-centralization of authority is satisfactory" ranked third. "Employees are encouraged to participate in decision-making and formulation of organizational goals" (3.59) is rated the fourth. The attribute "allows open and free flow of communication" ranked sixth.

The above analysis reveals that the variables such as Management philosophy of the organization helps to utilize human resource effectively, encourages the practice of self motivation and commitment, team spirit in the organization, and Decentralization of authority are dominant influential factors in APSRTC in maintaining good organizational structure and climate. To attain maximum output from the employee the corporation has to incorporate innovative strategies for maintaining healthy organizational structure and culture, which can ultimately help in reaching the organizational goals.

Regression Analysis: Organization Structure and Culture *versus* Demographic factors of the responded employees

H_{02}: Organizational structure & culture doesn't have significant impact on the employee's performance.

Table 5.17: Shows the regression analysis between demographic factors and Organizational Structure & Culture

Predictor	Coefficient	SE Coefficient	T-value	P-value
Constant	2.4750	0.6263	3.95	0.000
Qualification	0.02546	0.05119	0.50	0.620
Age	-0.06269	0.05643	-1.11	0.269
Gender	0.1237	0.1532	0.81	0.421
Designation	0.2448	0.1398	1.75	0.083
Department	*0.21158*	*0.09023*	*2.34*	*0.021*
Monthly Income	0.00001180	0.00000700	1.69	0.094
Length of service	0.03441	0.05652	0.61	0.544
Marital status	*-0.4737*	*0.1644*	*-2.88*	*0.005*
Nature of work	-0.0359	0.1011	-0.36	0.723

Source: Compiled and Computed from Primary Data

R-Sq = 13.0% P-value: 0.041

For the dimension Working Environment MLR analysis was carried out to study to establish the relationship between the demographic factors of respondents and Organization structure and climate being adopted in an organization. A regression analysis was conducted with the dependent variable Organization structure & climate and the independent demographic variables such as qualification, age, Gender, Designation, Department, Monthly Income, Length of Service, marital status and Nature of work. Two variables out of nine contributed significantly to the equation at 5 percent level. For these variables further ANOVA test is conducted as follows to know the significant difference in the average opinion scores among the categories of Department and marital status. The R-square value 13 percent divulges that there is a 13 percent of variation explained by the independent variables defined above towards the dependent variable Organization structure and climate. Further, two variables i.e., Designation and monthly income is significant at 10 percent level of significance.

Table 5.18: Shows ANOVA analysis of Department factor with
Organization Structure and Climate

Department	n	Mean	S.D	F- value	P-value	Decision
Technical	45	3.1778	.48841			
Non-Technical	58	3.3670	.69889	2.36	0.098	Not significant
Both	29	3.4729	.54945			

Source: Compiled and Computed from Primary Data

The table 5.18 reveals that there is a significant opinion score difference between the categories of the department of the managerial positions at 10 percent level as per the ANOVA test value 2.36 and its corresponding P-value 0.098. Further, the average opinion score of respondents who were from both technical and non-technical opined more positive than the remaining two categories and the score is nearer to "3.5" i.e., respondents from this category are nearer to satisfied option. The same is mentioned as a box plot in figure 5.13 with a few positive outliers as well as negative outliers i.e., respondents with optimistic and pessimistic opinion for their respective categories of the department respectively. The circled plus indicates the average values, upper end of the line indicates the highest value, the lower end of the line indicates the lowest value, the upper side of the box reveals the 75th percentile, the lower end of the box divulges the 25th percentile and the middle line relates to the median of the data.

Figure 5.13: Exhibits boxplot showing comparision of Organization Structure and Climate by Designation

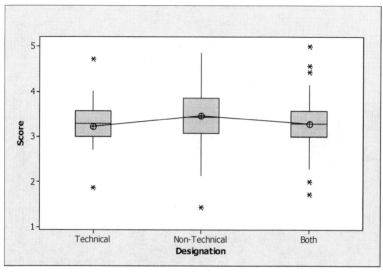

Source: Table 5.18

Table 5.19: Shows ANOVA analysis of Marital Status factor with Organization Structure and Climate

Marital Status	n	Mean	S.D	T- value	P-value	Decision
Married	117	3.69	0.572	1.24	0.233	Not significant
Unmarried/ Widowed	15	3.496	0.571			

Source: Compiled and Computed from Primary Data

The T-Test value 1.24 and P-value 0.233 reveals that there is no significant difference between the two categories of the marital status of the respondents. The average opinion score of the married respondents 3.69 have more fair opinion than the Unmarried/Widowed respondents 3.496 but the difference is not statistically significant at 5 percent level of significance for the dimension Organization structure and climate. The same is mentioned as a box plot in figure 5.14.

This indicates that the null hypothesis (H_{02}) that Organizational structure & culture doesn't have significant impact on the employee's performance is accepted.

Figure 5.14: Exhibits individual value plot showing comparision of Organization Structure and Climate by Marital Status

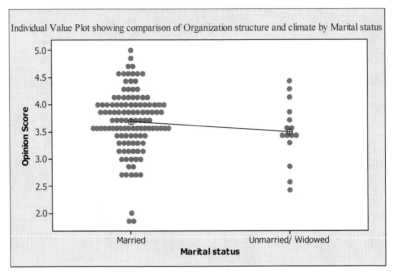

Source: Table 5.19

Dimension III: HRD Knowledge and Skills

Table 5.20: Shows the percentage analysis of employees perception on HRD Knowledge and Skills

Sl. No.	Statements on HRD Knowledge and Skills	Very much true	True	Partly true	Not so true	Not at all true
1.	Employees have knowledge on HRD practices	5.3	35.5	40.8	17.8	**0.7**
2.	Managers have enough skills for designing HRD	9.1	12.1	20.5	27.3	**31.1**
3.	Employees have leadership and initiative skills	9.9	54.6	32.9	2.6	
	Average Percentage	**8.09**	**34.04**	**31.38**	**15.89**	**10.59**

Source: Compiled and Computed from Primary Data

Attainment of knowledge, skills and acquiring better qualification should be the constant endeavour of employees to keep abreast with the developments in the business environment. Strong determination in employees to acquire knowledge and skills coupled with organizational help will serve the corporation to use those skills for higher productivity and effective accomplishment of organizational goals.

An enquiry in this study reveals that maximum of 34.04 percent and minimum of 8.09 percent employees admit that HRD Knowledge and Skills are true and very much true respectively. However, 31.38 percent employees opined as partly true, 15.89 percent opined as not so true and about 10.59 percent employees opined as not at all true.

The table 5.20 also exposes that maximun of 9.9 percent respondents accept that Employees have leadership and initiative skills and only 5.3 percent respondents admit that employees have knowledge on HRD Practices is very much true. On the other hand maximum of 54.6 percent respondents expressed that the employees have leadership and initiative skills is true and about 12.1 percent respondents expressed that managers have enough skills for designing HRD is true.

In a knowledge economy, optimizing human and intellectual capital is the biggest challenge faced by the organizations. Florence M Stone stated that "with escalating time pressure and constant change, upper management has their eye out for managers who can recruit capable employees, develop the skills they need to do today's jobs, and prepare them to handle tomorrow's jobs; who recognize their obligation to confront poor performers and who will work with these people to find a solution or make the tough decisions to terminate those who are dragging down the rest of the team; and who can keep their superstars shining even when there is little opportunity for advancement or dollars for increased performance[296]". Based on the above analysis, it is suggested that the corporation should chalkout an action plan to improve the knowledge and skills of the employees by providing required support and motivation to develop themselves. Every manager for the prosperity of the organization should have the skills of Open Communication, Team Approach and Value People. For this reason, corporation must offer human resource development professionals a valid instrument to develop effective managers.

Figure 5.15: Exhibits the Overall employees opinion on Training and Development

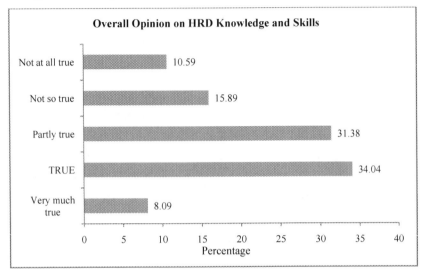

Source: Table 5.20

Friedman's Mean Rank Test:

Table 5.21: Shows the mean score of the statements on HRD Knowledge and Skills

Sl. No.	Statements on HRD Knowledge and Skills	MEAN	S.D	PERCENTAGE
1.	Employees have knowledge on HRD practices	3.2652	.82758	56.63
2.	Managers have enough skills for designing HRD	3.5758	.81138	64.395
3.	Employees have leadership and initiative skills	3.7197	.68031	67.9925
	Overall Mean Score	**3.519**	**0.772**	**63.005**

Source: Compiled and Computed from Primary Data

Table 5.21 reveals that the Friedman's mean rank test is arranged between 3.26 and 3.71. Employees have leadership and initiative skills - is the first preferred choice of the employees with mean score 3.71 followed by the attribute managers have enough skills for designing HRD Programmes which attained mean score 3.57. Employees have knowledge on HRD Practices is the third influencing factor of employee's skills in APSRTC with mean score 3.26.

To accomplish the objective of the corporation, managers should have the required HRD knowledge and skills for reorienting its HRD programmes.

Regression Analysis: HRD Knowledge and Skills *versus* Demographic factors of the respondents.

H$_{03}$: HRD knowledge & Skills doesn't have significant impact on the employee's performance.

Table 5.22: Shows the regression analysis between demographic factors and HRD knowledge & Skills

Predictor	Coefficient	SE Coefficient	T-value	P-valve
Constant	1.9131	0.7775	2.46	0.015
Qualification	0.01136	0.06355	0.18	0.858
Age	-0.08265	0.07006	-1.18	0.240
Gender	0.1580	0.1902	0.83	0.408
Designation	0.2140	0.1736	1.23	0.220
Department	-0.0356	0.1120	-0.32	0.751
Monthly Income	0.00000672	0.00000869	0.77	0.441
Length of service	*0.13675*	*0.07017*	*1.99*	*0.049*
Marital status	-0.0239	0.2041	-0.12	0.907
Nature of work	0.0978	0.1255	0.78	0.437

Source: Compiled and Computed from Primary Data

R-Sq = 6.9% P-value: 0.442

Since the P-value of the R-square is greater than 0.05, the level of significance and it is greater than 0.05, which make note that the variation between independent and dependent variables are not statistically significant at 0.05 level. Further, the independent variables (demographic factors) explain only 6.9 percent of variation on working relation. For this dimension knowledge skills a regression analysis was conducted with the dependent variable knowledge skills with the independent variables qualification, age, Gender, Designation, Department, Monthly Income, Length of Service, Marital status and Nature of work. Only one variable (length of service) out of nine contributed significantly to the equation at 5 percent level. For this variable, ANOVA test is conducted as follows to know the significant difference in the average opinion scores among the categories of length of service.

Table 5.23: Shows ANOVA analysis of Length of Service factor with HRD knowledge & Skills

Length of Service	n	Mean	S.D	F- value	P-value	Decision
0 - 10	31	2.8602	.75902	0.898	0.485	Not significant
11 - 15	5	3.1333	.64979			
16 - 20	15	3.1111	.84202			
21 - 25	49	3.1088	.71811			
26 - 30	22	3.0152	.56790			
Above 30	10	3.3667	.88122			

Source: Compiled and Computed from Primary Data

The table 5.23 reveals that there is no significant difference between six categories of the length of service of the respondents as per the ANOVA significance value 0.485 at 5 percent level of significance. Respondents who were having the experience above 30, opined more positively than the remaining categories followed by 11-15 years, whereas the experience category 0-10 opined pessimistically than the remaining five categories, but the difference in not statistically significant. The pictographic representation is shown as a box plot with more positive outliers for the service category 21-25 years and two negative outliers for the category below 10 years of experience which means that two respondents are opined more negatively belongs to this age category on the aspect "Knowledge skills". This indicates that the null hypothesis (H_{03}) that HRD knowledge & Skills doesn't have significant impact on the employee's performance is rejected and it is proved that there is a significant impact on employee performance.

Figure 5.16: Exhibits boxplot showing comparision of HRD Knowledge and Skills by Length of Service

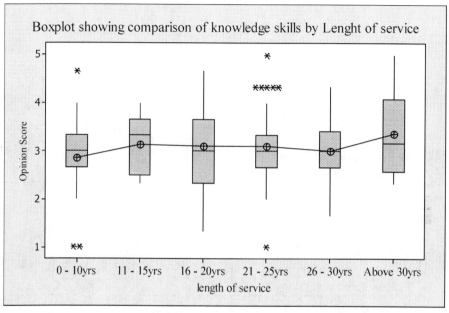

Source: Table 5.23

Dimension IV: HRD climate

Table 5.24: Shows the percentage analysis of employees perception on HRD Climate

Sl. No.	Statements on HRD climate	Very much true	True	Partly true	Not so true	Not at all true
1.	The top management of this organization goes out of its way to make sure that employees enjoy their work	4.5	22	18.9	32.6	22
2.	The top management believes that human resources are most valuable resource and that they have to be treated more humanly	21.1	53.3	18.4	6.6	0.7

3.	The top management is willing to invest a considerable part of their time and other resources to ensure development of employees	20.4	52.6	20.4	6.6	Nil
4.	People lacking competence in their jobs are helped to acquire competence rather than being left unattended	5.9	53.9	29.6	10.5	Nil
5.	The top management of the organization makes efforts to identify and utilize the potential of employee	14.5	52	26.3	5.9	1.3
6.	Employees are encouraged to experiment with new methods and try out creative ideas	6.1	24.2	16.7	27.3	25.8
7.	Weakness of employees are communicated to them in a non- threatening way	10.5	46.1	32.9	6.6	3.9
8.	When feedback is given to employees they take it seriously and use it for development	3.8	17.4	20.5	32.6	25.8
	Average Percentage	**10.85**	**40.18**	**22.96**	**16.08**	**9.94**

Source: Compiled and Computed from Primary Data

Human Resource Development Climate is considered as a pre-requisite of facilitating human resource development system in the organization. HRD is a continuous process, by which employees' capabilities are sharpened to realize their full potential and training is provided to them in handling the present and future jobs effeciently. To achieve these objectives there is a need for the organization to create conducive HRD climate.

In table 5.24, it is evident from average opinions of the respondents on HRD climate that a large chunk of employees 40.18 percent opined as true for the HRD climate in APSRTC and minimun of employees 9.94 percent felt as not at all true. Whereas, 22.96 percent employees opined as patly true, 16.08 percent employees admit as not so true and only 10.85 percent employees expessed as very much true.

From the table 5.24, it can also be visualized that maximum of 46.1 percent and minimum of employees 17.4 percent opine as true for the statements - Weakness of employees are communicated to them in a non- threatening way and when feedback is given to employees they take it seriously and use it for development respectively. Whereas same majority of employees 25.8 percent opined as not at all true for the statements, Employees are encouraged to experiment with new methods and try out creative ideas and when feedback is given to employees they take it seriously and use it for development. However, two statements obtained nil response i.e., the top management is willing to invest a considerable part of their time and other resources to ensure development of employees and people lacking competence in their jobs are helped to acquire competence rather than being left unattended are not at all true.

A competent employee is an asset to an organization and his retention and development largely depend on positive attitude of the management towards him. It motivates an employee to give his their best in performing their tasks by accepting the changes in the organization. Thus, favourable climate can highly influence the attitudes and perceptions of the employees. Purang (2008) through a survey on "Dimensions of HRD Climate Enhancing Organizational Commitment in Indian Organization" also pointed out that favourable climate directly influences the behaviour of managers in an organization which creates a sense of belongingness in them and also enables them to perform well. From the above analysis it is suggested that management of APSRTC should always develop and maintain dyadic relations at work, provide supportive guidance from the seniors to their juniors, improve welfare measures for the workforce and create a congenial working environment for better results and improved performance. This kind of positive working climate motivates employees to work tirelessly and enables them to perform better. However, from the survey results, it can be concluded that APSRTC had positive HRD Climate and has a positive influence on job performance of its employees. It is because of this reason that the corporation has its own culture, tradition and practices that affect their employees working pattern.

Figure 5.17: Exhibits the overall employees opinion on HRD climate

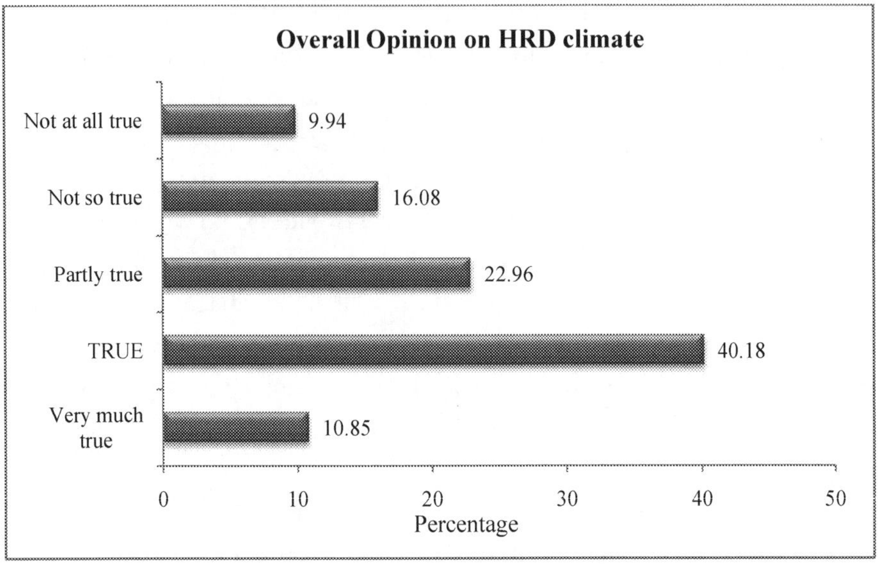

Source: Table 5.24

Friedman's Mean Rank Test:

Table 5.25: Shows the mean score of the statements on HRD Climate

Sl. No.	Statements on HRD Climate	MEAN	S.D	PERCENTAGE
1.	The top management of this organization goes out of its way to make sure that employees enjoy their work	3.4318	.81206	60.795
2.	The top management believes that human resources are most valuable resource and that they have to be treated more humanly	3.8712	.82337	71.78
3.	The top management is willing to invest a considerable part of their time and other resources to ensure development of employees	3.8409	.80863	71.0225
4.	People lacking competence in their jobs are helped to acquire competence rather than being left unattended	3.5606	.75420	64.015

5.	The top management of the organization makes efforts to identify and utilize the potential of employee	3.7348	.84582	68.37
6.	Employees are encouraged to experiment with new methods and try out creative ideas	3.6136	.85290	65.34
7.	Weakness of employees are communicated to them in a non- threatening way	3.5682	.86663	64.205
8.	When feedback is given to employees they take it seriously and use it for development	3.4242	.78265	60.605
	Overall Mean Score	**3.630**	**0.817**	**65.766**

Source: Compiled and Computed from Primary Data

It is evident from the table 5.25 that the attributes are ranked between 1 and 8 as per Friedman's mean rank test and values ranked between 3.42 and 3.87. The first rated attribute of managers regarding HRD climate is the top management believes that human resources are most valuable resource and that they have to be treated more humanly (3.87). The top management is willing to invest a considerable time and other resources to ensure development of employees is another influencing factor (3.84) that is chosen by the respondents. The third (3.73) and fourth (3.61) are, the top management of the organization makes efforts to identify and utilize the potential of employee and the fourth attribute is employees are encouraged to experiment with new methods and try out creative ideas. Weakness of employees are communicated to them in a non – threatening way (3.56) and people lacking competence in their jobs are helped to acquire competence rather than being left unattended (3.56) are ranked the fifth and sixth positions respectively. The top management of this organization goes out of its way to make sure that employees enjoy their work (3.43) and when feedback is given to employees they take it seriously and use it for development are the seventh and eighth persuading factors of HRD Climate to improve the productivity and performance of employees in APSRTC.

Thus, it is evident from the analysis that the most influencing factors of APSRTC are the top management believes that human resources are most valuable resource and that they have to be treated more humanly, the top management is willing to invest a considerable part of their time and other resources to ensure development of employees, and organization makes efforts to identify and utilize the potential of employee. It is also observed that the respondents do not have equal levels of opinions for all the attributes related to the HRD Climate in APSRTC.

Regression Analysis: HRD Climate *versus* Demographic factors of the responded employees

H_{04}: HRD Climate doesn't have significant impact on the employee's performance.

Table 5.26: Shows the regression analysis between demographic factors and HRD Climate

Predictor	Coefficient	SE Coefficient	T-value	P-value
Constant	2.3847	0.6127	3.89	0.000
Qualification	*0.10065*	*0.05008*	*2.01*	*0.047*
Age	0.03859	0.05520	0.70	0.486
Gender	0.1259	0.1499	0.84	0.403
Designation	0.1117	0.1368	0.82	0.416
Department	-0.03205	0.08827	-0.36	0.717
Monthly Income	0.00000745	0.00000685	1.09	0.279
Length of service	-0.00588	0.05529	-0.11	0.765
Marital status	-0.0482	0.1608	-0.30	0.765
Nature of work	-0.01408	0.09886	-0.14	0.887

Source: Compiled and Computed from Primary Data

R-Sq = 7.9% P-value: 0.320

Since the P-value of the R-square is 7.9 percent greater than 0.05, the level of significance which exemplifies that the variation between independent variables (demographic factors) and dependent variable (HRD Climate) are statistically significant at 0.05 level. Further, the independent variables (demographic factors) explain that only 7.9 percent of variation on this aspect.

A regression analysis was conducted with the dependent variable HRD Climate with the demographic factors. Only one variable (Qualification) out of nine contribute significantly to the regression equation at 0.05 level of statistical significance. For this variable, ANOVA test is conducted as follows to know the significant difference in the average opinion scores among the categories of qualification.

Table 5.27: Shows ANOVA analysis of Qualification factor with HRD Climate

Qualification	n	Mean	S.D	F- value	P-value	Decision
PG	59	3.1271	.50080	1.87	0.138	Not significant
Diploma	43	3.2936	.63848			
any other	8	3.3281	.67128			
below graduation	22	3.4432	.58468			

Source: Compiled and Computed from Primary Data

ANOVA test value and its corresponding P-value 0.138 reveal that there is no significant difference in the opinion of the respondents belongs to difference qualifications mentioned are at 5 percent level of significance. Further, the Average opinion score of the respondents belongs to below graduation level opined more positively than the remaining categories followed by other qualification and Diploma holders and the Post graduation holders. The diagrammatic representation is shown 6.18 as a box plot. This indicates that the null hypothesis (H_{04}) that HRD Climate doesn't have significant impact on the employee's performance is rejected and it is proved that there is a significant impact on employee performance.

Figure 5.18: Exhibits boxplot showing comparision of HRD Climate by Qualification

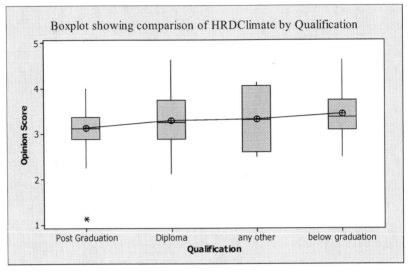

Source: Table: 6.27

Dimension V: Performance Appraisal

Table 5.28: Shows the percentage analysis of employees perception on Performance Appraisal

Sl. No.	Statements on Performance Appraisal	Very much true	True	Partly true	Not so true	Not at all true
1.	It has scope for correcting the bias or reporting officer through a review process	6.6	69.1	17.8	5.3	1.3
2.	The system provides for assessment of employee potential and enables him to select and pursue his future careers	6.8	21.2	20.5	26.5	25
3.	The system provides direction regarding potentials of the employees and helps the organization to plan for career and succession development	7.9	55.3	25.7	9.2	2

4.	The system has scope for helping each employee to discover his potential	5.3	50	30.3	11.8	2.6
5.	Provides an opportunity for each appraisee to communicate the support he needs from the superiors to perform his job effectively	4.5	24.2	18.2	28	25
6.	Performance appraisal system in the organization is transparent	13.2	49.3	28.9	5.9	2.6
	Average Percentage	**7.38**	**44.85**	**23.57**	**14.45**	**9.75**

Source: Compiled and Computed from Primary Data

Performance Appraisal is the evaluation of worth, quality or merit. Performance appraisal is "the process of observing and evaluating an employee's performance, recording the assessment and providing feedback to the employee" (Daft and Marcic, 1998). It is a structural formal interview between subordinate and superior that usually takes the form of periodic interview (annually or semi-annually) in which the work performance of the subordinate is examined and discussed, with the view to identify the weakness and strength as well as opportunity for skills and development (DECENZO and Robbins, 1995).

The survey reveals that the overall opinion of the respondents was maximum of employees, 44.85 percent opined that various performance appraisal practices in APSRTC are true and minimum of employees 7.38 percent opined as very much true. In addition, employees 23.57 percent expressed as partly true, 14.45 percent employees felt as not so true and only 9.75 percent employees opine as not at all true for the Performance Appraisal techniques adopted by the corporation.

The table 5.28 also portrays that maximum of respondents 69.1 percent expressed as true for the statement that it has scope for correcting the bias by the reporting officer through a review process and also minimum of respondents 21.2 percent expressed as true for the statement that the system provides for assessment of employee potential and enables him to select and pursue his future careers. Whereas, maximum of 13.2 percent respondents opined as very much true for the statement that Performance Appraisal system in the organization is transparent and only 4.5 percent respondents agreed as very much true for the statement that performance Appraisal provides an opportunity for each appraisee to communicate the support he needs from the superiors to perform his job effectively.

It is evident from the obtained results that the corporation's performance appraisal techniques are not bad. It is also observed from the analysis that majority of the respondents were of the opinion that Performance Appraisal system could not provide an opportunity for each appraisee to communicate the support he needs from the superiors to perform his job effectively and also could not provide assessment of employee potential and enable him to select and pursue his future careers. So the corporation should establish assessment center at zonal level to assess employee potential. This information helps in job rotation and enrichment.

The study on performance appraisal in APSRTC by Dr. B. Dharma Naik identified that performance appraisal ratings are based on appraisee's personal relationship with the immediate superiors. So it is necessary for APSRTC to take and provide counseling with the superiors to know the employee's drawbacks. For this the organization has to provide training to their executives in the performance appraisal techniques. Also in order to avoid bias, the performance Appraisal report should consist of quoting the reason for high appraisal and low appraisal. This method can also be more transparent and can be used for developmental, administrative decision-making, organizational maintenance and documentation.

Figure 5.19: Exhibits the overall employees
opinion on Performance Appraisal

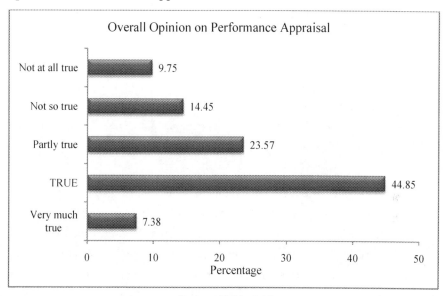

Source: Table 5.28

Friedman's Mean Rank Test:

Table 5.29: Shows the mean score of the statements
on Performance Appraisal

Sl. No.	Statements on Performance Appraisal	MEAN	S.D	PERCENTAGE
1.	It has scope for correcting the bias or reporting officer through a review process	3.7576	.67813	68.94
2.	The system provides for assessment of employee potential and enables him to select and pursue his future careers	3.6061	.78883	65.1525
3.	The system provides direction regarding potentials of the employees and helps the organization to plan for career and succession development	3.5606	.83124	64.015

4.	The system has scope for helping each employee to discover his potential	3.4394	.84941	60.985
5.	Provides an opportunity for each appraisee to communicate the support he needs from the superiors to perform his job effectively	3.6061	.75924	65.1525
6.	Performance appraisal system in the organization is transparent	3.6515	.87357	66.2875
	Overall Mean Score	**3.603**	**0.796**	**65.088**

Source: Field Survey

Friedman's mean rank test is used to identify the core Performance Appraisal dimensions which has significant influence on the employee's performance and the results are presented in table 5.28. It is clear from the table that among the six core performance appraisal dimensions, performance appraisal has scope for correcting the bias or reporting officer through a review process (3.75) is highly significant and ranked first, and followed by performance appraisal system in APSRTC is transparent (3.65) ranked second. The respondents jointly shared the third priority (3.60) for the attribute that the system provides for assessment of employee potential and enables him to select and pursue his future careers, and also for providing an opportunity for each appraisee to communicate the support he needs from the superiors to perform his job effectively. The performance appraisal system provides direction regarding potentials of the employees and helps the organization to plan for career and succession development (3.56), and the performance appraisal system has scope for helping each employee to discover his potential (3.43) are ranked fourth and fifth respectively.

It is evident from the fact that the dimensions of performance appraisal discussed in the 6.29 table are commonly employed performance appraisal techniques. To improve employee performance and achieve maximum productivity, the APSRTC has to introduce new innovative performance appraisal techniques. It can be concluded that the respondents do not have equal levels of satisfaction for all the dimensions of performance appraisal system which are adopted by the corporation.

Regression Analysis: Performance Appraisal *versus* Demographic factors of the responded employees

H_{05}: Performance Appraisal doesn't have significant impact on the employee's performance.

Table 5.30: Shows the regression analysis between demographic factors and Performance Appraisal

Predictor	Coefficient	SE Coefficient	T-Value	P-Value
Constant	2.9206	0.8525	3.43	0.001
Qualification	0.04894	0.06968	0.70	0.484
Age	0.03793	0.07681	0.49	0.6
Gender	-0.0151	0.2086	-0.07	0.943
Designation	0.0749	0.1904	0.39	0.695
Department	-0.0491	0.1228	-0.40	0.690
Monthly Income	0.00000737	0.00000953	0.77	0.441
Length of service	0.00186	0.07693	0.02	0.981
Marital status	0.0004	0.2237	0.00	0.999
Nature of work	-0.0974	0.1376	-0.71	0.480

Source: Compiled and Computed from Primary Data

R-Sq = 4.9% P-value: 0.711

For the dimension Performance Appraisal MLR analysis was carried out to establish the relationship between the demographic factors of respondents and Performance Appraisal being espoused in an organization. No demographic factors will influence the dependent variable at 5 percent level. This indicates that the null hypothesis (H_{05}) that Performance Appraisal doesn't have significant impact on the employee's performance is rejected and it is proved that there is a significant impact on employee performance.

Dimension VI: Counseling

Table 5.31: Shows the percentage analysis of employees
perception on Counseling

Sl. No.	Statements on Counseling	Very much true	True	Partly true	Not so true	Not at all true
1.	Enriches the understanding capabilities of the counselee regarding the possible short comes and enables to take precautions	7.9	55.3	32.2	4.6	
2.	Helps to acquire new technical, managerial and behavioral skills and knowledge in the course of discussions	13.2	53.9	29.6	3.3	
3.	Helps in learning the skills of formulating objectives, framing controlling techniques and the methods of self control	9.1	21.2	22	25.8	22
	Average Percentage	**10.06**	**43.44**	**27.91**	**11.23**	**7.33**

Source: Compiled and Computed from Primary Data

A counseling session is a meeting between the supervisor and the employee which may focus on a specific incident, a particular aspect of an employee's performance which the supervisor has identified as needing improvement, or the employee's overall performance or conduct. The counseling process is initiated and executed at the department level by the supervisor. It is a face-to-face communication between the supervisor and the employee, conducted in private, and is intended to have a constructive goal of providing feedback to the employee to correct the problem.

The table 5.31 reveals the average opinion on various counseling brushworks executed by APSRTC to improve their employee's performance. The table discloses that maximum of 43.44 percent and minimum of 7.33 percent agree that various counseling brushworks taken up by the corporation are true and not at all true respectively. Whereas, 27.91 percent respondents felt as partly true, 11.23 percent respondents opine as not so true and only 10.06 percent employees expressed as very much true.

The table also unveils that a large proportion of employees i.e. 55.3 percent agree as true for the statement that counseling enriches the understanding capabilities of the counselee regarding the possible short comes and enables to take precautions and least proportion of 21.2 percent employees admit as true for the statement that counseling helps in learning the skills of formulating objectives, framing controlling techniques and the methods of self control. The table also exposes that large chunk of 13.2 percent employees opine as very much true for the statement that counseling helps in learning the skills of formulating objectives, framing controlling techniques and the methods of self control and also minor chunk of 7.9 percent respondents agreed as very much true for the statement that counseling enriches the understanding capabilities of the counselee regarding the possible short comes and enables to take precautions.

It can be concluded that APSRTC is not ignoring the practice of counseling to its employees on par with the other HRD Practices. For better results from the counseling it is suggested that the management of APSRTC should speak to the employee, on a timely basis and describe specific, observable, measurable and/or unacceptable conduct. While conducting counseling, managers should be prepared, have the facts in hand before they meet the employees. The effect of the problem on the work environment or on the employee's performance should be stated clearly. Employee's problem should be known by encouraging them to speak freely and candidly and listening to the information with an open mind. Employees should be asked for potential solutions after managers have explained what work is acceptable. Consider all options. If you think it is necessary, they can add their own ideas. Give the employee a reason to improve work attitude. Offer suggestions to help the employee improve/change conduct. Reach an understanding on a corrective action. Management and the employee have to know what is expected of each other. Identify follow-up steps and dates. Meet again with the employee to review performance. Recognize improvements that have occurred.

Figure 5.20: Exhibits the overall employees opinion on Counseling

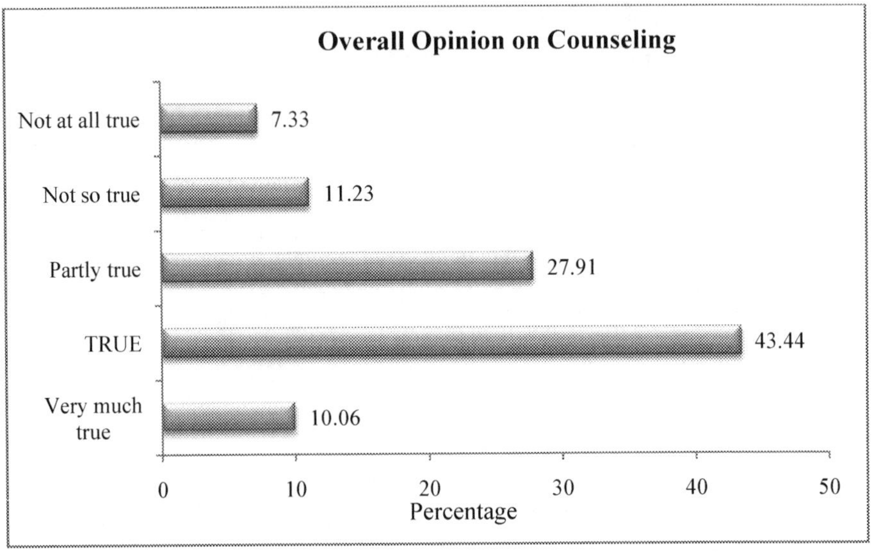

Overall Opinion on Counseling

Category	Percentage
Not at all true	7.33
Not so true	11.23
Partly true	27.91
TRUE	43.44
Very much true	10.06

Percentage (0, 10, 20, 30, 40, 50)

Source: Table 5.32

Friedman's Mean Rank Test:

Table 5.32: Shows the mean score of the statements on
Performance Appraisal

Sl. No.	Statements on Counseling	MEAN	S.D	PERCENTAGE
1.	Enriches the understanding capabilities of the counselee regarding the possible short comes and enables to take precautions	3.6742	.69344	66.855
2.	Helps to acquire new technical, managerial and behavioral skills and knowledge in the course of discussions	3.7803	.71317	69.5075
3.	Helps in learning the skills of formulating objectives, framing controlling techniques and the methods of self control	3.6591	.70796	66.4775
	Overall Mean Score	**3.704**	**0.704**	**67.613**

Source: Compiled and Computed from Primary Data

The table 5.32 exhibits the values of Friedman's mean rank test that are arranged between 66.47 and 69.50. The first preferred choice of the attributes of counseling in APSRTC is Counseling Helps to acquire new technical, managerial and behavioral skills and knowledge in the course of discussions (3.78) followed by counseling enriches the understanding capabilities of the counselee regarding the possible short comes and enables to take precautions (3.67), and counseling helps in learning the skills of formulating objectives, framing controlling techniques and the methods of self control (3.65) which are ranked second and third respectively.

The results reveal that the most significant attribute is counseling helps to acquire new technical, managerial and behavioral skills and knowledge in the course of discussions. Therefore, it can be concluded that the responses vary as per different satisfaction levels of APSRTC's managerial staff.

Regression Analysis: Counseling *versus* Demographic factors of the responded employees

H_{06}: Counseling doesn't have significant impact on the employee's performance.

Table 5.33: Shows the regression analysis between demographic factors and Counseling

Predictor	Coefficient	SE Coefficient	T-value	P-value
Constant	3.6622	0.8826	4.15	0.000
Qualification	-0.04346	0.07214	-0.60	0.548
Age	0.03666	0.07953	0.46	0.646
Gender	-0.0416	0.2160	-0.19	0.847
Designation	0.0956	0.1971	-0.48	0.629
Department	-0.0981	0.1272	-0.77	0.442
Monthly Income	*-0.00001250*	*0.00000987*	*-1.98*	*0.049*
Length of service	0.04266	0.07965	0.54	0.593
Marital status	0.1787	0.2316	0.77	0.442
Nature of work	0.0161	0.1424	0.11	0.910

Source: Compiled and Computed from Primary Data

R-Sq = 4.0% P-value: 0.821

Since the p-value of the R-square is greater than 0.82, the level of significance, which exemplifies that the variation between independent variables and dependent variable are not statistically significant at 5 percent level. Further, the independent variables (demographic factors) explain that only 4 percent of variation on working relation. Except one demographic factor (Monthly Income), all variables are not statistically significant on the counseling at 5 percent level. For this variable, ANOVA test is conducted as follows to know the significant difference in the average opinion scores among the categories of Monthly income.

Table 5.34: Shows ANOVA analysis of Monthly Income factor with Counseling

Monthly Income	n	Mean	S.D	F- value	P-value	Decision
Below 15000	14	3.4524	.66161	1.412	0.234	Not significant
15000-25000	27	3.4444	.88675			
25000-35000	44	3.0833	.88667			
35000-45000	15	3.1778	.73319			

Source: Compiled and Computed from Primary Data

The Average opinion Score of the respondents belonging to below 15000 opined more positively rather than the remaining categories of the income followed by 15000-25000 on the aspect counseling. Further, as per the ANOVA test value 1.412 and its significance value 0.234 does not give significant difference opinion on this aspect. This indicates that the null hypothesis (H_{06}) that Counseling doesn't have significant impact on the employee's performance is rejected and it is proved that there is a significant impact on employee performance.

Dimension VII: Career Planning and Development

Table 5.35: Shows the percentage analysis of employees perception on Career Planning and Development

Sl. No.	Statements on Career Planning and Development	Very much true	True	Partly true	Not so true	Not at all true
1.	Organization disseminates career option information	4.6	46.7	39.5	5.9	3.3
2.	Organization provides facility of assessment center to assist employees potentialities	5.3	20.5	15.2	34.1	25
3.	Organization provides career counseling and development workshops for career development	9.9	40.8	30.9	15.1	3.3
	Average Percentage	**6.60**	**36.00**	**28.53**	**18.37**	**10.53**

Source: Compiled and Computed from Primary Data

Career Development is vital for an individual and an organization to achieve personal and organizational objectives. Career Development refers to the plans set for proper career advancement to achieve targets in the given time. According to Prof. T.V. Rao, most young executives coming to the organizations are career minded, ambitious and looking for fast growth. Career advancement for most managers is the prime motivating factor. They want to know where they would be going in the organization after three, five, ten years from their joining. It will be to the advantage of the organization to work out a meaningful career planning system based on potential appraisal. Career planning and Development can become an effective tool for development of the employee and a key factor in the HRD system.

The table 5.35 visualizes the overall opinion of the passengers on the methods of career planning and development adopted by APSRTC. It is clear from the table that maximum of employees 36 percent agreed that career planning and Development methods of APSRTC were true and minimum of employees 6.60 percent expressed as very much true. However, 28.53 percent,

18.37 percent, and 10.53 percent respondents opine that the methods of career planning and development are partly true, not so true, and not at all true respectively.

The table 5.35 also depicts that maximum of employees 46.7 percent admit as true for the statement that organization disseminates career option information and minimum of employees 20.5 percent agreed as true for the statement that organization provides facility of assessment center to assist employees potentialities. Maximum of employees 9.9 percent opined as very much true for the statement that organization provides career counseling and development workshops for career development and only 4.6 percent employees admit as very much true for the statement that organization disseminates career option information.

Career development are personal development plans created and maintained for each individual, organization provides every employee with opportunities to choose a career path to suit the individual's core competence, an individual's development plan and activities are periodically reviewed, individuals have clear career paths within the organization, APSRTC has created a learning environment for both professional and personal growth and job rotation in organization facilitates employee development. Pareek and Rao mentioned that "while career development means the development of general and technical and managerial career in the organization, career planning implies planning of specific career paths of the employees in the foreseeable future in the organization with the help of the reporting officer. From the table it is also obvious that majority of the respondents in the corporation are disappointed about the statement that organization provides facility of assessment center to assist employee's potential. So there is a need for APSRTC to provide an assessment center for the employees to assist and assess their potentialities. In summary, it can be understood that APSRTC is not at all less in practicing positive career planning and developing its employees.

Figure 5.21: Exhibits the overall employees opinion on Career Planning and Development

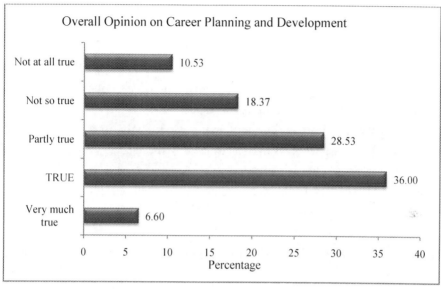

Overall Opinion on Career Planning and Development

Source: Table 5.36

Friedman's Mean Rank Test:

Table 5.36: Shows the mean score of the statements on Career Planning and Development

Sl. No.	Statements on Career Planning and Development	MEAN	S.D	PERCENTAGE
1.	Organization disseminates career option information	3.4394	.79365	60.985
2.	Organization provides facility of assessment center to assist employees potentialities	3.2576	.96204	56.44
3.	Organization provides career counseling and development workshops for career development	3.3712	.96824	59.28
	Overall Mean Score	**3.355**	**0.907**	**58.901**

Source: Compiled and Computed from Primary Data

Friedman's mean rank test is used to rank the Career Planning and Development dimensions prevailing in APSRTC that have significant influence on the level of satisfaction and the results of the test are presented in table 5.36. It is clear from the table that Organization disseminates career option information (3.43) ranked first. Organization provides career counseling and development workshops for career development (3.37), and Organization provides facility of assessment center to assist employee's potentialities (3.25) are stood in second and third positions respectively.

A careful observation on the above analysis sheds light on expectations and perception of the corporation's managerial staff with regard to the influence of Career Planning and Development variables that are adopted in APSRTC. The results indicate that the respondents do not have equal opinion on the Career Planning and Development practice adopted in APSRTC.

Regression Analysis: Career Planning and Development *versus* Demographic factors of the responded employees

H_{07}: Career Planning & Development doesn't have significant impact on the employee's performance.

Table 5.37: Shows the regression analysis between demographic factors and Career Planning and Development

Predictor	Coefficient	SE Coefficient	T-value	P-value
Constant	3.9476	0.7985	4.94	0.000
Qualification	0.02672	0.06527	0.41	.683
Age	*-0.15228*	*0.07194*	*-2.12*	*0.036*
Gender	-0.3214	0.1954	-1.65	0.102
Designation	-0.0606	0.1783	-0.34	0.734
Department	-0.1389	0.1150	-1.21	0.230
Monthly Income	0.00000001	0.00000893	0.00	0.999
Length of service	0.10688	0.07206	1.48	0.141
Marital status	-0.1491	0.2096	-0.71	0.478
Nature of work	0.1402	0.1289	1.09	0.279

Source: Compiled and Computed from Primary Data

R-Sq = 6.9% P-value: 0.439

Since the P-value 0.439 of the R-square 6.9 percent is greater than 0.05, the level of significance which exemplifies that the variation between independent variables (demographic factors) and dependent variable (Career Planning and Development) are statistically significant at 5 percent level. Further, the independent variables (demographic factors) explain that only 6.9 percent of variation on this aspect. Only one variable (Age) out of nine contributed significantly to the equation at 5 percent level. For these variables, ANOVA test is conducted as follows to know the significant difference in the average opinion scores among the age categories of the respondents on Career Planning and Development.

Table 5.38: Shows ANOVA analysis of Age factor with Career Planning & Development

Age	n	Mean	S.D	F- value	P-value	Decision
25 - 30	18	3.1111	.92178	0.199	0.962	Not significant
31 - 35	13	3.1795	.72795			
36 - 40	10	2.9667	.65640			
41 - 45	27	3.0741	.78628			
46 - 50	37	3.0090	.82584			
Above 50	27	2.9753	.54636			

Source: Compiled and Computed from Primary Data

The P-value 0.962 in the table 5.38 doesn't show statistical significance at 5 percent level, so it is concluded that there is no significant difference between age categories of the respondents. Further, the age group 46-50 shows positive opinion than other categories followed by 41-45 years of age groups on Career Planning and Development. This indicates that the null hypothesis (H_{07}) that Career Planning & Development doesn't have significant impact on the employee's performance is rejected and it is proved that there is a significant impact on employee performance.

Figure 5.22: Exhibits boxplot showing comparision of Career Planning and Development by Age

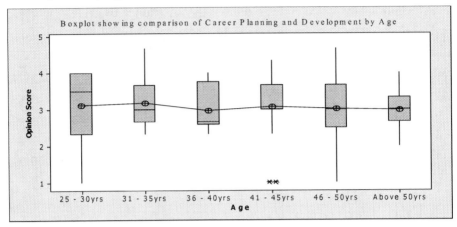

Source: Table 5.38

Mean Score, Percentage and Standard Deviation of dimensions of HRD Practices in APSRTC at Vizianagaram zone:

Table 5.39: Ranks of the dimensions of HRD practices
at APSRTC-Vizianagaram zone with Mean Score,
Percentage and Standard Deviation

Sl. No.	Dimensions of HRD Practices	Mean Score	S.D	Percentage Score	Rank
1.	Training and Development	3.614	0.822	65.368	4
2.	Organization Structure and Climate	3.667	0.836	66.693	2
3.	HRD Knowledge and Skills	3.519	0.772	63.005	6
4.	HRD Climate	3.630	0.817	65.766	3
5.	Performance Appraisal	3.603	0.796	65.088	5
6.	Counseling	3.704	0.704	67.613	1
7.	Career Planning and Development	3.355	0.907	58.901	7

Source: Compiled and Computed from Primary Data

From the Friedman's Mean Rank test of all the overall mean scores of the dimensions of the HRD practices, it can be understood that counseling practice has attained the highest rank that is one on the basis of 3.704 of human resource development of APSRTC in Vizianagaram zone. Overall mean score of HRD Practice, organization structure and climate is 3.667 with rank two. HRD Climate has attained third rank with 3.630 overall mean score; Training and Development has attained fourth rank with 3.614 overall mean score; Performance Appraisal has attained fifth rank with 3.603 overall mean score; HRD Knowledge has attained fifth rank with 8.603 overall mean score; HRD Knowledge and Skills has attained sixth rank with 3.519 overall mean score and Career Planning and Development has attained seventh rank with 3.355 overall mean score. It is evident that the overall mean score of Performance Appraisal Practice, Managers HRD Knowledge and Skills and Career Planning and Development have attained low ranks which indicate further scope for improvement in the organization. The overall mean score of all these organizations show satisfactory HRD Practices were prevailing in the organization at zonal level. The same is supported by the mean score 3.6388 of the overall HRD practices which is satisfactory score.

Section C: Overall level of satisfaction in the organization through HRD practices

Table 5.40: Shows the percentage analysis of employees satisfaction on Overall HRD Practices

Sl. No.	Statements on Overall level of satisfaction in the organization through HRD practices	Highly satisfied	Satisfied	Uncertain	Dissatisfied	Highly dissatisfied
1.	Learning environment in the organization	14.5	72.4	9.2	3.9	
2.	Training and Development practices	13.2	72.4	11.2	2.6	0.7
3.	Promotion policy and reward system	11.4	23.5	19.7	25	20.5
4.	Working conditions in the organization	9.2	64.5	15.1	7.2	3.9
5.	Compensation and welfare facilities	15.9	28	15.9	21.2	18.9
6.	Job description, role clarity are well defined	20.4	52.6	17.1	7.9	2
7.	Information sharing amongst employees	11.2	63.8	17.1	5.9	2
8.	Employee participation in finalization of tasks and targets	5.3	31.1	29.5	18.2	15.9
9.	Career planning opportunities	4.5	25	35.6	22	12.9
10.	Co-operation among superiors, peers and sub-ordinates	10.5	59.2	17.8	11.8	0.7
11.	Your association with the organization	23.7	65.8	8.6	2	
12.	Work culture in the organization	13.8	61.2	13.8	9.9	1.3

13.	Leadership at different levels in the organization	11.8	65.1	12.5	8.6	2
14.	HRIS facilitates HRD practices	10.5	44.7	34.9	8.6	1.3
15.	Library facilities in the organization	1.5	15.9	20.5	25	37.1
	Average Percentage	**11.83**	**49.68**	**18.57**	**11.99**	**7.95**

Source: Compiled and Computed from Primary Data

The constant support of the organization through HRD Practices increases the level of job enrichment and accordingly affects the level of job involvement and consequently affects the performance of the managers[297].

The table 5.40 shows that maximam of employees, 49.68 percent agreed that average percentage of opinion of the respondents on overall satisfaction level of HRD Practices were satisfactory and minimum of employees 7.95 percent expressd they are highly dissatisfied. Nearly 18.57 percent respondents were as uncertain, 11.99 percent employees are dissatisfied and only 11.83 percent respondents expressed that they are highly satisfied with various HRD practices that are adopted by APSRTC.

In the table 5.40, it can also be observed that an equal number of 72.4 percent respondents were satisfied with the learning environment and Training & Development practices of the organization. About only 15.9 Percent employees were satisfyed with library facilities in the organization. Maximum of respondents, 37.1 percent expressed high dissatisfaction for the library facilities in the organization. Where-as no respondent expressed high dissatisfaction towards learning environment and their association with the organization. From the analysis it can be inferred that the library facilities in the organization was not up to the mark. It is because of the reason that employees in their busy job schedule do not find time to spend in the libraries located at zonal offices. For updating knowledge the managers need to use library, so the management of APSRTC for easy accessability of books and articles, research projects etc., it should maintain digital library for its employees.

Successful organizations pay adequate attention to their HRD practices. According to Prof. T.V. Rao, "HRD practices should not be thought of in isolation. They are designed to work together in an integrated system, although any of them may exist in an organization that does not have an overall HRD plan"[298]. So for the full benefit of HRD to be experienced, APSRTC must implement it as an integrated system. In addition, top management's commitment to employ HRD practices and willingness to invest time and other resources is crucial, top management must make it obvious that the corporation's human resources are its most important resources. The value of HRD practices should be recognized by every member of the organization. If implemented properly, HRD Practices can significantly contribute to increased performance and increased organizational productivity.

Figure 5.23: Exhibits the overall Opinion on level of satisfaction in the organization through HRD practices

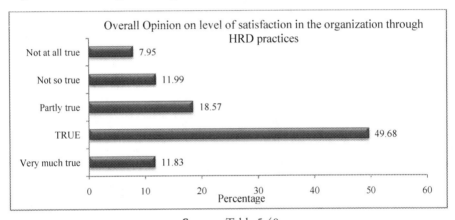

Source: Table 5.40

Friedman's Mean Rank Test:

Table 5.41: Shows the mean score of the statements on overall level of satisfaction of employees in the organization through HRD practices

Sl. No.	Statements on Overall level of satisfaction in the organization through HRD practices	MEAN	S.D	PERCENT-AGE
1.	Learning environment in the organization	3.9394	.63915	73.485
2.	Training and Development practices	3.9167	.65431	72.9175

3.	Promotion policy and reward system	3.6364	.95128	65.91
4.	Working conditions in the organization	3.6742	.87803	66.855
5.	Compensation and welfare facilities	3.9091	.79555	72.7275
6.	Job description, role clarity are well defined	3.7803	.92723	69.5075
7.	Information sharing amongst employees	3.7273	.82045	68.1825
8.	Employee participation in finalization of tasks and targets	3.5606	.80321	64.015
9.	Career planning opportunities	3.2803	.87645	57.0075
10.	Co-operation among superiors, peers and sub-ordinates	3.6288	.85073	65.72
11.	Your association with the organization	4.0909	.63552	77.2725
12.	Work culture in the organization	3.7652	.83675	69.13
13.	Leadership at different levels in the organization	3.7879	.81053	69.6975
14.	HRIS facilitates HRD practices	3.5379	.81405	63.4475
15.	Library facilities in the organization	2.1970	1.14878	29.925
	Overall Mean Score	**3.6288**	**0.8294**	**65.72**

Source: Compiled and Computed from Primary Data

Friedman's mean rank test identifies the significant influence on the overall satisfaction level of the respondents regarding the HRD Practices adopted in APSRTC. Employee association with the organization is the most significant factor (4.09) followed by learning environment in the organization (3.93) and Training and Development Practices (3.91) are ranked the second and third influential practices respectively. Compensation and welfare facilities (3.90), Leadership at different levels in the organization (3.78) as well as job description, role clarity are well defined (3.78) are rated fourth, fifth and sixth ranks respectively. For all the remaining statements the Friedman's mean rank values are ranged between 3.76 and 2.19. Work culture in the organization (3.76) and library facilities in the organization (2.19) are two extremes which are placed in seventh and fifteenth positions respectively.

Information sharing amongst employees (3.72), working conditions in the organization (3.67), promotion policy and reward system (3.63), Co-operation among superiors, peers and subordinates (3.62) and employee participation in finalization of tasks and targets (3.56) stood at eighth, ninth, tenth, eleventh and twelfth positions respectively. HRIS facilities HRD Practices (3.53) and Career Planning opportunities (3.28) are least preferred practices ranked thirteenth and fourteenth positions respectively.

The results indicate that the respondents do not have equal satisfaction levels for all the HRD Practices incorporated in APSRTC. The above analysis reveals that the HRD practices variables viz., employee association with the organization and learning environment in the organization are two dominant satisfying HRD practices of APSRTC. Hence, there is a dire need that the corporation should seriously act upon the dissatisfying practices that have less focus towards improving the employee's performance.

Regression Analysis: Overall HRD Practices *versus* Demographic factors of the responded employees

H_{08}: Overall level of satisfaction on HRD Practices doesn't have significant impact on the employee's performance.

Table 5.42: Shows the regression analysis between demographic factors and overall satisfaction of employees on HRD Practices

Predictor	Coefficient	SE Coefficient	T-value	P-value
Constant	3.6030	0.5366	6.71	0.000
Qualification	0.06905	0.04386	1.57	0.118
Age	-0.10043	0.04835	-2.08	0.040
Gender	0.1277	0.1313	0.97	0.333
Designation	0.1104	0.1198	-0.92	0.359
Department	0.02529	0.07731	0.33	0.744
Monthly Income	0.00000105	0.00000600	0.18	0.861
Length of service	0.07956	0.04843	1.64	0.103
Marital status	-0.1103	0.1408	-0.78	0.435
Nature of work	-0.02682	0.08659	-0.31	0.757

Source: Compiled and Computed from Primary Data

R-Sq = 7.9% P-value: 0.325

It was concluded that there is no linear relationship between the demographic factors extracted above and their probability of association with various HRD practices studied. A regression analysis was conducted with the dependent variable HRD Practices and the demographic factors. Only one variable (age) have impact on the HRD practices out of nine demographic factors at 5 percent level. For this variable further ANOVA test is conducted as follows

Table 5.43: Shows ANOVA analysis of Dimensions of Age factor with overall satisfaction of employees on HRD Practices

Age	n	Mean	S.D	F- value	P-value	Decision
25 - 30	18	3.5074	.60245	0.331	0.893	Not significant
31 - 35	13	3.3487	.49077			
36 - 40	10	3.3800	.35284			
41 - 45	27	3.4765	.37289			
46 - 50	37	3.4162	.55387			
Above 50	27	3.3506	.56647			

Source: Compiled and Computed from Primary Data

The age category in between 25-30 years opined more optimistically than the remaining categories followed by the category 41-45 years. The ANOVA test value and its corresponding significant P-value reveals that there is no significant difference in the opinion of the respondents on HRD practices among the mentioned age categories. The graphical representation is shown as a box plot in figure 5.24. This indicates that the null hypothesis (H_{08}) that Overall level of satisfaction on HRD Practices doesn't have significant impact on the employee's performance is rejected and it is proved that there is a significant impact on employee performance.

Figure 5.24: Exhibits boxplot showing comparision of Overall satisfication of respondents on HRD Practices by Age

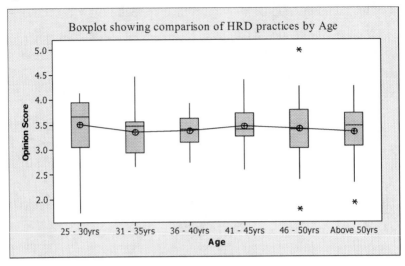

Source: Table 5.43

ANOVA test of employee's opinion on Overall HRD Practices:

H_{09}: HRD practices don't have significant impact on the designation i.e. level of management.

Table 5.44: Shows ANOVA analysis of Dimensions of HRD Practices factor with Designation

Dimensions of HRD Practices	Designation	n	Mean	S.D	F-value	P-value	Decision
Training and Development	Senior Scale Officer	27	3.503	0.6677	0.95	0.388	Not significant
	Junior Scale Officer	37	3.5943	0.5648			
	Low level Manager	68	3.6701	0.4722			
Organizational Structure and Climate	Senior Scale Officer	27	3.5126	0.6818	3.30	0.04	significant
	Junior Scale Officer	37	3.8573	0.5458			
	Low level Manager	68	3.6259	0.5208			
HRD Knowledge and Skills	Senior Scale Officer	27	3.4322	0.6047	1.08	0.342	Not significant
	Junior Scale Officer	37	3.4419	0.6433			
	Low level Manager	68	3.5978	0.6220			

HRD Climate	Senior Scale Officer	27	3.6689	0.5601	0.34	0.709	Not significant
	Junior Scale Officer	37	3.6781	0.5624			
	Low level Manager	68	3.5944	0.5472			
Performance Appraisal	Senior Scale Officer	27	3.6059	0.5620	0.57	0.568	Not significant
	Junior Scale Officer	37	3.6849	0.4839			
	Low level Manager	68	3.5591	0.6274			
Counseling	Senior Scale Officer	27	3.5804	0.6307	0.83	0.44	Not significant
	Junior Scale Officer	37	3.7392	0.6244			
	Low level Manager	68	3.7351	0.4972			
Career Planning and Development	Senior Scale Officer	27	3.1359	0.7760	1.52	0.222	Not significant
	Junior Scale Officer	37	3.4146	0.7007			
	Low level Manager	68	3.4124	0.7382			
Overall HRD Practices	Senior Scale Officer	27	3.6907	0.3992	1.15	0.319	Not significant
	Junior Scale Officer	37	3.7011	0.4561			
	Low level Manager	68	3.5668	0.5408			

Source: Compiled and Computed from Primary Data

Numerous studies have verified that the managerial effectiveness is influenced by both HRD climate and HRD Practices. HRD practices have become an important variable to influence the managerial effectiveness[299].

The above table 5.44 exemplifies the ANOVA test values indicating the association between Designation categories of the employees to the dimension of HRD Practices. The test shows that except for the dimension "Organization structure and climate", the remaining dimensions does not show significant difference among the three categories of the designations which the respondents have opined.

The ANOVA test shows that Training and Development P-value (0.388), HRD Knowledge and Skills P-value (0.342), HRD Climate P- Value (0.709), Performance Appraisal P- Value (0.568), Counseling P-value (0.44), Career Planning and Development P-value (0.222) and Overall HRD Practices P-value (0.319) with the designation categories of the employees does not show significant association. The ANOVA test value (3.30) and its corresponding P- value (0.04) reveal that organization Structure and Climate doesn't show significant difference among the three categories of the designations of the employees. The same is mentioned as a multiple bar diagram in figure 5.25. This indicates that the null hypothesis (H_{09}) that HRD practices don't have significant impact on the designation i.e. level of management is accepted in organizational structure and climate dimension. It proves that organization structure doesn't have a significant association to the designation categories of the employees in APSRTC at managerial level.

Figure 5.25: Exhibits comparison of HRD Practices by designation

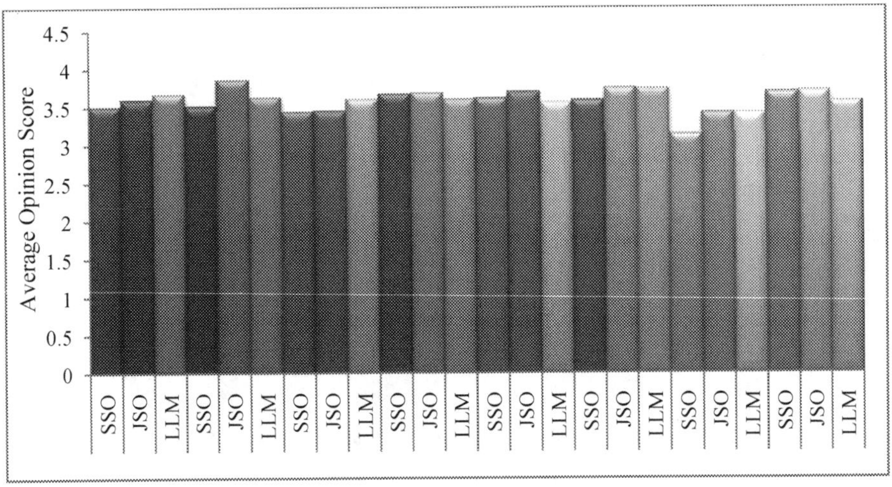

Source: Table 5.44

CONCLUSION

The percentage method of analysis on HRD Practices in APSRTC, Vizianagaram zone reveal as satisfactory. From the Friedman mean rank test of over mean scores of dimensions of the HRD practices, it is understood that counseling practice has attained the first rank and organization structure and climate attained the second rank. However, HRD climate, Training & Development practices attained third and fourth rank. The overall mean score of performance appraisal, HRD Knowledge and skills of the managers, career planning and development have attained lowest ranks i.e. fifth, sixth and seventh ranks respectively, and they indicate further scope for improvement in those practices to attain better performance from the employees of the organization. Further, the ANOVA test reveals that there is no significant association between designation of the employees with that of the organizational structure and climate dimension of the HRD practices implemented in APSRTC, Vizianagaram zone. It is for this reason that APSRTC is providing training to their managerial personnel at the apex level in Hyderabad without taking the organizational climate and structural aspects into consideration. So it is advised to the management of APSRTC, to look into this aspect by developing strategies of taking zonal climatic aspects and organizational aspects into consideration while providing training to their managerial personnel. The organization is advised to study the organizational climatic changes in every zone by conducting surveys every now and then and designing the training program according to their needs, so that it can give better results in the performance of the employees.

HRD practices instead of satisfactory performance is not showing any impact on the financial performance on APSRTC in Vizianagaram zone. In Vizianagaram zone of the corporation, financial records reveal that the zone is in loses of Rs. 53.97 crore. In this zone there are 2900 buses operating to various places and generating an income of Rs. 2.3 crore a day, which is below the expectations of the authorities[300]. To overcome loses and to shore up revenues, APSRTC is experimenting with a lot of options including giving packages to student', traders, pilgrims, ladies, employees etc. In-spite of taking all these measures, APSRTC could not improve in respect of insulating the corporation from loses. As implementation of HRD practices is an expensive method, if the corporation overcomes the prevailing loses, better HRD practices can be executed. As a result employee performance and organizational productivity can be maximized.

CHAPTER - VI

SUMMARY AND SUGGESTIONS

The previous chapter presented the empirical investigation of the HRD practices prevailing in Andhra Pradesh State Road Transport Corporation (APSRTC) – A Case study with reference to the Vizianagaram Zone. The Researcher conducted an exploratory survey of the employees of APSRTC at managerial level to get the clear picture regarding the status of Human Resource Development Practices prevalent in the selected zone of APSRTC. The responses of the employees of the corporation at the managerial level are converted into percentage form to interpret them in easy terms. The hypothesis for study framed on seven different dimensions of HRD Practices and two hypotheses were designed on overall HRD Practices in APSRTC. The present chapter has been prepared to discuss the findings of the study analyzed by the researcher and to offer suggestions for improving the pattern of HRD Practices in State Road Transport Corporation of Andhra Pradesh. The Direction for Future Research in the respective area of concern has also been given at the end.

India is one of the fastest growing economies across the globe and transport sector is one among the different sectors which has been developing at a rapid rate contributing a major share in nation's development. The growing importance of this service sector has attracted the attention of the researcher for selecting the APSRTC for her study. In this present section the researcher deals with the description of the research thesis, findings of the work and suggestions which are being proposed for pursuing the future research in the respective direction. The main objective of the present research study is to identify the HRD Practices prevalent in APSRTC. The researcher conducted an investigation for checking the degree of positivity in the implementation of HRD Practices at managerial level in Vizianagaram zone of APSRTC. The study divides the project into six chapters; A brief outlook of the integral thesis at a glance is presented below to overview the whole work compiled by the researcher.

Chaper I: Introduction to HRD: Conceptual Exposition

Human Resource is the most strategic resource of every organization in the form of its employees. Dynamic people build dynamic organizations. As such organizations continuously ensure that dynamism, competency, motivation, and effectiveness of the employees remain at higher levels.

Researchers, Academicians and organizations have recognized the importance of human resources in the organizations with the advent of science and technology. The development and growth of any organization or nations linked with the development of its people. In today's world this very resource of production has occupied the pivotal significance across the globe. This part is designed to assimilate with the term human resource development. According to Prof. T.V. Rao, HRD is a process by which employees of an organization are continuously helped in a planned way[301].

1. To acquire capabilities (knowledge, perspective, attitudes, values and skills) required to perform tasks or functions associated with their present or future expectations;

2. To develop their general enabling capabilities as individuals so that they are able to discover and utilize their own inner potential for their own or organizational development purpose;

3. To develop an organizational culture where superior subordinate relationships, team work and collaboration among different sub-units are strong and contribute to the organizational health, dynamism and pride of employees.

4. It is primarily concerned with developing employees through training, feedback, and counseling by the senior officers and other developmental officers (Udai Pareek and T.V. Rao)

This definition is found to be the most significant and comprehensive definition of HRD from the organizational point of view. Based on the above definition, it can be concluded that the HRD activities in the organization should begin right from the time the employee joins the organization and continue throughout his/her career regardless of his/her level or position in the organization. However, this definition provides a broad horizon for understanding the terminology of HRD.

In this chapter, the concept of HRD, its theoretical foundations, emergence, etc is discussed along with its historical back ground. There are certain practices through which the HRD operates its functioning. These practices have been discussed and out of it the dimensions of the present work have been selected for developing the questionnaire of the survey. The researcher has also added up the discussions including a talk over the role of government in HRD and its implementation in future. The chapter also observed a critical perception of HRD at all levels without exception.

Chapter II: Literature Review

In this part, the entire spectrum of the study has been discussed. The researcher has presented the literature relating to the field of HRD and transport sector, its different aspects with different perspectives, have been reviewed to know the work patterns, to clarify the concepts and to estimate the research gap for the study. The estimated research gap in review of literature enabled the objective assessment of the study. The objective of the study is to identify the existing HRD Practices and to examine its influence in APSRTC. The scope of the study is designed by the researcher by considering certain focal dimensions of the HRD; in that direction an attempt has been made in that direction to trace out the existing HRD practices in APSRTC. However, if they are available then up to what extent? On what attributes the managerial personnel agree as true, on what attributes they feel as not at all true, on what HRD practices employees feel satisfied and on what HRD practices they are dissatisfied. The perceptions of employees toward the prevailing HRD practices had been tested by the researcher with the help of the hypothesis. The hypothesis for study was framed on seven different dimensions of HRD Practices and two hypotheses were designed on overall HRD Practices in APSRTC. These are the factors that paved way for taking up the research in this direction.

Chapter III: Glimpses of Road Transport Sector in India.

This chapter provides observations from the study and also suggestions for policy prescription for improved operational and performance environment of Road Transport Sector, particularly State Transport Undertakings (STUs) in the direction of turnaround from the observation scenario.

❖ Summary of observations:

In the early fifties, Road Transport primarily served as a mode complimentary to the railways. However in course of time it became competent with the railways. The share of Road Transport to the GDP in 2008-09 is at 4.8 percent[302].

Road Transportation plays a pivotal role in India in bringing about greater mobility both within and between rural and urban areas through increased mobility it also contributes immensely to social, economical and cultural development of different regions of the country. India's road network consists of 70,934 kms national highways, 154522 kms of State Highways, Major and other District Roads constitute 3417000 kms. National Highways comprise 1.7 percent of total length of the road and carry over 40 percent of total traffic across the length and breadth of the country.

Roads are the dominant mode of transportation in India today. They carry almost 90 percent of the countries passenger traffic and 65 percent of its freight with substantial shift from rail to road has been observed over the years (source). Despite such an impressive growth, it is increasingly being recognized that there is a wide gap between the demand for and supply of road transport services both from qualitative as well as quantitative perspective.

Srtus Inception:

The Road Transport Act, 1950 enable State governments in India to take initiative to form the Road Transport Corporation under section 3 of the Act. APSRTC is one among the established SRTUs which were established under the Act. At present, there are 38 public sector undertakings consist of 133823 bus fleet, providing employment to 728,569 people and carry about 252,716.1 passengers. The daily passenger KMS operated by APSRTC is 5368332.6

The STUs in the country are set up under four forms.

i) Departmental Undertakings directly under State Governments
ii) Municipal undertakings owned and controlled by the Municipal Corporations
iii) Companies formed under the Indian Companies Act, 1956.
iv) Road Transport Corporations formed under the Road Transport Act, 1950.

Performance of SRTUs:

The present study brings out the performance of STUs across the Country during 2003-04 to 2012-13. It deals with the overall share of STUs in public transport, their financial position, operational performance together with the analysis of cost components, re-structure of business modes for tapping non traffic revenue sources and monitoring of top management. The study provides clear picture of public transport in India, which helps the policy makers to analyze the performance of STUs and infuse desired improvements in the State Road Transport undertakings in India.

STUs were caught between two opposite corporate objectives - one is commercial considerations and the other is social obligations, which situation leads the STUs to a state of quandary. As a consequence SRTUs ceased to operate in uneconomical routes depriving rural masses of access to various goods, services and facilities. This situation has been exploited by the private operators charging more fares while operating passenger transport buses, cabs and autos to the rural villages. The table 3.2 shows that the percentages of public sector buses are below 50 percent during 1961-2012.

In this context, the study throws light upon the utility of rural bus transport services and makes strategies to turn around the weak SRTUs to give a policy orientation and convince the State Governments of its Constitutional obligation of the need to give all physical support for the continuation of such services.

Physical Performance of SRTUs:

The performance evaluation is broadly divided into two components viz., Physical and Financial. Physical Performance includes fleet utilization, Occupancy Ratio (OR), Staff bus Ratio (SBR), Staff Productivity (Km/Staff/

Day) etc. Financial performances constitute reimbursement of concessional travel benefits, total costs, net profit and loss etc.

Over the years, there has been a steady improvement in the performance of STUs in respect of several parameters like occupancy ratio (OR), staff strength, vehicle bus ratio, fuel efficiency and tyre life. Some parameters of physical performance were discussed to support the above statement as satisfactory.

- ➢ The fleet strength of reporting SRTUs increased from 98090 during 2003-04 to 133823 during 2012-13.
- ➢ The total number of accidents declined from 20445 in 2002-03 to 19464 in 2012-13.
- ➢ Average vehicle productivity increased from 296.2 in 2002-03 to 312.9 in 2012-13.
- ➢ The Occupancy Ratio (OR) was rose from 61.60 during 2002-03 to 68.90 in 2012-13.

Thus, an in depth review of growth and development of the corporation was studied and analyzed with the help of tables, graphs and charts.

Financial Performance of SRTUs:

The study reveals that the financial performance of SRTUs in the period under review is not satisfactory. The performance of STUs in financial terms is dismal, but the burden borne by them is rarely appreciated. In spite of their poor earning, the STUs in general are not neglecting in securing physical infrastructure which is necessary for their performance. Barring few corporations, most of the corporations are in loss making. This loss is being attributed to high M.V. Tax, Concessions, Spiraling fuel prices, Sticky un-remunerative fares, and Cost barring social obligations. The poor financial performance also may be because of policies of the Government and failure in implementing HRD practices at managerial level in STUs is also added to the above attributions.

In this context, some SRTUs like Maharastra State Road Transport Corporation (MSRTC), Banglore Metropolitan Transport Corporation (BMTC), Karnataka State Road Transport Corporation (KSRTC), Odissa State Road Transport Corporation (OSRTC) managed to make profits on the face of all these handicaps. The below discussed aspects will support the claim of researcher on the financial performance of reporting SRTUs.

➢ The total revenue of reporting SRTUs increased from Rs. 1481714.11 crore in 2003-04 to Rs. 4208937.40 crore in 2012-13.

➢ The total cost of reporting SRTUs increased from Rs. 1624981.65 crore in 2003-04 to Rs. 4938131.85 crore in 2012-13.

➢ Loss of reporting SRTUs increased from Rs. 143267.54 crore to Rs. 726966.84 crore in the review period, 2003-04 to 2012-13.

Thus, an in depth review of growth and development of the corporation was reviewed and analyzed with the help of tables, graphs and charts.

Chapter IV: APSRTC – An Overview

In this chapter, the researcher has endeavored to put forward the growth of APSRTC in the background of HRD Practices along with physical and financial aspects of the corporation. The chapter is presented in two sections – Section 'A' & 'B'. The profile, organization structure, physical and financial performance, impact of illegal private operators and impact agitations and state bifurcation were discusses in Section 'A'. The HRD practices in APSRCT – A study of its implication is discussed in Section 'B' covering practices like Training and Development, Performance Appraisal, Incentives etc.

Section A portion of the chapter comprised of the profile of APSRTC with ups and downs in its functioning as service organization since from its inception – 1958. The origin of APSRTC dates back to June 1932, when it was first established as Nizam State Rail and Road transport department (NSR-RTD) – a wing of Nizam State Railways in the erstwhile Hyderabad State with 27 buses and 166 employees. It has become significant especially in the recent times because of the Andhra Pradesh State has a predominantly agriculture – oriented economy, and depends upon road transport for the movement of its agricultural produce, and raw and finished material. To review the present scenario of the APSRTC, the researcher referred the annual reports of APSRTC, Annual reports of performance of STUs – Ministry of Road Transport & Highways – Government of India, Performance indicator reports by CIRT – Pune, ASRTU reports, several articles, and newspapers etc., related to APSRTC

The profile, vision, functional setup, organizational structure, historical background of APSRTC along with physical and financial performance of the corporation is discussed in depth with the help of tables, graphs and charts.

* **Physical performance of APSRTC:** Researcher finds in her study that the physical performance of APSRTC has been improving over the years especially during 2003-04 to 2012-13. Some parameters of physical performance were discussed to support the above statement as satisfactory.

  ➤ The fleet strength of APSRTC increased from 19108 to 22402 during the period under review i.e., 2003- 04 to 2012-13.

  ➤ The Total staff strength increased from 122358 in the year 2003 – 04 to 123871 in the year 2012 – 13.

  ➤ The staff productivity of the Corporation increased to 60 kms/ staff/ day in 2012-13 from 50 kms/ staff/ day in 2003 – 04.

  ➤ The fleet utilization shows a marginal increase of 99.66 percent in 2012-13 compared to that of 99.27percent in 2003-04.

  ➤ Occupancy ratio raised from 60 percent during the 2003 – 04 to 69 percent during the year 2012 -13.

  ➤ High Speed Diesel consumption remained almost at the same level 5.37 KMPL during 2003-04 and 5.15 KMPL during 2012-13.

  ➤ Average tyre life increased from 1.66 KMPL in 2003-04 to 1.71 KMPL in 2012-13.

  ➤ The number of road accidents reduced from 0.10 in 2003-04 to 0.09 in 2012 – 13.

  ➤ Revenue Earning Kilometers increased from 22666.0 lakh kilometers in 2003-04 to 29783.0 lakh kilometers in 2012-13.

Thus, an in depth review of growth and development of the corporation was reviewed and analyzed with the help of tables, graphs and charts.

* **Financial Performance of APSRTC:**

The improved physical performance of APSRTC is not getting translated into positive financial performance. This is being attributed to Government policies, spiraling fuel prices, sticky un-remunerative fares, concessions and cost barring social obligations. State Government is continuously failing to reimburse the concession in fare to the targeted groups like freedom fighters, students, journalists etc., which is due to the corporation as promised earlier. It was about Rs 750 crore[303]. The below discussed aspects will support the claim of researcher on the financial performance of APSRTC.

> Illegal operation of private bus services is mainly a setback for the Corporation's revenue earnings, which are ultimately pushing APSRTC into loses. About 1500 private buses are operating illegally as stage carriers with a tacit support from politicians and some officers of the corporation[304]. Contract carriers, tourist services, cabs, and autos etc., vehicles under the guard of various names are operating on paying routes. The private vehicles are eating away more than 50 percent of profit which may accrue to the corporation. On an average Rs. 2 crore a day, loss is being incurred by APSRTC because of illegal private transport operations[305].

> Increase in fuel cost, time and again because of Central Government Policy is adding to the crisis in financial performance of the corporation during the period under study. Corporations expenditure on fuel is 26.24 percent out of its total cost Rs. 5720.81 crore in 2009-10[306].

> Because of the discriminatory policies of the state and Central Government, APSRTC is paying crores of rupees towards taxes like M.V. Tax, Sales Tax, VAT etc., to the Government. It is evident in the practice that APSRTC is paying 14 percent VAT as against organizations like Transco, Zenco which are paying only 4 percent VAT. Bias of the State and Central Governments was proved with a levy of 23 percent VAT on fuel towards APSRTC, as against 4 percent VAT levied to the airlines and railways.

> The total revenue of APSRTC increased from Rs. 3121 crore in 2003-04 to Rs. 7639.18 crore in 2012-13.

> The total cost of APSRTC increased from Rs. 3163.22 crore in 2003-04 to Rs. 7719.90 crore in 2012-13.

> Loss of APSRTC increased from Rs. 42.02 crore to Rs. 8071.06 crore in the review period, 2003-04 to 2012-13.

> Swell in size of people opting for personalized transport viz., cars, two wheelers.

Thus, an in depth review of growth and development of the corporation was studied and analyzed with the help of tables, graphs and charts.

In section B, the chapter also endeavors to put forward various HRD practices in APSRTC that are in vogue. Human Resource Development according to Armstrong is about enhancing and widening the skills of the employees by training, by helping people to grow within the organization and by enabling them to make better use of their skills and abilities.

In the post liberalization period with several businesses being threatened by global competition, the focus of HRD has shifted to establish direct links with business improvements. If the corporation doesn't survive, there is little it can do to take care of its employees. There will be no career, no rewards, no job rotation, no training and in fact no fresh recruitment. Hence, business survival has become a significant and non-negotiable goal and all HRD efforts have to be re-directed towards business goals. The relevance of HRD is more today than before. Therefore, to meet the above challenges, APSRTC is implementing HRD practices like Recruitment, Selection, Training and Development, Performance Appraisal, Incentive Schemes, and Participative Management. These practices have been discussed in detail in this present chapter 4. To meet the fundamental purpose of HRD – to help the personnel to develop skills and abilities, it is important to take some important modifications in the implementation of its practice to suit the present times.

Chapter V: Data Analysis – HRD Practices in APSRTC – An empirical study with reference to Vizianagaram.

The chapter presents the analysis of the survey conducted by the researcher. The present research is based upon an empirical survey of HRD practices in APSRTC with special reference to Vizianagaram zone. The glimpses of road transport sector in India and profile of APSRTC have been discussed in third and fourth chapters respectively. The total number of employees considered for the survey is 132. The total 132 respondents chosen are managerial and supervisory cadre employees in APSRTC of Vizianagaram zone. The instrument developed for administering the survey was based on the questionnaire. To elicit the information from the respondents, questionnaire was designed by practices of HRD as variables on a five point Likert Scale, with 1 for "Not at all true", 2 for "Not so true", 3 for "partly true", 4 for "True" and 5 for "very much true". The questionnaire was divided into three sections. Section A was designed to obtain demographic information of the respondents.

It covers qualification, age, gender, present designation, Department, monthly salary, length of service, marital status and nature of work. Section B measures the seven most important dimensions, HRD practices like Training and Development, Organizational structure and culture, HRD Knowledge and Skills, HRD climate, Performance Appraisal, Counseling, and Career planning and Development. Section C estimates the overall satisfaction of the respondents towards HRD practices in the organization. In Section C various aspects of HRD practices are measured on a five point Likert Scale, with 1 for "Highly Dissatisfied", 2 for "Dissatisfied", 3 for Neutral", 4 for "Satisfied" and 5 for "Highly Satisfied". On the basis of these three sections in the questionnaire, the HRD practices have been judged in APSRTC and analysis has been made. In the present study, item – wise average values of the HRD Practices in APSRTC are calculated, in order to make the interpretations easy the mean scores have been converted into percentage scores. To test the validity of the results, the researcher used Regression analysis and ANOVA analysis. Whereas, ANOVA analysis is used to test further significance levels of those items in HRD practices that are resulted as significant in regression analysis.

Chapter VI: Findings and Suggestions

It is the present chapter that comprises of the summary of the whole research and deals with the findings, pragmatic recommendations in the form of suitable suggestions. Several auxiliary research directions are also offered by the researcher in detail for future implications on the subject. In a nut shell, this chapter provides an overview of the manner in which the general HRD Practices are prevalent in APSRTC.

FINDINGS OF THE STUDY

The main findings of the study are as follows:

(a)The General Characteristics of employees Covered in the Survey:
> ➤ From analysis it is understood that more than 50 percent of the respondents who are selected for the study have P.G and Ph.D with either technical or Non- technical skills.

> The survey results reveal that the corporation maintains a good ratio of all age groups of employees. It can also be analyzed that proportionate number of managerial staff of age between 25-35 years and above 50 years are employed in APSRTC. So this can be considered as a positive sign in the organization to design and implement HRD Practices with right proportion of young and experienced minds.

> The investigation reveals that female managerial staffs are lower when compared to male staff in APSRTC at managerial and supervisory cadre. So to enhance the prevailing female managerial staff, the organization must give some percentage of priority for women in promotions in addition to the existing women reservation exercised in recruitment.

> The study reveals that most of the respondents in APSRTC entered the organization at lower positions and have grown to higher positions depending on the length of service and educational qualifications. Only few respondents were appointed directly in executive cadre.

> It can be observed from the analysis that majority of 43.9 percent managerial staff in APSRTC belong to non-technical departments. However, corporation consists of both technical and non-technical departments; it has to maintain a good balance of technical and non-technical managerial staff. The study also reveals that the corporation needs more technical staff to perform better on par with their counterparts.

> Majority of 33.3 percent managerial staff salaries fall in between 25000-35000.

> Majority of 37.1 percent of the respondents are having 21-25 years of experience. As the organization under study is an age old organization, it is expected to have more experienced managerial staff. But the survey reveals that a good composition of youth and experienced managerial staff were placed and employed at managerial level in APSRTC.

> A vast majority of 88.6 percent managerial staff are married. So it can be concluded that marriage is not a barrier for employees to perform better. The pictographic representation is shown below.

> It is observed that majority of 46.2 percent employees were engaged in non technical work. Nature of work depends on employees educational

qualification. For an employee to perform well they should be placed in job that suit their educational qualifications and skills. Hence, for an employee to work efficiently educational qualification should match the nature of work performed in the organization.

(b) Dimension wise study findings of Human Resource Development Practices in APSRTC, Vizianagaram zone:

The present study attempts to explore employee's perception of the adequate and effective, implementation of human resource development practices in the APSRTC, Vizianagaram zone.

Dimension 1: Training & Development

In the present study, the table 5.11 reveals that the overall average opinions of the employees reveal that maximum 45.52 percent of the employees felt that the statements on training and development are true and only 5.81 percent employees opined as not at all true. Where as nearly 28.02 percentage of employees opined as partly true, 9.84 percent employees felt as very much true and about 10.80 percent employees felt that training and development practices are not so true.

Dimension 2: Organization structure & climate

A peep into the average opinions of the respondents on organizational structure and climate in table 5.14 demonstrate that maximum of 40.51 percent employees opined as true and minimum of 7.90 percent employees opined as not at all true. However 25.99 percent employees expressed as partly true, 13.05 percent employees felt not so true and about 12.55 percent employees expressed as very much true.

Dimension 3: HRD Knowledge and Skills

An enquiry in this study reveals that maximum of 34.04 percent and minimum of 8.09 percent employees admit that HRD Knowledge and Skills are true and very much true respectively. However, table 5.20 also exhibits that 31.38 percent employees opined as partly true, 15.89 percent opined as not so true and about 10.59 percent employees opined as not at all true.

Dimension 4: HRD climate

In table 5.23, it is evident from average opinions of the respondents on HRD climate that a large chunk of 40.18 percent employees opined as true for the HRD climate in APSRTC and minimun of 9.94 percent employees felt as no at all true. Whereas, 22.96 percent employees opined as patly true, 16.08 percent employees admit as not so true and only 10.85 percent employees expessed as very much true.

Dimension 5: Performance Appraisal

The survey results in table 5.28 that the overall opinion of the respondents was maximum of 44.85 percent employees opine that various performance appraisal practice in APSRTC are true and minimum of 7.38 percent employees opine as very much true. In addition, 23.57 percent employees expressed as partly true, 14.45 percent employees felt as not so true and only 9.75 percent employees opine as not at all true for the Performance Appraisal techniques adopted by the corporation.

Dimension VI: Counseling

The table 5.30 reveals the average opinion on various counseling brushworks executed by APSRTC to improve their employee's performance. The table discloses that maximum of 43.44 percent and minimum of 7.33 percent agree that various counseling brushworks taken up by the corporation are true and not at all true respectively. Whereas, 27.91 percent respondents felt as partly true, 11.23 percent respondents opine as no so true and only 10.06 percent employees expressed as very much true.

Dimension VII: Career Planning and Development

The table 5.34 visualizes the overall opinion of the passengers on the methods of career planning and development adopted by APSRTC. It is clear from the table that maximum of 36 percent employees agree that career planning and Development methods of APSRTC were true and minimum of 6.60 percent employees express as very much true. However, 28.53 percent, 18.37 percent, and 10.53 percent respondents opine that the methods of career planning and development are partly true, not so true, and not at all true respectively.

Overall HRD Practices

The table 5.38 shows that maximam of 49.68 percent employees agree that average percentage of opinion of the respondents on overall satisfaction level of HRD Practices were satisfactory and minimum of 7.95 percent employees express they are highly dissatisfied. Nearly 18.57 percent respondents were as uncertain, 11.99 percent employees are dissatisfied and only 11.83 percent respondents expressed that they are highly satisfied with various HRD practices that are adopted by APSRTC.

Dimension wise mean score ranks have ben assigned to the HRD Practices. The highest-rated dimension has been ranked one, the second highest rated rank two and so on until lowest rated rated dimention that is given rank 7. The mean score of all item for each dimension gives the dimension score and the total of all the means gives the total human resource development score of the organization.

Friedman's Mean Rank test of all the overall mean scores of the dimensions of the HRD practices, it can be understood that counseling practice has attained the highest rank that is one on the basis of 3.704 of human resource development of APSRTC in Vizianagaram zone. Overall mean score of HRD Practice, organization structure and climate is 3.667 with rank two. HRD Climate has attained third rank with 3.630 overall mean score; Training and Development has attained fourth rank with 3.614 overall mean score; Performance Appraisal has attained fifth rank with 3.603 overall mean score; HRD Knowledge and Skills has attained sixth rank with 3.519 overall mean score and Career Planning and Development has attained seventh rank with 3.355 overall mean score. It is evident that the overall mean score of Performance Appraisal Practice, Managers HRD Knowledge and Skills and Career Planning and Development have attained low ranks which indicate further scope for improvement in the organization. The overall mean score of all these organizations show satisfactory HRD Practices were prevailing in the organization at zonal level. The same is supported by the mean score 3.6388 of the overall HRD practices which is satisfactory score.

The regression analysis and further ANOVA test for significance between HRD practices and demographic factors reveals that except training and development practice and organizational structure and climate practice in gender and department respectively, have no significant impact on HRD practice in APSRTC at managerial level at 10 percent level of significance. On the other hand, it is also proved that for all the remaining HRD Practices viz., HRD knowledge and skills, HRD Climate, Performance Appraisal, Counseling, and Career Planning and Development practices dimensions have no significant impact on employee's performance.

Also the ANOVA test for significance between HRD Practices and designations of the employees reveal that except for the dimension "Organization structure and climate" the remaining dimensions does not show significant difference among the three categories of the designations.

➤ The survey results reveal that the managerial staff follow up towards trained employees is neglected, not measured and utilized properly.

➤ It is observed that teamspirit is high in the corporation.

➤ It is identified that from the analysis that corporation fails to encourage the practice of self motivation and commitment.

➤ The study identifies that the employees of the corporation have good initiative and leadership skills.

➤ It is observed that most of the managerial staff despite the experience still lacks enough skills for designing HRD

➤ It is observed that when feedback is given to employees they don't take it seriously and use it for self development.

➤ It is observed that Performance Appraisal system doesn't provide an opportunity for each appraisee to communicate the support he needs from the superiors to perform his job effectively.

➤ Also it is evident that the performance appraisal system failed to assess the employee potential in order to enables him to select and pursue his future careers.

➤ It is observed that corporation provides good number of counseling sessions to its employees for their development.

➤ It is observed that counseling lacks in helping the employees to learn the skills of formulating objectives, framing controlling techniques and the methods.

➤ It is found that Organization fails to provide facility of assessment center to assist employee's potentialities.

➤ It is found that employees in APSRTC are very much dissatisfied about the existing Library facilities in the organization.

➢ Also it is observed that there is some amount of dissatisfaction regarding the Promotion policy and reward system adopted in APSRTC.

➢ As a whole it is identified that the HRD Practices adopted by the corporation are satisfactory.

SUGGESTIONS

Based on the research results and critical analysis, the researcher identified some gaps in the HRD practices in APSRTC. The following suggestions are being given to APSRTC administration to improve its HRD systems and practices so as to enable to improve its administrative strength and also compete in the present day competitive environment. Suggestions are being given specifically on each dimension of HRD so that the administration can think systematically to improve its efficiency. Suggestions are also given in general which will help the organization to have good organizational culture. These suggestions are also reflect the perceptions of sample respondents and their opinion on various dimensions of HRD systems and practices being implemented in APSRTC.

1. Since APSRTC is spending huge amount in providing training to their employees, the course content of the training programme should be framed in consonance with the duties and responsibilities discharged by them as well as to the organizational goals. The content should also take care of the changing technological and behaviour aspects.

2. The study reveals that HRD programs for managerial staff is conducted at apex level, so it is suggested for the corporation to conduct training programs for managers exclusively by taking organization structure, culture and climate of zones into consideration for improving the productivity of the employees.

3. Training and development program needs should be identified periodically by taking latest developmental aspects into consideration. Also necessary interventions should be made while designing the training and development programmes to enhance managerial, technical and non technical skills of the employees.

4. Computer based training technique which does not require face to face interation with human trainer and role plays should be encouraged

to combat the situations like strikes in factory, managing conflict between two parties and scheduling vacation days etc. It is necessary for the management of APSRTC to measure the impact of training and that information can be used in drafting further programmes.

5. The analysis reveals that the corporation fails to encourage the practice of self motivation and commitment. Therefore, it is suggested that corporation must promote employees to try out new methods in accomplishing their tasks and such methods may be rewarded as a token of appreciation.

6. APSRTC should take initiatives to improve HRD Climate at zonal level. This in turn develop employees in building their competencies like leadership skills, open communication and self motivation.

7. As the channels of communication between the departments is not satisfactory in APSRTC, it is advised to ensure proper communication and coordination among various departments for better team spirit and interpersonal relations amongst the employees.

8. Recent HRD trends must be adopted at all levels in the organization and aggressive leadership qualities at the managerial level should be improved to establish leadership pipeline. A strong leadership motivates the people in doing a better job.

9. It is suggested that the corporation should chalk out an action plan to improve the HRD knowledge and skills of the employees by providing awareness programmes at frequent intervals.

10. Managers should be governed to practice team approach to become more creative and innovative at their work.

11. Feedback from the lower level employees, who have direct interaction with the passengers, is suggested to be seriously considered. While making decisions related to the policies of the organization and its goals. So the bottom level employees should also be involved in contributing their ideas while framing the policies of the corporation.

12. The study reveals the establishment of assessment centers at zonal level to appraise employee potential. This information helps in job rotation and job enrichment.

13. New performance appraisal techniques like 720 degree performance appraisal must be adopted so that the gaps in old techniques can be

covered. The 720 degree performance appraisal can be stated as twice the application 360 degree performance appraisal: once when the appraisal is done and the targets are set feedback is measured and the second basing on the feedback given the boss gives tips to achieve the goals. Hence, there is a pre and a post round of feedback is analyzed.

14. In order to avoid bias, the performance Appraisal report should be more transparent and that information can be used for developmental, administrative decision-making, organizational maintenance and documentation.

15. Management of APSRTC should monitor the employee at frequent intervals and evaluate his behavior. If his behavior requires any support, that can be extended by counseling.

16. Managers should be given training on counseling techniques, so that the counseling can be conducted effectively with good results. The Goodie bag and other fun and informative stuff help make a counseling session an occasion for joy, as well as for additional learning.

17. Employees of the corporation must be provided with mentors in order to clarify their work related doubts and to provide feedback about their performance.

18. Managers should conduct periodical training and counseling for behavioural change in drivers and conductors must be organized for better interaction with the passengers and to avoid accidents. Counseling must be given to the drivers to avoid the use of mobile phones and intoxication while driving.

19. Promotion channel should be strengthened at all levels. Individual tasks and targets need to be given and performance based promotions should be encouraged.

20. It is advised that corporation must implement talent management practices right from the recruitment stage onwards. While recruiting employees, care should be taken to hire good talented and skilled employees.

21. Employee welfare measures should be increased so as to motivate employees and maximize productivity of the organization. It is suggested that the children of the deceased employees must be provided employment in RTC as a welfare measure.

22. It is suggested to extend pension benefits to its employees after retirement as in the case of government employees. This action of the corporation board will ensure security to the employees and can result in maximizing the employee productivity.

23. To keep pace with the highly changing fast communicative internet world, MIS (Management Information System) must be further strengthened in the corporation to achieve paperless communication with the help of computerization.

24. Too much pressure regarding targets on employees must be reduced. To overcome this work pressure, refreshments like tea or snakes may be arranged at regular basis to re-energize employees from the routine work.

25. For updating knowledge the managers need to use library, but the library facility is centralized at zonal level only. So it is suggested that need for library at the depot level and digital library may facilitate their easy access and add more convenience for the employees.

26. Bus staff ratio must be maintained properly to reduce the personnel cost of the corporation. APSRTC is advised to implement voluntary retirement scheme to reduce its burden of overstaffing as well as to retain better performing employees rather than old and sick employees.

CONCLUSION OF THE STUDY

The foregoing account of APSRTC reveals that there has been progress from rudiments – Nizam State Rail and Road transport department to full-fledged APSRTC. Viewed from 1932, over this long period, APSRTC has been gradually made more service oriented and responsible to its passengers. With the nationalization of Railways, Road Transport came under the government of Hyderabad State on 1st November, 1951 and functioned as Road Transport Department until taking the present corporation form in 1958. Superintendent was the in charge of the road transport department in the beginning, who was replaced by the present corporation board during 1958-65. In place of divisional setup regional set up was established to overcome the existing inherent defects in the system during 1978-94.

APSRTC registered a steady growth from 27 buses to 22507 buses and 166 employees to 1.23 lakh employees; seen from 1932, it is clear that organizational improvements along with satisfactory operational performance have been made in APSRTC till now. But the fact is that organizational and operational improvements have not been matched with improvements in poor financial performance of the corporation. Training imparted to managers for their skills development as part of HRD practices in APSRTC has shown no impact in arresting financial losses to the corporation. In the present study, the survey results indicate that the HRD practices prevailing in APSRTC are satisfactory. HRD practices inspite of satisfactory performance are not showing any impact on the financial performance of APSRTC in Vizianagaram zone. In the Vizianagaram zone of the corporation, financial records reveal that the zone is in loses to the tune of Rs. 53.97 crore during 2011-12. In this zone there are 2900 buses operating to and from various places and generating an income of Rs. 2.3 crore a day which is way below the expectations of the authorities[307]. To overcome these loses and to shore up revenues, APSRTC is experimenting with various options including giving packages to students', traders, pilgrims, Ladies, employees etc. Inspite of taking all these measures, APSRTC could not show any improvement in respect to insulating the corporation from loses. To offset RTC from making losses, better HRD Practices in tune with the needs of the organization may be useful. Implementation of which may be a costly affair, this action will result in improved performance of the employees combined with organizational productivity. However, the bad performance of APSRTC in financial matters is not due to lapses in HRD practices or operational performance but due to fallacies in both central and state government policies.

With the internationalization of oil prices, the diesel prices are increasing time and again which badly affects the financials of APSRTC. The cancellation of subsidies on diesel to public undertakings by the Ministry Of Oil And Natural Gas, the financial performance of the corporation has come from bad to worst position. This policy of petroleum ministry added an additional burden of Rs. 12 per litre diesel. Hitherto diesel price from oil companies to APSRTC was Rs. 51. Now it was Rs. 63 after the lifting of subsidy on diesel which adds to Rs. 720 crores burden to the corporation per year. Private operators have benefited from the policy of Oil and Natural Gas Ministry.

Illegal operations of private buses are also affecting 30% revenue income of the corporation per year, which adds to the prevailing losses of the corporation. Interest on loan is a major concern for APSRTC than the prevailing loss of Rs. 4200 crore because of the fear that interest will exceed the principle amount over the years to come.

To overcome the grim financial scenario, the corporation should be given independent status in certain areas of decision making such as recruitment of workforce at various levels, fare revision, new buses purchase in place of condemned buses and also take decisions in linking to local retail bunks for purchase of fuel by top-up method in place of bulk purchase. In addition to the above government interference should be reduced to minimum for efficient functioning of the corporation.

SCOPE OF FUTURE RESEARCH

The present study was an empirical study of HRD Practices in APSRTC with reference to Vizianagaram zone. Whereas there could be different aspects as well that could be taken for future research like instead of studying the whole of HRD practices. Research can be done on its distinctive variables like Training and Developmental practices in APSRTC, or a study on organization structure and climate of APSRTC, or a study on Employee Planning and Development Practices in APSRTC etc. The same kind of study could also be undertaken in various SRTUS. Likewise, there are many other variables that could be undertaken for further analysis. As this study has analyzed the managerial perspective of HRD practices of APSRTC at Vizianagaram zone, the other perspective of study could be a comparative analysis of HRD Practices in APSRTC with special reference to Vizianagaram and Vijayawada zones, or with special reference to Hyderabad and Karimnagar zone, etc. Similarly several zones can be taken for comparative analysis. Study of HRD Climate could also be considered for investigation in the same corporation or in different corporations. Several case studies with larger sample size could also be conducted with different aspects in same corporation i.e. APSRTC or this study can be extended to the whole state. Moreover, this same line of study could also be undertaken in future in some other industries.

The conclusion of this research paves the way for several research areas and has the potential of becoming a base for auxiliary research. As the study is empirical in nature, the conclusion has been drawn on the basis of employee's views and perceptions on APSRTC. The results of every research in different industries and different sample of study will end up in diverse results. HRD according to Prof. C.S. Sanker (1984) is "a development oriented planning efforts in the personnel area which is basically concerned with the development of human resources in the organization for improving the existing capabilities and acquiring new capabilities for achievement of the corporate and individual goals". Hence, this chapter also ends up with the discussions and conclusions of the study.

Bibliography

THESIS BOOKS

1. **Arvind Kumar Purohit**, "HRD in Life Insurance Corporation of India (LIC)", Dundelkhand University, Jhansi, 1996.
2. **Atluri Bala Saraswathi**, "Human Resource Development and Organizational effectiveness - A case study of Hindustan Petroleum Corporation Limited (HPCL) Visakha Refinery an Exploratory Study", Andhra university, 2013.
3. **Chaturvedi M C**, "Operational Efficiency of State Road Transport Industry in India: A Case Study of Rajasthan State Road Transport Corporation", Unpublished Thesis, University of Rajasthan, 1979.
4. **Deepakshi Gupta**, "HRD Practices in Information Technology (IT) Industry in India", Guru Nanak Dev University, 2010.
5. **Ganagadhar Rao M**, "Human factor in APSRTC - A focus on conductors", Andhra University, 1987.
6. **Gangappa K**, "Performance Of Urban Passenger Road Transport-A Case Study Of Twin City Services Of Hyderabad And Secunderabad of APSRTC", Ph.D. Thesis, Sri Krishnadevaraya University, Anantapur, 1991.
7. **Kondayya K V N R S**, "HRD in APSRTC – A Study with reference to Managerial Personnel', Andhra University, Visakhapatnam 530003.
8. **Jawahar Suresh U**, "Human Resource Planning in Andhra Pradesh State Road Transport Corporation (APSRTC) – A Study of Karimnagar Zone of Andhra Pradesh", Ph.D. Thesis, Sri Krishnadevaraya University, Anantapur, 2012.
9. **John Wesly G**, "Trade Unions And Politics In The Light Of Economic Reforms: A Socio-Legal Study With Special Reference To Andhra Pradesh

State Road Transport Corporation (APSRTC), A.P, India", Department of Legal Studies, Acharya Nagarjuna University, Guntur, Andhra Pradesh 522510, 17ᵗʰ April, 2013.

10. **Phaniswara Raju B**, "Materials Management in APSRTC", Ph.D Thesis, Sri Krishnadevaraya University, Anantapur, 1986.

11. **Pi-Chi Han**, "Developing Global Workforce: An Integrative Intercultural Effectiveness Model for International Human Resource Development", University of Missouri-St. Louis, 2013

12. **Pollappa J**, "Industrial Relations – Need to have Effective Grievance Handling Machinery – A Case Study of Cuddapah Zone of APSRTC – 2000", Unpublished Thesis, Sri Krishnadevaraya University, Anantapur, A.P., 2000.

13. **Rahi Kishore**, "Performance of Public and Private Transport undertakings -A case study of Punjab Roadways and Ambala Bus Syndicate Pvt. Ltd.", M.Phil dissertation, Punjab University, Chandigarh, 1977.

14. **Sastry**, "Physical and Financial Performance of some State Road Transport Undertakings in India", Ph.D Thesis, Unpublished, JNTU, 1974.

15. **Sheema Tarab**, "HRD in Telecom Industry in India with special reference to the public and private sector companies", Aligarg Muslim University, 2013.

16. **Sheema Tarab**, "Human Resource Development (HRD) in telecom industry in India with special reference to the public and private sector companies", Aligarh Muslim University, 19ᵗʰ September, 2013.

17. **Satyanarayana B** (Ph.D. Guide), "Organizational Climate in State Road Transport Corporation", 2006.

18. **Trinath Babu M**, "Marketing Operations of APSRTC A Study With Reference To Vizianagaram Zone", Department of Commerce and Management Studies, Andhra University, 2012.

19. **Srinivasa Rao S**, "Human Resource Management in Andhra Pradesh State Transport Corporation: A Study on Vizianagaram Zone", Andhra University, 13ᵗʰ May, 2013.

20. **Srinivas D**, "Performance Evaluation of A. P. State Transport Corporation (APSRTC) with a Perceptional focus on turn around", Andhra University, 13ᵗʰ May, 2013.

21. **Vaidya S C**, "Inter-State Road Passenger Transport in India, with special reference to Punjab – A study in Cost Organisation and Operations", Ph.D Thesis, Punjab University, 1983.

22. **Udai S Mehta**, "Research Study of the Road Transport Sector in India", Research submitted to The Ministry of Corporate Affairs, Govt. of India, 25th January, 2012.

23. **Vishnuprasad Nagadevara and Ramanayya, T V**, "Factors Affecting Passenger Satisfaction Levels – A Case Study of Andhra Pradesh State Road Transport Corporation", Indian Institute of Management, Bangalore, India, 2007.

JOURNALS:

1. Advances in Developing Human Resources
2. African Journal of Business Management
3. Asia Pacific Journal of Human Resources
4. Asia Pacific Journal of Research
5. Asia Pacific Journal of Research in Business Management
6. Asian Journal of Business Management
7. Asia-Pacific Journal of Business Administration,
8. Ethiopian Journal of Health Development
9. EuroMed Journal of Business
10. European Journal of Training and Development
11. Gian Jyoti E-Journal
12. Human Resource Development International
13. Human Resource Development Review
14. Indian Journal of Commerce
15. Indian Journal of Social Work,
16. International Business Research
17. International Journal of Human Resource Management,
18. International Journal of Information Technology and Computer Sciences Perspectives
19. International Journal of Innovation, Management and Technology
20. International Journal of Management and Business Studies
21. International Journal of Marketing and Management Research

22. International Journal of Organizational Behaviour & Management Perspectives
23. International Journal of Public Sector Management
24. International Journal of Training and Development
25. International Journals of Marketing and Technology
26. Journal of European Industrial Training
27. Journal of Health Management
28. Journal of Information Science
29. Journal of Managerial Psychology
30. Journal of NIMHANS
31. Journal of Public Transportation
32. Journal of Research In Commerce & Management
33. Journal of Social Science
34. Journal of Transport Management
35. Osmania Journal of Management
36. Paripex - Indian Journal of Research
37. Prime Journal of Social Science
38. The IUP Journal of Operations Management
39. The Journal of Indian Management & Strategy
40. The Journal of Institute of Public Enterprise
41. The Journal of Knowledge Economy & Knowledge Management,
42. Universal Journal of Management and Social Sciences

TEXT BOOKS

1. **Agarwal A K**, "Analysis of Financial Statement Jaipur: University Book House Pvt, Ltd", 1992.

2. **Aswathappa K**, "HR and personnel Management, Text and Cases", Third Edition., Tata Mc Graw Hill Publishing Company Limited, New Delhi, 1984.

3. **Bhatia S K**, "Training and Development Concepts and Practices, Emerging Developments, Challenges and Strategies in HRD, Deep & Deep Publication Private Ltd, New Delhi.

4. **Deb T**, "Human Resource Development Theory and Practice", Ane Books Pvt., LTD, New Delhi.

5. **Desimone L and Harris**, "Human Resource Development", The Dryden Press, New York, 1998.

6. **Elig Ginzberg Man and His worm**, edited by Dale S Beach, "Managing People at work", Macmillan Publishing Co., Inc., New York, 1980,

7. **Florence M Stone**, "Coaching, Counseling And Mentoring: How To Choose & Use The Right Technique To Boost Employee Performance", AMACOM Books, 2nd Edition, Newyork, 2007.

8. **Gibb S J**, "Human Resource Development: Processes, Practices and Perspectives", Palgrave Macmillan, Basingstoke, 2011.

9. **Gundam Rajeswari**, "Public Sector Performance of State Road Transport Corporation: A Case Study of Andhra Pradesh", APH, 1998.

10. **Gupta S and Gupta S**, "HRD Concepts and Practices" Deep and Deep Publications Pvt. Ltd. New Delhi, 2008.

11. **Jane Weightman**, "Managing Human Resources", Amazon Publication, UK, 30th May, 2005. (www.amazon.co.uk.)

12. **Khurana A, Khurana P, and Sharma H L**, "Human Resource Management", V.K. Enterprises, New Delhi, 2009.

13. **Krishnaveni, R.**, "Human Resource Development-a researcher's Perspective", Excel Books.

14. **Kulshresta D K**, "Management of State Road Transport in India", Mittal Publications, New Delhi, 1989.

15. **Lincoln, Yvonna S, Lynham and Susan A**, "Criteria for Assessing Good Theory in Human Resource Development and Other Applied Disciplines from an Interpretive Perspective", Krieger Publishing, 2007.

16. **Manorama** Year Book, 2012, 2013.

17. **Megginson Leon C**, "Personnel And Human Resource Administration", 1977.

18. **Menta M M**, "Human Resource Development planning (with special reference to Asia and Far East)", The Macmillan Co. of India, New Delhi, 1976.

19. **Miller V A**, "The History of Training" in R. L. Cruig (Ed), Training & Development Handbook, McGraw Hill, New York, 1967.

20. **Myrdal Gunnar**, Asian Drama, Penguin Books Ltd., Middlesex, 1968.

21. **Nadler L and Nadler**, "Developing Human Resource", San Francisco, Jossey – Boss, 1969.

22. **Nadler L**, "Developing Human Resource and (Ed) Learning Concept", University Associates, San Diego, 1979.

23. **Pareek and Rao**, "Pioneering HRD; the L & T system, Amedabad, Academy of HRD", 1988.

24. **Ramanadham V V**, "Nationalized Road Services in Hyderabad", Orient Publishing Company, Madras, 1955.

25. **Rao T V and E Abraham S J**, "HRD Climate in Organization", 2008.

26. **Rao T V**, "HRD Audit: Evaluating the HR Function for Business Improvement", Sage Publications, 1999.

27. **Rao, T. V. and Abraham S J**, "Recent Experiences in HRD", Oxford and IBH Publishing Co.Pvt. Ltd. New Delhi, reprinted, 1989.

28. **Rensis likert**, "The Human Organisation: Its Management and Value", McGraw Hill, Kogha Kusha, Tokyo, 1996.

29. **Ritva Laakso-Manninen and Riitta Viitala**, "Competence management and human resource development-A theoretical framework for understanding the practices of modern Finnish organizations", HAAGA-HELIA Publication, 2007.

30. **Satyanarayana J**, "The working of the Andhra Pradesh State Road Transport Corporation", CESS and Concept Publishing Co., New Delhi, 1985.

31. **Saxena A S**, "Financial Management in SRTC's", Kaniska Publishers and Distributers, New Delhi, 1994.

32. **Singh S K**, "Human resource Development", Atlantic Publishers Pvt. Ltd., New Delhi, 2008.

33. **Srinivasulu Y**, "Marketing of Transport Services-A Case Study of Passenger Road Transport Services by Andhra Pradesh State Road Transport Corporation", Service Marketing in India.

34. **Sudarsanam Padam**, "Changing Imperatives of HRD: A Case of Passenger Road Transport Industry", in Rao T V et. al.(Eds.), "HRD in the New Economic Environment", Tata McGraw Hill, New Delhi, 1994.

35. **Sudarsanam Padam**, 'Bus Transport in India', Ajanta Publications, Delhi, 1990.

36. **Swarajayalakshmi C**, "Human Resource Development", Sultan Chand and Sons, New Delhi.

37. **Venkata Ratnam C S**, "Economic Liberalization and Transformation of Industrial Relations Policies in India" in Verma A, Kochan T A and Lansbury R D (eds) "Employment Relations in the growing Asian Economics, London: Routledge, 1995.

REPORTS

APSRTC Physical Audit Annual Reports 2009-10 to 2011-12.
APSRTC Physical Performance Annual Reports 2003-04 to 2011-12
Ministry of Roads and Highways Annual Reports 2003-04 to 2011-12

WEBSITES

www.ehow.com
cistupiisc.ernet.in
en.wikipedia.org
www.ap.gov.in
www.apsrtc.gov.in
www.businessdictionary.com
www.morth.nic.in
www.postnoon.com
www.siamonline.in
www.wikipedia.com
www.xavier.edu

NEWS PAPERS

Andhra Bhoomi Daily News Paper, 2011, 2012, 2013, 2014
Business Line Daily News Paper, 2011, 2012, 2013, 2014
Eenadu Daily News Paper, 2011, 2012, 2013, 2014
The Hindu Daily News Paper, 2011, 2012, 2013, 2014

VISUAL MEDIA

TV9 – Discussions' on APSRTC
CVR News - Discussions' on APSRTC

Annexure

QUESTIONNAIRE

Dear sir/madam,

This is to inform you that I am pursuing Doctor of philosophy (Ph.D) under the supervision of Prof. M.Sandhya sridevi, Department of Commerce and Management Studies, Andhra University, on the topic entitled "HRD practices in APSRTC – A case study in Vizianagaram Zone of A.P".

Hence, I request you to kindly share and express your views through this schedule for enabling me to consolidate the report. Further, the information gathered is meant for academic purpose and high confidentiality will be maintained.

Thanking you sir,

Yours sincerely,

(Santosha pavani tammineni)

HRD Practices in APSRTC
(A case study in Vizianagaram Zone of A.P)

A. Personal information:

1) Name (optional):
2) Qualification:
   i. Graduation
   ii. Post graduation
   iii. Pl. specify if any other_____

3) Age (years):
        i. 25-30   ii. 31-35   iii. 36-40
        iv. 41-45   v. 46-50   vi. above 50

4) Gender: i. Male   ii. Female

5) Present designation/grade:

6) Department:

7) Monthly salary(approximately):

8) Length of service(in years):
        i. 0-10   ii. 11-15   iii. 16-20
        iv. 21-25   v. 26-30   vi. Above 30

9. Marital status:
        i. married   ii. Unmarried   iii. Widowed   iv.Divorsed

10) Nature of your work:
        i. Technical   ii. Non technical   iii. Both

B. Perception on HRD practices:

Please indicate your response on the HRD practices followed in your organization by rating each statement using the following five point scale.

5-very much True;   4-True;   3-Partly True;

2-Not so true;   1-Not at all true

1. Training and development

SL. NO	STATEMENT	VERY MUCH TRUE	TRUE	PARTLY TRUE	NOT SO TRUE	NOT AT ALL TRUE
1.	employees perception towards training is satisfactory					
2.	Managers are sponsored to training programs on the basis of carefully identified training needs					
3.	Management recognizes performers and creates facilities for non performers to improve					
4.	Organizations training programs are evaluated and improved upon every year					
5.	Significant improvement is observed in performance of the managers after training					
6.	Job rotation is practiced widely to help people develop their potential in new areas					
7.	Change in the output of the employees returning from training is measured and utilized					

2. Organizational structure and climate

SL. NO	STATEMENT	VERY MUCH TRUE	TRUE	PARTLY TRUE	NOT SO TRUE	NOT AT ALL TRUE
1.	De-centralization of authority is satisfactory					
2.	Management philosophy of the organization helps to utilize human resource effectively					
3.	Employees are encouraged to participate in decision-making and formulation of organizational goals					
4.	Encourages the practice of self motivation and commitment					
5.	Allows open and free flow of communication					
6.	Team sprit is high in the organization					
7.	Officers maintain good human relations with their employees					

3. HRD Knowledge and Skills

SL. NO	STATEMENT	VERY MUCH TRUE	TRUE	PARTLY TRUE	NOT SO TRUE	NOT AT ALL TRUE
1.	Employees have knowledge on HRD practices					
2.	Managers have enough skills for designing HRD					
3.	Employees have leadership and initiative skills					

4. HRD climate

SL. NO	STATEMENT	VERY MUCH TRUE	TRUE	PARTLY TRUE	NOT SO TRUE	NOT AT ALL TRUE
1.	The top management of this organization goes out of its way to make sure that employees enjoy their work					
2.	The top management believes that human resources are most valuable resource and that they have to be treated more humanly					
3.	The top management is willing to invest a considerable part of their time and other resources to ensure development of employees					
4.	People lacking competence in their jobs are helped to acquire competence rather than being left unattended					
5.	The top management of the organization makes efforts to identify and utilize the potential of employee					
6.	Employees are encouraged to experiment with new methods and try out creative ideas					
7.	Weakness of employees are communicated to them in a non- threatening way					
8.	When feedback is given to employees they take it seriously and use it for development					

5. Performance Appraisal

SL. NO	STATEMENT	VERY MUCH TRUE	TRUE	PARTLY TRUE	NOT SO TRUE	NOT AT ALL TRUE
1.	It has scope for correcting the bias or reporting officer through a review process					
2.	The system provides for assessment of employee potential and enables him to select and pursue his future careers					
3.	The system provides direction regarding potentials of the employees and helps the organization to plan for career and succession development					
4.	The system has scope for helping each employee to discover his potential					
5.	Provides an opportunity for each appraisee to communicate the support he needs from the superiors to perform his job effectively					
6.	Performance appraisal system in the organization is transparent					

6. Counseling

SL. NO	STATEMENT	VERY MUCH TRUE	TRUE	PARTLY TRUE	NOT SO TRUE	NOT AT ALL TRUE
1.	Enriches the understanding capabilities of the counselee regarding the possible short comes and enables to take precautions					
2.	Helps to acquire new technical, managerial and behavioral skills and knowledge in the course of discussions					
3.	Helps in learning the skills of formulating objectives, framing controlling techniques and the methods of self control					

7. Career Planning and Development

SL. NO	STATEMENT	VERY MUCH TRUE	TRUE	PARTLY TRUE	NOT SO TRUE	NOT AT ALL TRUE
1.	Organization disseminates career option information					
2.	Organization provides facility of assessment center to assist employees potentialities					
3.	Organization provides career counseling and development workshops for career development					

C. Overall level of satisfaction in the organization through HRD practices:

Please give your assessment by rating the following statements using the following five point scale.

HS-Highly satisfied   **S**-Satisfied   **UC**-Uncertain
DS-Dissatisfied   **HD**-Highly Dissatisfied

SL. NO	STATEMENT	HS	S	UC	DS	HD
1.	Learning environment in the organization					
2.	Training and Development practices					
3.	Promotion policy and reward system					
4.	Working conditions in the organization					
5.	Compensation and welfare facilities					
6.	Job description, role clarity are well defined					
7.	Information sharing amongst employees					
8.	Employee participation in finalization of tasks and targets					
9.	Career planning opportunities					
10.	Co-operation among superiors, peers and sub-ordinates					
11.	Your association with the organization					
12.	Work culture in the organization					
13.	Leadership at different levels in the organization					
14.	HRIS facilitates HRD practices					
15.	Library facilities in the organization					

Please feel free to give your suggestions on the policies to be taken to improve your organizational excellence keeping in view the changing business environment:

Thank You for your kind cooperation

Endnotes

1   Rensis likert, "The Human Organisation: Its Management and Value", McGraw Hill, Kogha Kusha, Tokyo, P.1, 1996.

2   Megginson Leon C, "Personnel And Human Resource Administration", P. 4, 1977.

3   Menta M M, "Human Resource Development planning (with special reference to Asia and Far East)", The Macmillan Co. of India, New Delhi, P.1, 1976.

4   Galbraith J K, "Men and Capital", Saturday Evening Post, P. 32, 5th March, 1960.

5   Nadler L, "Developing Human Resource and (Ed) Learning Concept", University Associates, San Diego, 1979.

6   Khan M N, "HRD in Modern Technological Structure", Indian Journal of Commerce, XL No. 150-51, P.83, 1987.

7   Gupta S and Gupta S, "HRD Concepts and Practices" Deep and Deep Publications Pvt. Ltd. New Delhi, 2008.

8   Singh S K, "Human resource Development", Atlantic Publishers Pvt. Ltd., New Delhi, 2008.

9   http://www.ehow.com/about_5417857_introduction-hrd.html

10 Ibid

11 Kelly D, "Dual Perceptions of HRD: Issues for Policy: SME's, Other Constituencies, and the Contested Definitions of Human Resource Development", 2001.

12 Xavier University HRD Program. http://www.xavier.edu/hrd

13 Desimone L and Harris, "Human Resource Development", The Dryden Press, New York, 1998.

14   Miller V A, "The History of Training" in R. L. Cruig (Ed), Training & Development Handbook, McGraw Hill, New York, PP. 3-18, 1967.

15   Ibid.

16   Balasubramanian A G, "Evolution of Personnel Function in India: A re-examination.(part I) Management and Labour Studies, Vol. 19, No. 4, PP. 197-210, 1994.

17   Balasubramanian A G, "Evolution of Personnel Function in India: A re-examination.(part II) Management and Labour Studies, Vol. 20, No. 1, PP. 5-14, 1995.

18   Aswathappa K, "HR and personnel Management, Text and Cases", Third Edition., Tata Mc Graw Hill Publishing Company Limited, New Delhi, P.16, 1984.

19   Pareek and Rao, "Pioneering HRD; the L & T system, Amedabad, Academy of HRD", P. 24, 1988.

20   Ashok Kumar, "Human Resource Development: An Interdisciplinary Approach", (Ed) Annual Publications, New Delhi, Vol. 1, 1991.

21   Venkata Ratnam C S, "Economic Liberalization and Transformation of Industrial Relations Policies in India" in Verma A, Kochan T A and Lansbury R D (eds) "Employment Relations in the growing Asian Economics, London: Routledge, 1995.

22   Ramaswamy E A and Schiphorst F B, "Human Resource Management, Trade Union and Empowerment: Two Cases from India", International Journal of Human Resource Management, Vol. 11, No. 4, 2000

23   Rao, T. V. and Abraham S J, "Recent Experiences in HRD", Oxford and IBH Publishing Co.Pvt. Ltd. New Delhi, PP. 20-42, reprinted, 1989.

24   Krishnaveni, R., "Human Resource Development-a researcher's Perspective", Excel Books, PP. 5-15.

25   Kcith Sission, editor, International Journal of Human Resources Management – IJHRM, Harvard, United States, November, 1996.

26   Jane Weightman, "Managing Human Resources", Amazon Publication, UK, P. 99, 30th May, 2005. (www.amazon.co.uk.)

27   Rao T V, "HRD Audit: Evaluating the HR Function for Business Improvement", Sage Publications, P. 35, 1999.

28   Khurana A, Khurana P, and Sharma H L, "Human Resource Management", V.K. Enterprises, New Delhi, 2009.

29 Bhatia S K, "Training and Development Concepts and Practices, Emerging Developments, Challenges and Strategies in HRD, Deep & Deep Publication Private Ltd, New Delhi.

30 Nadler L and Nadler, "Developing Human Resource", San Francisco, Jossey – Boss, 1969.

31 Adelman I, "The Role of Government in Economic Development", Working Paper No. 890, California Agricultural Experiment Station Giannini Foundation of Agricultural Economics.

32 Swarajayalakshmi C, "Human Resource Development", Sultan Chand and Sons, P.5, New Delhi.

33 Sheema Tarab, "Human Resource Development (HRD) in telecom industry in India with special reference to the public and private sector companies", Aligarh Muslim University, 19th September, 2013.

34 Alexander E Ellinger and Andrea D Ellinger, "Leveraging human resource development expertise to improve supply chain managers' skills and competencies", European Journal of Training and Development, Vol. 38 Issue 1/2, PP. 118 – 135, 2014.

35 Anushree Banerjee, "Human Resource Development in Tourism Industry in India: A Case Study of Jet Airways India Ltd", Journal of NIMHANS, Vol. 1, Issue 1, January, 2014.

36 Peter McGraw, "A Review of Human Resource Development Trends and Practices in Australia Multinationals, Locals, and Responses to Economic Turbulence", Advances in Developing Human Resources, Vol. 16, No. 1, PP. 92-107, February, 2014.

37 Clíodhna MacKenzie, Thomas N Garavan and Ronan Carbery, "The Global Financial and Economic Crisis Did HRD Play a Role?", Advances in Developing Human Resources, Vol. 16, No. 1, PP. 34-53, February, 2014.

38 Maura Sheehan, "Investment in Training and Development in Times of Uncertainty", Advances in Developing Human Resources, Vol. 16, No. 1, PP. 13-33, February, 2014.

39 Jie Ke and Greg G Wang, "China's Ethical Dilemmas Under Globalization and Uncertainty Implications for HRD", Advances in Developing Human Resources, Vol. 16, No. 1, PP. 74-91, February, 2014.

40 Saul Carliner, "Human Performance Technology and HRD", New Horizons in Adult Education and Human Resource Development, Vol. 26, Issue 1, PP. 33–41, Winter, 2014.

41 Dr Leigh Burrows, "Spirituality at Work: The Contribution of Mindfulness to Personal and Workforce Development", Workforce Development, PP. 303-316, 2014.

42 Dr. Jim Stewart and Dr. Sally Sambrook, "Critical Perspectives on Workforce Development", Workforce Development, PP. 329-349, 2014.

43 Melinde Coetzee and Dries (A.M.G.) Schreuder, "Career Anchors as a Meta-Capacity in Organizational Career Development", Psycho-social Career Meta-capacities, PP 139-154, 2014

44 Atluri Bala Saraswathi, "Human Resource Development and Organizational effectiveness - A case study of Hindustan Petroleum Corporation Limited (HPCL) Visakha Refinery an Exploratory Study", Andhra university, 2013.

45 Asad Abbas and Ali Madni, "A Business Process Approach to Human Resource Development", International Journal of Academic Research in Business and Social Sciences, Vol. 3, No. 1, January 2013.

46 Sheema Tarab, "HRD in Telecom Industry in India with special reference to the public and private sector companies", Aligarg Muslim University, 2013.

47 Bhaskar Purohit and R K Verma, "A Study of Human Resource Development Climate in Government Health Centres in India", Journal of Health Management, Vol. 15, No. 3, PP. 431-443, September, 2013.

48 Hee Sung Lee and Jeong Rok Oh, "A Conceptual Model for Community of Practice and Its Implications for Human Resource Development Practice", Learning and performance quartely, Vol. 2, No. 1, 2013.

49 Dan Li, "Study on the Strategy of Young Retirees' Human Resource Development", International Academic Workshop on Social Science, IAW-SC-13, September, 2013.

50 Pi-Chi Han, "Developing Global Workforce: An Integrative Intercultural Effectiveness Model for International Human Resource Development", University of Missouri-St. Louis, 2013

51 Dr. Rinku Sanjeev, Dr. Anita Singh and Dr. Sanjeev Kumar Singh, "Training And Development In FMCG Company: An Investigation",

International Journal of Organizational Behaviour & Management Perspectives, Vol 2, No. 4, 2013.

52 Deepakshi Gupta and Neena Malhotra, "Human Resource Development Climate in Information Technology Organizations", Gian Jyoti E-Journal, Vol. 2, Issue 3, July – Septemper, 2012.

53 Daniel Eseme Gberevbie, "Impact Of Human Resource Development and Organizational Commitment on Financial Sector Employees In Nigeria", VERSITA, Scientific Annals of the Alexandru Ioan Cuza, University of Iași Economic Sciences, Vol. 59, No. 2, PP. 29-41, 2012.

54 Akintayo DI, "Human resource development programmes and workers' job security in work organizations in Nigeria", Prime Journal of Social Science (PJSS), Vol. 1, No. 2, PP. 19-26, 19th June, 2012.

55 Gary N Mc Lean, Min-Hsun (Christine) Kuo, Nadir N.Budhwani and Busaya Virakul, "Capacity Building for Societal Development: Case Studies in HRD", 17th May, 2012.

56 Clíodhna A MacKenzie, Thomas N Garavan and Ronan Carbery, "Through the looking glass: challenges for human resource development (HRD) post the global financial crisis – business as usual?", Taylor & Francis Journal, Vol. 15, Issue 3, PP. 353-364, 2012.

57 Tami S Moser and Michael Williams, "Considering A Market-Driven Human Resource Development Approach in Small Business: Succession Management Systems for Strategic Continuity and Excellence", Paper for the 2012 Conference, C12040.

58 Peter Stokes and Ewan Oiry, "An Evaluation of the Use of Competencies In Human Resource Development – A Historical And Contemporary Recontextualisation", EuroMed Journal of Business, Vol. 7, Issue 1, PP.4 – 23, 2012.

59 Thumwimon Sukserm and Yoshi Takahashi, "Self-Efficacy as A Mediator Of The Relationships Between Learning And Ethical Behavior From Human Resource Development In Corporate Social Responsibility Activity", Asia-Pacific Journal of Business Administration, Vol. 4, Issue 1, PP. 8 – 22, 2012.

60 Nada Trunk Sirca, Katarina Babnik and Kristijan Breznik, "The Relationship between Human Resource Development System and

Job Satisfaction", Management, Knowledge Learning, International conference, 2012.

61 Julie Gedro, Frances Mercer and Jody D. Lodice, "Recovered Alcoholics and Career Development: Implications for Human Resource Development", Human Resource Development Quarterly, 19th March, 2012.

62 Ellen Scully Russ, "Human resource development and sustainability: beyond sustainable organizations", Human Resource Development International journal, Vol. 15, Issue 4, PP. 399-415, 13th August, 2012.

63 Greg G Wang and Judy Y Sun, "Theorizing Comparative Human Resource Development: A Formal Language Approach", Sage Journal, 2012.

64 Namhee Kim, "Toward the Use of Human Resource Development for Societal Development Issues, Challenges, and Opportunities", Vol. 14, No. 3, PP. 345-354, 2012.

65 Muhammad Tariq Khan, Naseer Ahmed Khan and Khalid Mahmood, "An Organizational Concept of Human Resource Development – How Human Resource Management Scholars View 'HRD' - Literature Review", Universal Journal of Management and Social Sciences, Vol. 2, No. 5, May, 2012.

66 Vilmante Kumpikaite and Kestutis Duoba, "The Role of Acculturization for Cross-Cultural Human Resource Development", The Journal of Knowledge Economy & Knowledge Management, Vol. 7, 2012.

67 James M. Kilika, Peter O K'Obonyo, Martin Ogutu and Justus M Munyoki, "Towards Understanding the Design of Human Resource Development Infrastructures for Knowledge Intensive Organizations: Empirical Evidence from Universities in Kenya", The Africa Management Review is published quarterly, Department of Business Administration, School of Business, University of Nairobi Vol. 2, No. 2, 2012.

68 Sylvia N Naris and Wilfred I Ukpere, "Evaluation of Human Resource Development And Training At A Higher Educational Institution in Namibia', African Journal of Business Management Vol. 6, No. 49, PP. 11859-11864, 12th December, 2012.

69 Akinyemi Benjamin, "Human Resource Development Climate as a Predictor of Citizenship Behaviour and Voluntary Turnover Intentions in the Banking Sector", International Business Research, Vol. 5, No.1, 2012.

70 Gibb S J, "Human Resource Development: Processes, Practices and Perspectives", Palgrave Macmillan, Basingstoke, 2011.

71 Myungweon Choi and Wendy E A Ruona, "Individual Readiness for Organizational Change and Its Implications for Human Resource and Organization Development", Human Resource Development Review, Vol. 10, No. 1, PP. 46-73, March, 2011.

72 Raavi Radhika, "HRD Processes at Singareni Collieries Company Limited Kothagudem (A.P)", International Journal of Innovation, Management and Technology, Vol. 2, No. 1, February, 2011.

73 Deepakshi Gupta, "HRD Practices in Information Technology (IT) Industry in India", Guru Nanak Dev University, 2010.

74 Thomas N Garavan and David McGuire, "Human Resource Development and Society: Human Resource Development's Role in Embedding Corporate Social Responsibility, Sustainability, and Ethics in Organizations", Advances in Developing Human Resources, Vol. 12, No. 5, PP. 487-507, October, 2010.

75 Peter Kuchinke K, "Human Development As A Central Goal For Human Resource Development", Human Resource Development International, Vol. 13, Issue 5, PP. 575-585, 2010.

76 Thomas G Reio Jr and Rajashi Ghosh, "Antecedents and outcomes of workplace incivility: Implications for human resource development research and practice", Human Resource Development Quarterly, Vol. 20, Issue 3, PP. 237–264, Autumn (Fall), 2009.

77 Ronald L Jacobs and Yoonhee Park, "A Proposed Conceptual Framework of Workplace Learning: Implications for Theory Development and Research in Human Resource Development", Human Resource Development Review, Vol. 8, No. 2, PP. 133-150, June, 2009.

78 Laura L Bierema, "Critiquing Human Resource Development's Dominant Masculine Rationality and Evaluating Its Impact", Human Resource Development Review, Vol. 8, No. 1, PP. 68-96, March, 2009.

79 Mustapha M Achoui, "Human resource development in Gulf countries: an analysis of the trends and challenges facing Saudi Arabia", Human Resource Development International, Vol. 12, Issue 1, PP. 35-46, 2009.

80 Irakli Gvaramadze, "Human Resource Development Practice: The Paradox of Empowerment and Individualization", Human Resource Development International, Vol. 11, Issue 5, PP. 465-477, 2008.

81 Alan Clardy, "The strategic role of Human Resource Development in managing core competencies", Human Resource Development International, Vol. 11, Issue 2, PP. 183-197, 2008.

82 Dingie HCJ van Rensburg, Francois Steyn, Helen Schneider and Les Loffstadt, "Human Resource Development And Antiretroviral Treatment In Free State Province, South Africa", Human Resources for Health, Vol. 15, No. 6, 28th July 2008.

83 Thomas N Garavan and Alma Mc Carthy, "Collective Learning Processes and Human Resource Development", Advances in Developing Human Resources, Vol. 10, No. 4, PP. 451-471, August, 2008.

84 Tara Fenwick and Laura Bierema, "Corporate Social Responsibility: Issues For Human Resource Development Professionals", International Journal of Training and Development, Vol. 12, Issue 1, PP. 24–35, March, 2008.

85 Greg G Wang and Richard A Swanson, "Economics and Human Resource Development: A Rejoinder", Human Resource Development Review, Vol. 7, No. 3, PP. 358-362, September, 2008.

86 Jens Rowold, "Multiple Effects of Human Resource Development Interventions", Journal of European Industrial Training, Vol. 32 Issue 1, PP. 32 – 44, 2008.

87 Brian Nicholson and Sundeep Sahay, "Human Resource Development Policy In The Context Of Software Exports Case Evidence From Costa Rica", Progress in Development Studies, Vol. 8, No. 2, PP. 163-176, April, 2008.

88 Alan Clardy, "Human Resource Development and the Resource-Based Model of Core Competencies: Methods for Diagnosis and Assessment", Human Resource Development Review, Vol. 7, No. 4, PP. 387-407, December, 2008.

89 Lynn Perry Wooten and Erika Hayes James, "Linking Crisis Management and Leadership Competencies: The Role of Human Resource Development", Advances in Developing Human Resources, Vol. 10, No. 3, PP. 352-379, June, 2008.

90 Holly M Hutchins and Jia Wang, "Organizational Crisis Management and Human Resource Development: A Review of the Literature and Implications to HRD Research and Practice", Advances in Developing Human Resources, Vol. 10, No. 3, PP. 310-330, June, 2008.

91 Anne H Reilly, "The Role of Human Resource Development Competencies in Facilitating Effective Crisis Communication", Advances in Developing Human Resources, Vol. 10, No. 3, PP. 331-351, June 2008.

92 Xiaohui Wang and Gary N McLean, "The Dilemma of Defining International Human Resource Development", Human Resource Development Review, Vol. 6, No. 1, PP. 96-108, March, 2007.

93 Peter Holland, Cathy Sheehan and Helen De Cieri, "Attracting and retaining talent: exploring human resources development trends in Australia', Human Resource Development International, Vol. 10, Issue 3, PP. 247-262, 2007.

94 Abdullah H, Rose R C and N Kumar, "Human resource development strategies: The Malaysian scenario", Journal of Social Science, Vol. 3, Issue 4, PP. 213-222, 2007.

95 Lincoln, Yvonna S, Lynham and Susan A, "Criteria for Assessing Good Theory in Human Resource Development and Other Applied Disciplines from an Interpretive Perspective", Krieger Publishing, 2007.

96 Ritva Laakso-Manninen and Riitta Viitala, "Competence management and human resource development-A theoretical framework for understanding the practices of modern Finnish organizations", HAAGA-HELIA Publication, 2007.

97 Salvatore Parise, "Knowledge Management and Human Resource Development: An Application in Social Network Analysis Methods", Advances in Developing Human Resources, Vol. 9, No. 3, PP. 359-383, August, 2007.

98 Kenneth J. Zula and Thomas J. Chermack, "Integrative Literature Review: Human Capital Planning: A Review of Literature and Implications for Human Resource Development", Human Resource Development Review, Vol. 6, No. 3, PP. 245-262, September, 2007.

99 Carole Tansley and Sue Newell, "Project Social Capital, Leadership and Trust: A Study Of Human Resource Information Systems Development", Journal of Managerial Psychology, Vol. 22, Issue 4, PP. 350 – 368, 2007.

100 Grugulis and Irena, "Skills Training And Human Resource Development: A Critical Text", Vocedplus, National Centre for Vocational Education Research (NCVER), 2007.

101 Jonathon R B Halbesleben and Denise M. Rotondo, "Developing Social Support in Employees: Human Resource Development Lessons From Same-Career Couples", Advances in Developing Human Resources, Vol. 9, No. 4, PP. 544-555, November, 2007.

102 Andreas Schmidt and Christine Kunzmann, "Sustainable Competency-Oriented Human Resource Development with Ontology-Based Competency Catalogs", Cunningham and Cunningham: eChallenges, Den Haag, 2007.

103 Thomas N Garavan, David O'Donnell, David McGuire and Sandra Watson, "Exploring Perspectives on Human Resource Development: An Introduction", Advances in Developing Human Resources, Vol. 9, No. 1, PP. 3-10, February, 2007.

104 Girma S, Yohannes A G, Kitaw Y, Ye-Ebiyo Y, Seyoum A, Desta H and Teklehaimanot A, "Human Resource Development for Health in Ethiopia: Challenges of Achieving the Millennium development Goals", Ethiopian Journal of Health Development, Vol. 21, No. 3, PP. 216-231, 2007.

105 Claire Valentin, "Researching human resource development: emergence of a critical approach to HRD enquiry", International Journal of Training and Development, Vol. 10, Issue 1, PP. 17–29, March, 2006.

106 Barry-Craig P Johansen and Gary N McLean, "Worldviews of Adult Learning in the Workplace: A Core Concept in Human Resource Development", Advances in Developing Human Resources, Vol. 8, No. 3, PP. 321-328, August, 2006.

107 Liam Brown, Eamonn Murphy and Vincent Wade, "Corporate eLearning: Human Resource Development Implications For Large And Small Organizations", Human Resource Development International, Vol. 9, Issue 3, PP. 415-427, 2006.

108 Jia Wang and Greg G Wang, "Exploring National Human Resource Development: A Case of China Management Development in a Transitioning Context", Human Resource Development Review, Vol. 5, No. 2, PP. 176-201, June 2006.

109 Arif Hassan, Junaidah Hashim, Ahmad Zaki Hj Ismail, "Human resource development practices as determinant of HRD climate and quality orientation", Journal of European Industrial Training, Vol. 30, Issue 1, PP. 4 – 18, 2006.

110 Kit Brooks and Fredrick Muyia Nafukho, "Human resource development, social capital, emotional intelligence: Any link to productivity?", Journal of European Industrial Training, Vol. 30, Issue 2, PP.117 – 128, 2006.

111 Ani B Raidén and Andrew R J Dainty, "Human Resource Development In Construction Organisations: An Example Of A Chaordic Learning Organisation?", Vol. 13, Issue 1, PP. 63 – 79, 2006.

112 Noordeen Gangani, Gary N McLean and Richard A Braden, "A Competency-Based Human Resource Development Strategy", Wiley periodicals, Performance Improvement Quarterly, Vol. 19, Issue 1, PP. 127–139, March, 2006.

113 Tracy Wilcox, "Human Resource Development as an Element of Corporate Social Responsibility", Asia Pacific Journal of Human Resources, Vol. 44, Issue 2, PP. 184–196, August, 2006.

114 Susan A Lynham and Peter W Cunningham, "National Human Resource Development in Transitioning Societies in the Developing World: Concept and Challenges", Advances in Developing Human Resources, Vol. 8, No. 1, PP. 116-135, February, 2006.

115 Mary E Graham and Lindsay M Tarbell, "The Importance Of The Employee Perspective In The Competency Development Of Human Resource Professionals", Human Resource Management, Special Issue: Developing and Assessing Professional and Managerial Competence, Vol. 45, Issue 3, PP. 337–355, Autumn (Fall), 2006.

116 Andreas Schmidt and Christine Kunzmann, "Towards a Human Resource Development Ontology for Combining Competence Management and Technology-Enhanced Workplace Learning", Springer Berlin Heidelberg, Vol. 4278, PP. 1078-1087, 2006.

117 Consuelo L Waight, "Exploring Connections Between Human Resource Development and Creativity", Advances in Developing Human Resources, Vol. 7, No. 2, PP. 151-159, May, 2005.

118 Greg G Wang and Elwood F Holton III, "Neoclassical and Institutional Economics as Foundations for Human Resource Development Theory",

Human Resource Development Review, Vol. 4, No. 1, PP. 86-108, March, 2005.

119 Susan K Lippert and Paul Michael Swiercz, "Human resource information systems (HRIS) and technology trust", Journal of Information Science, Vol. 31, No. 5, PP. 340-353, October, 2005.

120 Greg G Wang and Dean R Spitzer, "Human Resource Development Measurement and Evaluation: Looking Back and Moving Forward", Advances in Developing Human Resources, Vol. 7, No. 1, PP. 5-15, February, 2005.

121 Jinyu Xie, "Human Resource Development Roles In The People's Republic Of China: Investigation From Seven Provinces", International Journal of Training and Development, Vol. 9, Issue 1, PP. 32–45, March, 2005.

122 Darlene Russ-Eft and Hallie Preskill, "In Search of the Holy Grail: Return on Investment Evaluation in Human Resource Development", Advances in Developing Human Resources, Vol. 7, No. 1, PP. 71-85, February, 2005.

123 Sarah A Hezlett and Sharon K Gibson, "Mentoring and Human Resource Development: Where We Are and Where We Need to Go", Advances in Developing Human Resources, Vol. 7, No. 4, PP. 446-469, November 2005.

124 Greg G Wang and Jia Wang, "Human Resource Development Evaluation: Emerging Market, Barriers, and Theory Building", Advances in Developing Human Resources, Vol. 7, No. 1, PP. 22-36, February, 2005.

125 Richard J Torraco, "Work Design Theory: A review and critique with implications for human resource development", Human Resource Development Quarterly, Vol. 16, Issue 1, PP. 85–109, Spring, 2005.

126 Colin Fisher Dr, "HRD Attitudes: Or the Roles and Ethical Stances of Human Resource Developers", Human Resource Development International, Vol. 8, Issue 2, PP. 239-255, 2005.

127 Laird D McLean, "Organizational Culture's Influence on Creativity and Innovation: A Review of the Literature and Implications for Human Resource Development", Advances in Developing Human Resources, Vol. 7, No. 2, PP. 226-246, May, 2005.

128 Kimberly S McDonald and Linda M Hite, "Reviving the Relevance of Career Development in Human Resource Development", Human Resource Development Review, Vol. 4, No. 4, PP. 418-439, December, 2005.

129 Norma D'Annunzio-Green and Helen Francis, "Human resource development and the psychological contract: Great expectations or false hopes?", Human Resource Development International, Vol. 8, Issue 3, PP. 327-344, 2005.

130 Dr Beverly Dawn Metcalfe and Christopher J Rees, "Theorizing advances in international human resource development", Human Resource Development International, Vol. 8, Issue 4, PP. 449-465, 2005.

131 Aahad M Osman-Gani and Ronald L Jacobs, "Technological Change and Human Resource Development Practices in Asia: A Study of Singapore-Based Companies", International Journal of Training and Development, Vol. 9, Issue 4, PP. 271–280, December, 2005.

132 Jon E Lervik, Bjorn W Hennestad, Rolv Petter Amdam, Randi Lunnan and Solvi M Nilsen, "Implementing Human Resource Development Best Practices: Replication or Re-Creation?", Human Resource Development International, Vol. 8, Issue 3, PP. 345-360, 2005.

133 Arvind Kumar Purohit, "HRD in Life Insurance Corporation of India (LIC)", Dundelkhand University, Jhansi, 1996.

134 Sanjay K Singh, "An Inquiry In to the Cost Structure of State Transport Undertakings in India", Transport Policy, Vol. 32, PP. 1–8, March, 2014.

135 Paul Dhinakaran D and Dr Rajarajan M, "Passengers' Perception towards Service Quality in Tamilnadu State Transport Corporation (Kumbakonam) Limited, Kumbakonam", Asia Pacific Journal of Research, Vol. I Issue XIII, January, 2014.

136 Srinivas D, "Performance Evaluation of A.P. State Road Transport Corporation (APSRTC) with a perceptional focus on turnaround", Andhra University, 2013.

137 Srinivasa Rao S, "HRM Practices in APSRTC - A Study on Vizianagaram zone", Andhra University, 2013.

138 Reddy P C, Sai Prasad Reddy C S and Samanth Reddy P, "Information System in Andhra Pradesh State Road Transport Corporation: A Study", International Journal of Information Technology and Computer Sciences Perspectives, Vol 2, No. 2, 2013.

139 Narasimha Rao V, "Turnaround Management in Andhra Pradesh State Road Transport Orporation – A Case Research Study", Paripex - Indian Journal of Research, Vol. 3, Issue 4, May, 2013.

140 TarakeswaraRao S, "Working of Trade Unions in APSRTC in Srikakulam Region of Andhra Pradesh State", The SIJ Transactions on Industrial, Financial & Business Management (IFBM), Vol. 1, No. 1, March-April, 2013.

141 Chandran Vijaya, "Impact of Employee Satisfaction And Union – Management Relation On Enhanced Customer Satisfaction- Regression Analysis - A study of Andhra Pradesh State Road Transport Corporation", ZENITH International Journal of Multidisciplinary Research, Vol. 3, Issue 4, 2013.

142 Srinivasa Rao S, "Human Resource Management Practices In Andhra Pradesh State Road Transport Corporation: A Study on Vizianagaram Zone", Andhra University, 13th May, 2013.

143 John Wesly G, "Trade Unions And Politics In The Light Of Economic Reforms: A Socio-Legal Study With Special Reference To Andhra Pradesh State Road Transport Corporation (APSRTC), A.P, India", Department of Legal Studies, Acharya Nagarjuna University, Guntur, Andhra Pradesh 522510, 17th April, 2013.

144 Dharma Naik B, "Performance Appraisal in APSRTC", Osmania Journal of Management, Osmania University, Hyderabad, 2013

145 Anita D'Souza, "A Study on Employee Satisfaction (With Special Reference to A.P.S.R.T.C Sangareddy Bus Depot)", Abhinav National Monthly Refereed Journal Of Research In Commerce & Management, Vol. 1, No. 1, Issue 7, 2012.

146 Trinath Babu M, "Marketing Operations of APSRTC A Study With Reference To Vizianagaram Zone", Department of Commerce and Management Studies, Andhra University, 2012.

147 Jawahar Suresh U, "Human Resource Planning in Andhra Pradesh State Road Transport Corporation (APSRTC) – A Study of Karimnagar Zone of Andhra Pradesh", Ph.D. Thesis, Sri Krishnadevaraya University, Anantapur, 2012.

148 Udai S Mehta, "Research Study of the Road Transport Sector in India", Research submitted to The Ministry of Corporate Affairs, Govt. of India, 25th January, 2012.

149 Sawinder Kaur and Navkiranjit Kaur, 'Growth and Pattern of Bus Service in Punjab', International Journal of Advanced Research in Management and Social Sciences, Vol. 1, No. 2, August, 2012.

150 Vijay V and Durga Prasad, "Passenger Amenities of Andhra Pradesh State Road Transport Corporation (APSRTC): A Study", Asian Journal of Business Management, IDOSI publications, Vol. 2, No. 2, PP. 76-83, 2011.

151 Kanagaluru Sai Kumar, "Consumption Pattern of Materials in APSRTC - A Study and Analysis", Asia Pacific Journal of Research in Business Management, Vol. 2, Issue 12, PP. 203-224, 2011.

152 Agarwal R K, and Pramod Bhargava, "Financial Distress Syndrome in State Transport Undertakings". IJTM 2011.

153 Prasada Rao and Bayyarapu, "Moving People - A Case of Andhra Pradesh State Road Transport Corporation APSRTC", International Association of Public Transport (Uitp), Rue Sainte Marie 6, Brussels Be-1080, Belgium, 2011.

154 Panduranga Murthy C, and Sathyavathi M, "Urban Passenger Awareness of the Marketing Schemes in APSRTC - An Assessment", Indian Journal of Transport Management, July – September, 2011.

155 Shivi Agarwal, Shiv Prasad Yadav, and Singh S P, "DEA Based Estimation of the Technical Efficiency of State Transport Undertakings in India", OPSEARCH, Vol. 47, No. 3, PP. 216–230, February, 2011.

156 Prakash B, Murthy C Panduranga and Sathyavathi M, "Rural Passenger Awareness of The Marketing Schemes In Apsrtc- An Assessment", International Journal of Marketing and Management Research, Vol. 2, Issue 7, 2011.

157 Sai Kumar K, "Scrap management in APSRTC – A study and analysis", International Journals of Marketing and Technology, Vol. 1, Issue 6, 2011.

158 Kumar K Sai, "Quality of Services in State Transport Corporations: A Study of APSRTC", The IUP Journal of Operations Management, Vol. 10, No. 3, PP. 27-38, August, 2011.

159 Rajesham A, "Improvement of Productivity through Incentive Schemes", Paper Presented On Management Development Programme, CIRT Pune, Feburary, 2009.

160 Prakash B, Ali Mohmed and Gayathri C, "Training in A.P.S.R.T.C (Andhra Pradesh State Road Transport Corporation)—An Empirical Study", The Journal of Indian Management & Strategy 8M, Vol. 13, Issue 1, 2008.

161 Ravichandran N, and Surya Prasad M V N, "Reviving Gujarat State Road Transport Corporation: An Agenda for Action", Indian Institute Of Management, Ahmedabad-380 015, W.P. No. 2007-03-05, March, 2007.

162 Vishnuprasad Nagadevara and Ramanayya, T V, "Factors Affecting Passenger Satisfaction Levels – A Case Study of Andhra Pradesh State Road Transport Corporation", Indian Institute of Management, Bangalore, India, 2007.

163 Satyanarayana B (Ph.D. Guide), "Organizational Climate in State Road Transport Corporation", 2006.

164 Metri Bhimaraya A, "Total Quality Transportation Through Deming's 14 Points", Journal of Public Transportation, Vol. 9, No. 4, PP. 35-46, 2006.

165 Kane and Tony, "Opening Session Welcome' in Performance Measures to Improve Transportation Systems: Summary of the Second National Conference", National Academy Press, Washington, D.C., 2005.

166 Kondayya K V N R S, "HRD in APSRTC – A Study with reference to Managerial Personnel', Andhra University, Visakhapatnam 530003.

167 Karne Manisha and Venkatesh, Anand, "Ananlysis of productivity and efficiency in MSRTC", Published in Working papers of the Department of Economics, PP. 1-26, 2003.

168 Pollappa J, "Industrial Relations – Need to have Effective Grievance Handling Machinery – A Case Study of Cuddapah Zone of APSRTC – 2000", Unpublished Thesis, Sri Krishnadevaraya University, Anantapur, A.P., 2000.

169 Sunil Kumar, "State Road Transport Undertakings in India: Technical Efficiency and Its Determinants", Benchmarking: An International Journal, Vol. 18, Issue 5, PP. 616 – 643, 1999.

170 Ghosh S K, "HRD Agenda for Future Strategies-The case of State Road Transport Undertakings", Manpower Journal, PP. 37-43, January-March, 1999; "Human Resource Development Climate in State Transport Undertakings", Indian Journal of Transport Management, C.I.R.T., Pune, PP. 411-416, June 1998 and "Training Effectiveness in State Road Transport

Undertakings", The Journal of the Institute of Public Enterprises, Vol. 20, No. 1&2, PP. 28-35, Hyderabad, 1997.

171 Gawhane S H and Sundaram padam, "Strategic Management Process of SRTUs-An Approach", The Journal of Institute of Public Enterprise, Vol. 1&2, PP. 64-76, Hyderabad, 1999.

172 Gundam Rajeswari, "Public Sector Performance of State Road Transport Corporation: A Case Study of Andhra Pradesh", APH, P. 125, 1998.

173 Made Gowda J, "Manpower Productivity in State Road Transport Undertakings-An Appraisal", The Journal of Transport Management, PP. 397-400, June, 1996.

174 Rama Rao K, "Rural Bus Transport Operations of APSRTC: A Study of their Impact on Socio-Economic Development of household in Visakhapatnam", 1996.

175 Saxena A S, "Financial Management in SRTC's", Kaniska Publishers and Distributers, New Delhi, 1994.

176 Prem Babu, "Human Resource Development in Greater Manchester Buses in UK.", Journal of Transport Management, CIRT, Pune, PP. 15-18, January, 1993.

177 Vaidya S C, "Inter-State Road Passenger Transport in India, with special reference to Punjab – A study in Cost Organisation and Operations", Ph.D Thesis, Punjab University, 1983.

178 Sudarsanam Padam, "Changing Imperatives of HRD: A Case of Passenger Road Transport Industry", in Rao T V et. al.(Eds.), "HRD in the New Economic Environment", Tata McGraw Hill, New Delhi, PP. 199-207, 1994.

179 Agarwal A K, "Analysis of Financial Statement Jaipur: University Book House Pvt, Ltd", 1992.

180 Gangappa K, "Performance Of Urban Passenger Road Transport-A Case Study Of Twin City Services Of Hyderabad And Secunderabad of APSRTC", Ph.D. Thesis, Sri Krishnadevaraya University, Anantapur, 1991.

181 Raman, "Tapping of Funds for Urban Bus Transport System", The Hindu, 23rd January, 1990.

182 Sudarsanam Padam,'Bus Transport in India', Ajanta Publications, Delhi, 1990.

183 Rama Mohan Rao, "Management of Change in a Public Enterprise - A Case Study of APSRTC", 1989.

184 Kulshresta D K, "Management of State Road Transport in India", Mittal Publications, New Delhi, 1989.

185 Mishra R K and Nandagopal R, "State Transport Undertakings in India: Reforms and Privatization Strategies", International Journal of Public Sector Management, Vol. 6, Issue 5, 1988.

186 Vijayaraghavan T A S, "Strategic options for state road transport undertakings in India", International Journal of Public Sector Management, Vol. 8, Issue 1, PP.48 – 67, 1988.

187 Ganagadhar Rao M, "Human factor in APSRTC - A focus on conductors", Andhra University, 1987.

188 Patankar P G, "Road Passenger Transport in India", Puna, Central Institute of Road Transport (Training and Research), 1986.

189 Phaniswara Raju B, "Materials Management in APSRTC", Ph.D Thesis, Sri Krishnadevaraya University, Anantapur, 1986.

190 Satyanarayana J, "The working of the Andhra Pradesh State Road Transport Corporation", CESS and Concept Publishing Co., New Delhi, 1985.

191 Santosh Sarma, "Productivity in Road Transport: A Study in Innovative Management New Delhi: ASRTU".

192 Mahesh Chand S, "Financial Performance of Public Road Transport Undertakings, Lok Udyog, April, 1982.

193 Jamwal J S, "Organization Structure of Transport Undertakings", Journal of Transport Management, PP. 18-19, April, 1978.

194 Rahi Kishore, "Performance of Public and Private Transport undertakings -A case study of Punjab Roadways and Ambala Bus Syndicate Pvt. Ltd.", M.Phil dissertation, Punjab University, Chandigarh, 1977.

195 Chaturvedi M C, "Operational Efficiency of State Road Transport Industry in India: A Case Study of Rajasthan State Road Transport Corporation", Unpublished Thesis, University of Rajasthan, 1979.

196 Sastry, "Physical and Financial Performance of some State Road Transport Undertakings in India", Ph.D Thesis, Unpublished, JNTU, 1974.

197 Krishna Murthy, "AP Road Transport – A Case Study", Journal of Transport Management, Vol. 9, No 18, PP.12-14, August, 1969

198 Ramanadham V V, "Nationalized Road Services in Hyderabad", Orient Publishing Company, Madras, 1955.

199 Mr Rajesh Pilot, Former Union Minister of Transport, "STUs Performance", Journal of Transport Management.

200 www.wikipedia.com

201 http://en.wikipedia.org/wiki/Census

202 www.wikipedia.com/road transport in india.

203 Central Statistical Organisation.

204 Sri Raman S, "Road Transport Development in India", Current Science, Vol.75, No. 8, 25th October, 1998.

205 Manorama Year Book, "Transport", P. 629, 2013.

206 Manorama Year Book, "Transport", P. 628-29, 2012 and 2013.

207 Manorama Year Book, "Transport", P. 629, 2013.

208 Ibid

209 www.wikipedia.com/ Transport in India

210 Ibid.

211 Sri Raman S, "Road Transport Development in India-special section-Transport-Current science", Vol.75, No.8, 25th October, 1998.

212 cistupiisc.ernet.in

213 www.morth.nic.in

214 www.ap.gov.in

215 http://en.wikipedia.org/wiki/Andhra_Pradesh

216 Srinivasulu Y, "Marketing of Transport Services-A Case Study of Passenger Road Transport Services by Andhra Pradesh State Road Transport Corporation", Service Marketing in India, P. 313.

217 www.apsrtc.gov.in

218 ibid

219 www.apsrtc.gov.in

220 ibid

221 www.apsrtc.gov.in

222 www.siamonline.in/SAFE-AC.../Raj%20Shekhar%20-%20**APSRTC**.pdf

223 Andhra Bhoomi Daily News Paper, "RTC three National Awards", 8th January, 2014.

224 Ravindra Prasadam D and Prasad V S, "Administrative Thinkers", chapter 7 edited by, Luther Gullick and Lyndal Urwick in S. P. Ranga Rao, P. 93, 1989.

225 Srinivas D, "Performance Evaluation of A. P. State Transport Corporation (APSRTC) with a Perceptional focus on turn around", Andhra University, 13th May, 2013.

226 Ibid

227 Srinivas D, "Performance Evaluation of A. P. State Transport Corporation (APSRTC) with a Perceptional focus on turn around", Andhra University, 13th May, 2013.

228 Srinivas D, "Performance Evaluation of A. P. State Transport Corporation (APSRTC) with a Perceptional focus on turn around", Andhra University, 13th May, 2013.

229 Srinivas D, "Performance Evaluation of A. P. State Transport Corporation (APSRTC) with a Perceptional focus on turn around", Andhra University, 13th May, 2013.

230 Srinivas Rao S, "Human Resource Management in Andhra Pradesh State Transport Corporation: A Study on Vizianagaram Zone", Andhra University, 13th May, 2013.

231 Srinivas D, "Performance Evaluation of A. P. State Transport Corporation (APSRTC) with a Perceptional focus on turn around", Andhra University, 13th May, 2013.

232 Ibid

233 Ibid

234 Ibid

235 Andhra Bhoomi Daily News Paper, PP. 1&7, 3rd October, 2013

236 The Hindu Daily News Paper, "With Leading - of burden and receding hope APSRTC"

237 Andhra Bhoomi, P. 7, 3rd October, 2013

238 The Hindu Daily News Paper, "Burden and Receding Hope for APSRTC", 10th October, 2013

239 Eenadu Daily News Paper, "Krungina pragathi chakram", P. 4, 30th April, 2013.

240 Eenadu Daily News Paper, 'Krungina pragathi chakralu', P. 4, 30th April, 2013.

241 The Hindu Daily News Paper, "Burden and receding hope for APSRTC", 10th October, 2013.

242 The Hindu Daily News Paper, "Splitting headache for APSRTC", P. 5, 29th August, 2013.

243 Eenadu Daily News Paper, "Krungina pragathi chakralu", P. 4, 30th April, 2013

244 The Hindu Daily News Paper, "Burden and receding hope for APSRTC", 10th October, 2013.

245 Andhra Bhoomi Daily News Paper, P. 7, 3rd October, 2013.

246 Srinivas Rao Chilumuri, "Financial Performance Evaluation of APSRTC", International Journal of Management and Business Studies, Vol. 3, Issue 1, January – March, 2013.

247 http://postnoon.com/2013/04/18/apsrtc-planning-to-design-and-build-its-own-buses/120506

248 The Hindu Daily News Paper, "Post-strike, 1300 RTC buses await fitness certificates", P. 4, 19th October, 2013.

249 www.apsrtc.gov.in

250 Eenadu Daily News Paper and Office Source, 2013.

251 www.apsrtc.gov.in

252 Ibid.

253 The Hindu Daily News Paper, "RTC to introduce tracking System", P. 5, 20th October, 2013.

254 Ibid

255 Andhra Bhoomi Daily News Paper, 30th May, 2013.

256 Andhra Bhoomi Daily News Paper, Editorial, P. 4, 7th November, 2013.

257 The Hindu Daily News Paper, "Kiritparikh Pannel wants diesel price hiked by Rs. 5", 29th October, 2013.

258 Andhra Bhoomi Daily News Paper, "No exception for Private Travellers", PP. 5-7, 5th November, 2013.

259 Ibid

260 Ibid

261 Ibid

262 Eenadu Daily News Paper, "Private Domination on APSRTC", 2013.

263 Ibid.

264 TV 9 News, "Private travelles Mafia – Discussion", at 7 Pm to 8 PM, 6th January, 2014.

265 A Report by IIM, Banglore – Andhra Bhoomi Daily news paper, "RTC Parirakshana", P. 7, 24th February, 2014.

266 C.V.R. NEWS, TV Discussion, "Maa Route aa Private", 9th January, 2014, 6:45 PM.

267 The Hindu, P. 4, 21st January, 2014.

268 Ibid - C.V.R News.

269 The Hindu Daily News Paper, P. 4, 11th October, 2013.

270 Andhra Bhoomi Daily News Paper, Srikakulam Distict Edition, PP. 1-2, 11th October, 2013.

271 The Hindu Daily News Paper, "Splitting headache for APSRTC", P. 5, 29th August, 2013.

272 Andhra Bhoomi Daily News Paper, P. 3, 11th September, 2013.

273 Ibid.

274 Ibid.

275 Ibid.

276 The Hindu, "Burden and receding hope for APSRTC", 10th October, 2013.

277 Andhra Bhoomi Daily News paper, P. 3, 17th October, 2013.

278 The Researchers experience when happened to travel during the RTC strike period.

279 The Hindu Daily News paper, "Burden and receding hope for APSRTC", 10th October, 2013.

280 Ibid.

281 Andhra Bhoomi Daily News paper, PP. 1 & 7, 3rd October, 2013.

282 Andhra Bhoomi Daily News paper, PP.1 & 7, 3rd October, 2013.

283 Reply to an RTI filed by a Social Activist –G. A. Raju.

284 Ibid.

285 Business Line Daily News Paper," APSRTC Plans to Shore up lost revenues makeup for loss Rs. 211 Crore during Strike phase", 21st October, 2011.

286 Reply to an RTI filed by a Social Activist –G. A. Raju.

287 Business Line Daily News Paper, "APSRTC Plans to Shore up lost revenues makeup for loss Rs. 211 Crore during Strike phase", 21st October, 2011.

288 Andhra Bhoomi Daily News Paper, "Adakatthera lo RTC", P. 4, 3rd March, 2014.

289 Ibid

290 Ibid

291 Ibid

292 http://en.wikipedia.org/wiki/SWOT_analysis

293 www.wikipedia.com

294 http://www.businessdictionary.com/definition/department.html

295 Nurs Educ J and Grigsby K A, "Perceptions of the Organizations Climate: Influenced by the organization's structure?", US National Library of Medicine, National Institutes of Health, Vol. 30, No. 2, PP. 81-8; February, 1991.

296 Florence M Stone, "Coaching, Counseling And Mentoring: How To Choose & Use The Right Technique To Boost Employee Performance", AMACOM Books, 2nd Edition, Newyork, 2007.

297 Parikshit Joshi and Anuj Srivastava, "Examining the HRD Practices in Indian PSUs – with special reference to IOC Mathura Refinery", SMS Varanasi, Vol. 8, No.2, December, 2012.

298 Rao T V and E Abraham S J, "HRD Climate in Organization", 2008.

299 Ibid, Parikshit Joshi

300 Andhra Bhoomi Daily News Paper, P.7, 17th January, 2014.

301 Prof Krishnaveni R, "Human Resource Development: A Researchers' Perspective", Excel Books, P. 5.

302 Srinivas D, "Performance Evaluation of A. P. State Transport Corporation (APSRTC) with a Perceptional Focus on Turn Around", Andhra University, 13th May, 2013.

303 Eenadu Daily News Paper

304 TV 9 News, "Private Travelles Mafia – Discussion", at 7 PM to 8 PM, 6th January, 2014.

305 Andhra Bhoomi Daily News Paper, Srikakulam District Edition, P.7, 11th April, 2013.

306 APSRTC Annual Reports.

307 Andhra Bhoomi, P.7, 17th January, 2014.